The Story of
SHREWSBURY

To all friends round the Wrekin

The Story of
SHREWSBURY

by
Mary de Saulles
ARIBA AADip FCSD FRSA

Logaston Press

LOGASTON PRESS
Little Logaston Woonton Almeley
Herefordshire HR3 6QH
logastonpress.co.uk

First published by Logaston Press 2012
Reprinted 2016
Copyright text © Mary de Saulles 2012
Copyright illustrations © as credited in the captions and acknowledgements

ISBN 978 1 906663 68 1

Typeset by Logaston Press
and printed and bound in Poland by
www.lfbookservices.co.uk

CONTENTS

FOREWORD   *vii*

ACKNOWLEDGEMENTS   *x*

PREFACE   *xi*

1   ORIGINS: THE UNSOLVED MYSTERY   1

2   THE SAXON BURGH (827-1066)   9

3   A NORMAN STRONGHOLD (1066-1150)   17

4   PLANTAGENET SHREWSBURY AND
          THE WELSH CONFLICT (1150-1400)   31

5   BATTLE, GUILDS AND PRINCES (1400-1485)   51

6   THE TUDOR TOWN (1485-1603)   65

7   STUART SHREWSBURY (1603-1642)   89

8   THE CIVIL WAR AND COMMONWEALTH (1642-1660)   97

9   RESTORATION SHREWSBURY (1660-1702)   107

10   GEORGIAN SHREWSBURY (1702-1837)   117

11   VICTORIAN TIMES (1837-1901)   159

12   EDWARDIAN INTERLUDE (1901-1914)   195

13   THE FIRST WORLD WAR (1914-1918)   203

14   THE INTER WAR PERIOD (1918-1939)   209

15   THE SECOND WORLD WAR (1939-1945)   219

16   THE POST-WAR YEARS (1945-1985)   225

17   'EXCEPTIONAL HERITAGE', LEADS TO THE FUTURE (1985-)   235

     APPENDIX: SOME SHREWSBURY STREET NAMES   249

     INDEX   253

A recent view of Shrewsbury –
'islanded by Severn stream' in the words of A.E. Housman
(webaviation)

Foreword

Although I was born and bred in Staffordshire, my association with Shropshire in general, and Shrewsbury in particular, goes back a long way. I have spent many happy years in the county, and have become increasingly involved in Shrewsbury life. She is a fascinating and ancient town, and for centuries has drawn many folk through her town walls every day, for trade, for work and for pleasure. Her residents have always had, and still have, an enviable reputation for both hospitality and charity.

Shrewsbury's architecture and general design and layout is most interesting. The mixture of new and old has not always been happily achieved, but the current emphasis by those who guide the destiny of Shropshire architecture is on promoting the use of old materials and preserving the beauty of the past while finding creative ways to satisfy the needs of the present. In creating their town, our ancestors excelled themselves, and it is good to see that in this day and age, their work is valued and enhanced with pride.

I am delighted and honoured to have been asked to write a Foreword to the *The Story of Shrewsbury*, which ends with some suggestions about how the town may move into the future. I am sure that all who pick up this book will find it an interesting and valuable account of one of our great county towns.

The Rt Hon the Earl of Shrewsbury and Waterford
September 2012

'Below: Prospect of ye Ancient & Beautiful Town of Shrewsbury c.1750.
(Courtesy of Shropshire Museums)

PROSPECT of ye
SHREW

To the Right Worship!
THE MAYOR RECORDER
ALDERMEN and BURGESSES
OF SHREWSBURY
This Prospect is humbly Dedicated &c
Presented by R. Marshall

Mercers Grocers Drapers Goldsmiths Ironmongers Barber Surgeons Apothecaries Upholsters

Masons Dyers Chandlers

Above: 'South West Prospect of Shrewsbury' by S. & N. Buck c.1732. (SA PR-3-260)

Acknowledgements

I would like to record my indebtedness to all those historians and other writers whose works over so many centuries have provided such fascinating reading – and tempting side tracks; to all those poets, artists, pictorial sculptors and photographers, from the earliest Welsh poets to the latest film crews, who have recorded facts and created images that linger in the memory; to all the craftsmen, architects and designers, together with the benefactors and administrators who made their work possible, for creating the physical town we all enjoy; and to all those researchers, map-makers, archaeologists, historians, curators, librarians and speakers who have discovered, stored, assembled, sorted and presented information. All these have made my task, in attempting to draw *The Story of Shrewsbury* together, despite all its problems, one of constant appreciation and delight.

I would like particularly to thank the staff at Shropshire Archives and Shropshire Museums for their help in providing images and information. Several of these images are included in colour, and these usually include an Archives' or Museum Service's reference number (prefaced by SA or SHYMS respectively); where images from the Archives have simply been reused from *The Book of Shrewsbury* (on which this book is based) the credit is simply to Shropshire Archives. Others who have been of great assistance in answering queries include Dr Nigel Baker, James Lawson, Rev. Ian Ross, and Michael Webb. I would also like to thank Mike Willmott for editing time in the early stages, and my son, Stephen for his constant support, his tutelage on all technology, his supply of many ideas, and for the generous contribution of his various professional photographic skills. Finally my thanks go to Andy and Karen Johnson for their ideas to develop the text and for their work in blending it all together.

Preface

It is readily acknowledged and recognized that Shrewsbury is a wonderful place to live and work and visit, but in the hustle and bustle of daily life we often fail to reflect on the richness of the town's heritage. With centuries of history, a wealth of architecture and fine buildings, the county town of Shropshire nestling in the loop of the River Severn, has much to offer.

Mary de Saulles' re-write of *The Book of Shrewsbury*, first published over a quarter of a century ago, whets the appetite for those wanting to know more about the town; it engenders a great sense of pride in Shrewsbury and a feeling that we are merely short-term guardians in the very long time-line of one of England's most splendid towns and we have much to be thankful for.

Helen Ball BA (Hons), FILCM
Town Clerk
September 2012

1 Origins: The Unsolved Mystery

'I had arms, men and horses; I had wealth in abundance; can you wonder that I was unwilling to lose them? The ambition of Rome aspires to universal domination; and must mankind, by consequence, stretch their necks to the yoke? I stood at bay for years. Had I acted otherwise where, on your part, would have been the glory of conquest, and where, on mine, the honour of a brave resistance? I am now in your power: if you are bent on vengeance, execute your purpose; the bloody scene will soon be over, and the name of Caratacus will sink into oblivion. Preserve my life, and I shall be to late posterity, a monument of Roman clemency.'

> From the address to the tribunal in Rome by Caratacus in AD 51.
> (The Emperor Claudius granted him and his family a free pardon.)

On the eve of the Roman invasion the present area of Shropshire was probably governed from a hill fort on the Wrekin, the administrative centre of the British tribe known as the Cornovii to the Romans when they reached this part of the country in about AD50. The site of the town of *Viroconium* (subsequently called *Wroeken* then *Wroecenseter* and finally Wroxeter) may have been a fortified camp when Caratacus, the last of the British princes to offer resistance, finally surrendered in about AD48.

The Wrekin (1,334ft), part of the oldest rocks in Shropshire, rises steeply from the surrounding plain, a most impressive landmark, and is capped by a well-preserved Iron Age fort, the original headquarters of the Cornovii. (Stephen de Saulles)

Soon afterwards an attempt was made to conquer Wales. It was probably then that the Headquarters of the XIVth Legion was moved forward from Wall, near Lichfield, to *Viroconium* where it remained for about 20 years. Later, Chester was seen as a more convenient military base, and *Viroconium* became a civilian settlement and one of the outposts of Roman civilisation. Excavations show that the Romans were developing it as a centre of civilian government, and after AD122, when the emperor Hadrian visited, the work appears to have accelerated.

The inscription on the front of the forum indicates a civilised and sophisticated people. It identified Wroxeter as *Civitas Cornoviorum*, the tribal capital of the Cornovii. The forum, at about 245 x 225 feet (75 x 69 metres), was large compared with others in Britain. The whole 200 acre (just over 80 ha) site represents the largest civil Roman city in Britain, and is unique in not having been built over since. The buildings included ornate plaster vaulting and decorative mosaic floors, as well as all normal Roman amenities such as central heating, and there is evidence of trade with continental Europe in luxury goods. The existence of a quay indicates a certain amount of river traffic.

Part of the mile-wide, 200-acre (just over 80 hectares) site of Wroxeter, more than half the size of Roman London. First a camp, then a legionary fortress, and later a mixed community of several thousand, Hadrian intended it as an outpost of Roman civilization on a grand scale. Thomas Telford, excavating the site in 1788, was probably the first to realize the significance of 'crop marks' in archaeology. Seen after periods of prolonged drought, they reveal the existence of old walls and other features below the surface.
(Cambridge University Collection, Crown Copyright reserved)

'In honour of the Emperor Caesar Trajanus Hadrianus Augustus, son of the deified Trajanus Parthicus, grandson of the deified Nerva, Pontifex Maximus, holding the tribunician power for the fourteenth year, consul for the third time, Father of his country, the Community of the Cornovii [erected this building]'. This inscription over the new forum, constructed as part of Hadrian's civic development of Wroxeter, shattered when the entrance collapsed. The inscription has been restored and is presently housed in Rowley's House Museum. It is one of the most remarkable examples of Roman lettering, equal to that on Trajan's column in Rome. The forum was constructed on the site of the unfinished baths as part of Hadrian's concept of establishing an important outpost of Rome's urban civilization. (Stephen de Saulles, courtesy of Shropshire Museums)

The city was probably partially inhabited by retired army personnel wanting to remain in this country. Aerial photographs reveal many surrounding farms and villas, and a certain amount of intermarrying probably took place. There just might have been an outlying farm on the site of Shrewsbury, though no evidence exists.

In about AD280 the first of a series of pirate Saxon raids began on the east coast. Thereafter, attacks from Saxons, Picts and Scots increased, and put pressure on the Romans to the extent that there was a gradual withdrawal from the area that became Shropshire. By 300 the baths had been abandoned and other civic buildings had fallen into disuse, but it appears that commercial activity continued. Where sites were cleared, timber-framed buildings with infill panels were constructed as opposed to ones of stone and brick as built by the Romans, though more substantial structures followed within a few decades, probably being the rulers' residences. Although in timber, the style was still Roman.

By 410 Rome itself had been attacked. Britain had become too difficult to hold, and the Roman armies withdrew, leaving Britain more open to assault. A French bishop, visiting in 429, reported that 'the islanders were still prosperous and defending themselves' but by 460 chroniclers record a general depression and collapse.

Over the years, as Saxon settlement gradually pushed westwards, some of the native British headed further west while others remained to often form separate settlements from their Saxon neighbours. However, the invaders seem to have been halted just to the east of the present Shropshire border, along the line of Roman Watling Street, perhaps with the help of mercenaries such as Cunorix, whose tomb was found near here.

The inscription on his funeral stone is CUNORIX MACUS MAQVI COLINE, which translates as 'Cunorix ('Hound-king') son of Maqui-Coline ('Son of the tribe of Holly')'. Cunorix is considered an Irish name and suggests he was a mercenary leader. It was quite usual for the Romans, and later the Saxons, to employ mercenaries.

For the 2-300 years after the Shropshire area ceased effectively to be ruled from Rome, it appears to have been governed by native British rulers, and to have retained a high degree of independence. It seems that, some time between 490 and 516, invaders moving west suffered a series of rebuffs, culminating in a great British victory at a place referred to as Mount Badon, (by legends, either near Bath, or Coalville in Leicestershire), under the leadership of a mysterious Christian hero known later as 'Arthur of Britain', who was to become a legendary figure across Europe. By the late 6th century it would appear that Shropshire was subject to the British king Urien of Reged, (c.530-590), a kingdom which extended from near Wroxeter in the south to Galloway in the north. About 590 he and his sons were assassinated, and much of his power passed to Aethelfrith, the English king of Bernicia (which was in north-east England). It was perhaps following

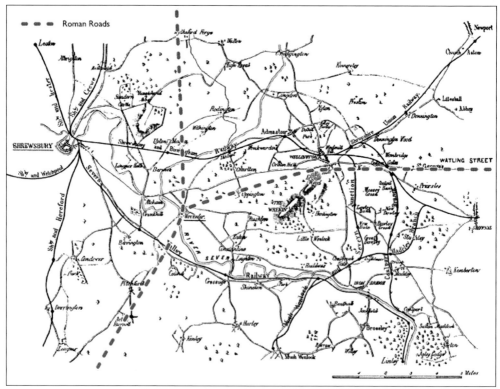

The principal Roman communication lines (bringing troops and supplies from the south-east to Wroxeter and beyond), superimposed on Hulbert's 19th-century map to show their relationship to Shrewsbury and the modern railway communications network. Wroxeter was sited where Watling Street met the Severn and whilst there is no evidence of a road towards Shrewsbury, it would have been accessible by river (a quayside was found during excavations at Wroxeter).

According to legend, when the long perimeter walls of Wroxeter became indefensible to the reduced 6th-century population, its rulers may have moved to a new fortified settlement known as the Berth (SJ 429236). Surrounded by marsh, it is about 8km north-west of Shrewsbury and near Baschurch. A 7th-century cauldron was found, which indicates that the site was occupied at that period. (SA 6001-198-97)

these upheavals that the area around Shrewsbury became part of the shadowy Celtic kingdom of Powys, the 'paradise of Wales' of Welsh poetry, and the lowland Cornovii moved to a site easier to defend against local raiders. This may have been to the Berth near Baschurch, although some say Atcham. In any case, Wroxeter was abandoned.

Another wave of Saxon raids penetrated from the Humber along the River Trent. As part of the process of resistance, a mosaic of small states was being brought together in the Midlands, forming the basis of the later kingdom of Mercia.

By about 600 half the island had been conquered and occupied, and small kingdoms had been founded, each under its own ruler. Interwoven with recorded facts are many legends. The poet Llywarch Hen tells us that he came from Northumbria to take refuge with Cynddylan, a kinsman and Prince of Powys, whose palace was at 'Pengwern'. This was Shrewsbury, according to some, but perhaps the Berth to others. Llywarch Hen laments the destruction of *Viroconium* and Pengwern and bids its maidens behold the 'habitation of Cynddylan wrapped in flames'. A few years earlier, Brochmael, Prince of Powys, had his palace there, allegedly on the hill where old St Chad's stood. Old Welsh poetry mentions a legendary re-occupation of Pengwern after the fire.

By a series of more factual battles, mergers, and conquests in these early centuries, the kingdom, (and now region), of Mercia gradually came into being, a name deriving from West Saxon mearc, a border. By 590 Staffordshire was already under the Mercian dynasty of Penda. Urien and his sons were assassinated, and much of his power passed back to the king of Bernicia in the north.

Aethelfrith, a pagan Bernician, became the first king of Northumbria, a kingdom formed by the merging of Bernicia, which lay north of the River Tees, with Deira to the south of the river, whose capital was York. Aethelfrith (596-616) first overcame Deira, whose Prince Edwin escaped to north Wales. In 613 Aethelfrith went on to defeat the joint armies of Gwynedd and Powys and those of the Cornovii led by Cyndrwyn, but Edwin escaped again, this time to East Anglia. Aethelfrith pursued him but was in turn defeated.

Edwin then took over Aethelfrith's authority in the north. (He married Ethelburga, sister of the king of Kent, and converted to Christianity. Thus St Augustine's Christianity was taken to Northumbria.) Edwin next attacked Cadwallon, Prince of Gwynedd, but the latter gained Penda of Mercia as an ally. Edwin was killed in battle in 633. This battle was an early step in the gradual rise of Mercian ascendancy, the Saxon kingdom centred on Tamworth – although the evidence of the Welsh poets suggests that the Cornovii still retained their independence during Penda's lifetime.

A Welsh poem, *Marwnad Cynddylan*, relates a story of Cynddylan, in which he refused to pay tribute to a Saxon king in about 655, and won a battle against a Saxon army near Lichfield. He was killed in the following year, however, perhaps in a battle against a Northumbrian army, and his body was taken to be laid in a church at 'Bassa', which suggests the present-day Baschurch near the Berth. His sons fled to Powys, and the Shropshire area came under the control of the Mercian kings at Tamworth.

Pagan Penda of Mercia was killed in the year 655 and was succeeded by his son Paeda. Mercia's power was reduced for a while but, when Penda's other son, Wulfere, became king in 658, its supremacy was restored. A Tribal Hidage census of Mercian territories in 661 included the Wreocensaetan people. These were the settlers around the Wrekin. The boundary between the bishopric sees of Lichfield and Hereford was between the 'Magonsaete' area to the south and the 'Wreocensaete' to the north. The same boundary still persists today.

Wulfere also took from the Welsh the area that was to become the diocese of Hereford. Wulfere's Ford, near Melverley, could be the site of a treaty made between the Mercian king and the rulers of Powys at that time.

The Mercians adopted Christianity in Wulfere's time. However, the dedication of a church at Cressage to St Samson, who was born in Wales and travelled as far as Cornwall and Brittany in the 6th century, suggests that he visited there, and that Christianity may have continued in Shropshire from the end of Roman rule. In the year 633, Lichfield was established as the bishopric for this area and, following the Synod of Whitby in 664, the Roman system of bishoprics, parishes and monasteries was initiated. It provided a pattern for future government.

By 720, Mercia was coming nearer to overall supremacy than any other kingdom since the departure of the Romans, a position strengthened under two strong kings who ruled for nearly 80 years without a break: first Aethelbald and then Offa, who ruled from 757-96. Offa took the Shrewsbury area from the Welsh, allegedly drove the Prince of Powys from his Pengwern palace, twice-devastated south Wales, and built the famous dyke between his kingdom and the Welsh. He made sure that, wherever possible, the better agricultural land was on his side throughout its hundred mile length. This now much-eroded structure lies approximately on the present boundary between England and Wales, and signifies Offa's great authority. His status as a monarch was reflected by the Emperor Charlemagne, the most powerful ruler in Europe at the time, who addressed him as an equal, and as 'king of Britain'. Apart from increasing trade, this was a time of cultural recovery. The barbarian invasions had halted for a while.

When Offa died in 796, he left a number of problems. There was deep resentment in the kingdoms he had subdued, an over-powerful church, and the Welsh frontier. From his palace in London, he had levied tolls on Frisian and Frankish merchants. He had annexed Essex and East Anglia, and made Wessex and Kent unwilling vassals. He 'centralised' power by nepotism, creating his own kin as earls over annexed provinces. A strong but despotic ruler, he left Mercia potentially weakened. His son, Ecgfrith died after ruling for only six months. Kent broke out in revolt; and an opportunity was provided for Egbert of Wessex, founder of a new Saxon dynasty, (and grandfather of Alfred the Great), who won a great battle over Mercia in 825. Kent and Essex acknowledged him, but not Northumbria or other independent dynasties in East Anglia. Unity was only brought about under the pressure of further invasions from the east. For Viking raiders began to take advantage of defenceless England, and continued their destruction for around two hundred years.

The evidence for any Saxon settlement at Shrewsbury during this period is very slight. Local archaeologist Nigel Baker, in his recent *Shrewsbury, An archaeological assessment of an English border town*, can only suggest 'indications'. For example, a quoin stone in the south-west corner of the west tower of St Mary's church shows evidence of having once been subjected to Roman building techniques, for it has the type of sunken holes into which hooks were inserted and attached to a scissor-like lifting gear used by the Romans. This stone may indicate that the Saxons used some Roman stonework to build their early church, which was then subsequently reused when St Mary's was built. Nigel Baker also mentions the existence of unexplained crop-marks seen in 1975 midway between Wroxeter and Shrewsbury, near Atcham, that are yet to be excavated and might be an important part of the story, – or possibly not. Sadly, archaeologists have found no tangible evidence to support the long-cherished legends of Shrewsbury's connections with the Berth, or Baschurch, or its identity with the Pengwern of Welsh poetry, but perhaps legends and folklore should be allowed to enjoy an independent life of their own.

There have been archaeological finds on the gravels south of Shrewsbury, at Bayston Hill and Meole Brace, which date from the late prehistoric period, whilst Bronze Age axes have been found in the High Street. The likely explanation for these is that there was probably an early trackway which crossed the peninsula made by the Severn on which Shrewsbury sits, making use of the fordable crossing points on either side. A few isolated, unenclosed, lowland Iron Age settlements have been found outside the river loop: one in Belle Vue, between the Rad and Rea Brooks, along a route towards *Viroconium*; also to the north, in Greenfields, and a little further out north at Berwick, at Alkmund Park Roman villa. These could have developed as farmsteads, perhaps providing for the needs of a larger settlement.

Apart from the above finds, the earliest positive evidence for post-Roman activity in the Shrewsbury area appears to be monastic. Steven Basset's research in 1991 suggested that the very large rural parishes of St Mary's and St Chad's indicate extensive royal grants of land in the middle Saxon period. Significantly, each minster was sited on one of the two 'hilltop' areas of the near-island site. He also considered that the founding of St Mary's by King Edgar in about 960 was more likely to have been a re-founding of a much earlier church, 'almost certainly as a royal foundation of middle Saxon date' probably in the late 600s or early 700s. New bishoprics had been created by around 680 at Hereford and Worcester, and a new minster church founded at Much Wenlock. Basset speculated that St Chad's could have been founded at around the same time to fulfil the role of head minster in Shrewsbury. Nigel Baker makes the further suggestion that the royal, ecclesiastical and administrative centres may then have been separate, a feature of many Saxon centres such as those at Hereford and Gloucester. St Mary's, later a collegiate church, was staffed by a dean and prebendaries, and St Chad's had certainly become an episcopal minster before the function was transferred to Chester in 1075. It belonged to the bishops of Lichfield, and was staffed by nearly 20 secular canons accommodated in houses near by, some of them around the present road called College Hill. These two substantial ecclesiastical communities, together with other lesser ones, would inevitably have provided a stimulus for the growth of a settlement.

So far, the archaeological evidence to determine the shape and size of this settlement is missing. Over the last half century, whilst pottery sherds have been revealed at several excavations, these Stafford-ware finds are not useful for chronological dating. They can only be dated to within a span of, some say, 150 years, others argue for 300 years, that is between about 850 or 700 and 1000.

Shrewsbury's eventual siting suggests that at least two factors were important: first, defence, for, like other Saxon towns such as Stafford or Worcester, it was surrounded by marshes. And second, the river, important for trading and communication, because by then the Roman roads would have been overgrown and probably forgotten.

Meanwhile, Charlemagne had died, having reigned and dominated Europe for nearly 50 years. For the year 827 the *Anglo-Saxon Chronicles* record that Ludeca, king of the Mercians, together with his five 'ealdormen', (a term that covers a possible regional governor to a local man of high standing, and from which the word 'aldermen' derives) were all killed. Then also, conveying the significance of events, in 829 they record 'the moon darkened on Christmas Eve' and that 'in the same year Ecgbryht [Egbert] overcame the Mercian kingdom and all lands south of the Humber'. With these portentous phrases, the context for Shrewsbury's story had been set.

2 THE SAXON BURGH

'The king went across the Thames into Shropshire and there received his food rents and Christmas entertainment. So much terror then arose from the force that men could not think nor conceive how they might be driven from the land, or how to hold the land against them ... The king began to discuss in earnest with his counsellors what seemed the most advisable to them all, how the land might be protected before being utterly destroyed ... For the good of all the nation, though it was hateful to them, all agreed that the force must be yielded tribute. Then the king sent message to the force.'

King Aethelred's decision to pay Danegeld, possibly made in Shrewsbury, as recorded in *The Anglo-Saxon Chronicle* for the year 1006.

Under the leadership of Egbert, king of Wessex (802-39), acclaimed the 'Bretwalda' or sole ruler of Britain, the seven kingdoms of the Saxon Heptarchy moved towards a system of single monarchy. This was hastened perhaps by the need for unity in the face of the new invaders, for it was near the end of Offa's reign in the 790s that the Vikings (Danes and Norsemen) began their hit-and-run raids. Initially targeting the coast, the raiders soon penetrated inland, plundering, murdering and devastating farmlands. By the middle of the 9th century the raiders were settling, bringing their families and making fortified camps in which to over-winter, and by the 860s the attacks had become more organised, with permanent settlement intended.

There was much fighting. In 871 Egbert's young grandson Alfred (later Alfred the Great), 'fighting like a wild boar', defeated the invaders at Ashdown, which was probably on the Ridgeway, between Aldworth and The Astons in the Berkshire Downs.

After defeating the Scandinavians again in battle, Alfred negotiated the Peace of Wedmore in 878, by which they agreed to keep within the north-eastern Danelaw territory allocated to them; he then set about reorganising the remainder of the country. Within a few months his elder brother was dead, and Alfred became king, fighting nine battles in the same year as the Danes sought once more to extend their territory. The Danes overran eastern Mercia and reached as close as Bridgnorth, wintering there in 895.

Having again come to terms with the Danish leaders, Alfred made peace with the Welsh, and bound the territories of Wessex and Mercia together, by marrying his daughter

Ethelfleda to Earl Aethelred, the most senior Mercian noble. He retained control of Wessex himself, and sent his daughter and son-in-law to rule western Mercia.

As well as designing superior longships and founding a navy, Alfred also reorganised the army and established 'burghs' modelled on the Danish examples he had seen in his youth. These were centres that served as bases for attack and retreat, created by fortifying existing towns, or by building new burghs where necessary. Local 'thegns', noblemen next in rank to an earl, would be required to organise the construction of each stronghold complete with ditch and stockade. A thegn would also be bound to maintain and command the garrison. Although Shrewsbury does not appear on the known list of ten burghs established in Mercia, there is a significant document evidencing its status. A charter dated 901 concerning Wenlock (now Much Wenlock), ends with the declaration *'acta est ... in civitate Scrobbensi* [Shrewsbury]'. This indicates that Shrewsbury was an officially defended site, the word *civitas* implying an administrative centre exercising authority over a wide area. 'Scrob' is often interpreted as meaning scrub or shrubs, but it could also be a personal name – it was a Richard, son of Scrob or Scrope, for example, who built Richard's Castle on the Shropshire/Herefordshire border.

A typical stronghold would have consisted of a timber tower erected on an earthen mound (the 'motte'), with a stockade at the narrow neck of land created by the loop of the river, where the castle now stands. The tower and motte was probably built where Laura's Tower, designed by the young Thomas Telford in the 18th century, now stands. Only about half of the later raised motte now remains, due to erosion and landslip on the riverside. The main purpose of the tower would have been as a look-out post, with a secondary role as a place of defence.

Anglo-Saxon coins minted in Shrewsbury. Athelstan was the first of 14 kings to have coins struck in the town. Illustrated: Athelstan (925-39) Nos 1 & 2; Edgar the Peaceable (959-75) No 3; Canute (1016-35) Nos 4-9. Saxon monarchs derived revenue from the issue of coinage by exacting payment for the use of the die on the obverse side of the king's image. To increase income, coin types were changed every six years and, from 973 all mints had to use identical dies.

When her husband died, Ethelfleda succeeded him as sole ruler in Mercia for seven years. According to tradition, she founded the church dedicated to St Alkmund, a prince of the royal house of Northumbria from which she was descended. She and her brother, King Edward the Elder of Wessex, continued to fight vigorously against the Danes, and she died in 918 while negotiating for the surrender of York.

In that same year the Danish leaders finally submitted to her brother and the land became one kingdom as far north as the Humber. After his death, Edward's three sons then ruled in turn. The first, Athelstan, re-conquered land further north, and so claimed to be the first Saxon king of Britain. In 925 he passed a law to unify coinage and specified the number of moneyers permitted in each selected and suitably fortified centre. Shrewsbury was allowed one moneyer, and examples of the coins minted in the town at that time still exist.

After nearly a century of violence, which had affected many parts of Europe, the Norsemen began to settle in France, the disruption lessened, at least for a while, and recovery began. Several improvements in agricultural methods made assarting (the clearing of woodland) easier. Improved harness and the use of horseshoes made possible the greater use of animals, and food production and population increased. From recent archaeological evidence, notably that from pottery sherds found at several sites within the river loop, it appears that occupation was already as extensive, if not as dense, as in the later medieval periods.

Surplus products would have led to barter, travelling merchants and the development of commerce. In Shrewsbury, the early market grew up in the space between where St Alkmund's and St Juliana's churches stood. A further market developed in the Pride Hill and Castle Street area. It is reasonable to suppose that the early merchants on the north side of the street were those whose trades were related to the grazing land behind, alongside the river, or perhaps to early trades based on the river itself – fish from the fishweir upstream, and products from local farms up or downstream.

In Saxon England's 'golden age of prosperity', the English language came to be written as well as spoken; coinage was standardised and so were weights and measures. In 957 St Dunstan was recalled by King Edgar from temporary exile in France, where he had been banished after an argument with the king's brother Edwy two years previously, and appointed first bishop of Worcester and then archbishop of Canterbury. In Shrewsbury, Edgar founded St Mary's church in about 960, or perhaps had it built on the site of an earlier church. (When central heating was being installed in 1864, it was found that the

Long thought to have been a Saxon pin, this object, about five inches long and dating from the 8th to 9th century, was found in 1889 while excavating the crypt of old St Chad's and is the earliest conclusive evidence of occupation. It has since been identified as a stylus for writing on wax tablets, with the flat end used as an eraser, after the discovery of a similar item in a monastery at Whitby. (Stephen de Saulles, courtesy of Shropshire Museums)

mid 12th-century walls were resting on walls of an earlier date. By tradition this was 'a Saxon church founded by King Edgar', but now there is possible reason to think that there was an even earlier building on the site.) He also re-founded St Alkmund's as a 'college', (with a dean and chapter, or group, of canons), under the direction of Dunstan, increasing its endowment.

The system of administration was improved. The whole country was divided into shires (Anglo-Saxon '*scire*' meaning division) and a shire reeve (sheriff) was appointed to each under the ealdorman, the most senior royal official in each shire or group of shires. Shires were divided into boroughs, boroughs into hundreds, and hundreds into hides (*c*.120 acres or 50 hectares), which were a taxable unit of land and property.

By the late 900s the settlement therefore included four churches: the late 8th-century St Chad's, St Alkmund's of *c*.920, St Mary's of *c*.960 and St Julian's, then dedicated to St Juliana, whose origin is uncertain. The Shrewsbury river loop was probably chosen for

Excavations of the crypt under the north transept of the medieval church of St Chad in 1889 found Saxon architecture and ancient graves suggesting an earlier Christian church.
The 'travelling bishop', St Chad, had converted the Mercians and was made bishop of Mercia in 670 at the head of the diocese of Lichfield. By Edward the Confessor's time the church was of considerable importance and owned extensive manors, as recorded in the Domesday survey. Llywarch Hen, the Welsh poet, a prince by birth, cousin to Urien, came from Cumberland to take refuge with a prince named Cynddylan 'whose palace was at Pengwern' (meaning marsh head or end). There has been a long-standing legend that St Chad later built his church on the site of this palace, destroyed by flames. (Shropshire Archives)

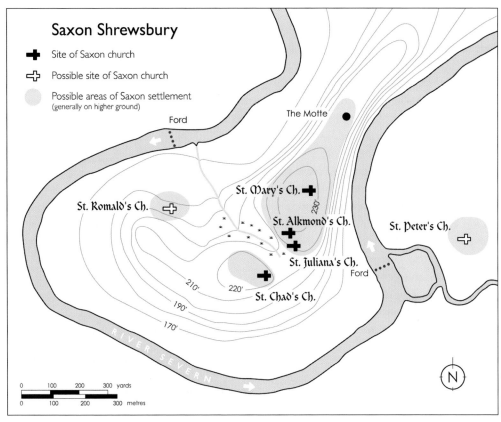

A map of the Saxon settlement areas and topography of the site. It shows a ridge with steep sides rising 60ft (over 18m) above the river which sweeps in a tight horseshoe to leave barely 300 yards (c.275m) across the neck. Two small hills within it were separated by a boggy pond, (now The Square) drained by a stream flowing out near Welsh Bridge. (Stephen de Saulles)

these early ecclesiastical foundations for very specific reasons. The hilltop siting within the river valley would give high visibility from a wide area round about. The surrounding river, and whatever defences existed at the time, afforded them protection but at the same time provided a transport route. The site would also have given a feeling of seclusion and perhaps, given its elevation, a special status.

There is evidence that the churches were built in stone from local quarries. St Alkmund's was the richest foundation. By Edward the Confessor's time the college owned 11 manors, which indicates the nature of the surrounding development outside the burgh, and some 4,000 acres (1,620 hectares) of land. There was another small timber church, outside the protection of the river loop, founded by Siward, a rich Saxon nobleman, the second biggest landowner in the county, on the site of the later Norman abbey and dedicated to St Peter. St Wulfstan, made bishop of Worcester in 1062, was chided by the townspeople for praying in this church on his journeys between Chester and Worcester, in preference to one of the 'finer churches' in the centre of town, which indicates that the churches were already built of stone.

This period of peace was not to last. Soon after Edgar died in 975, the Danes returned. They sacked Chester and created terror in the land again. Edgar's son, Edward the Martyr, was probably murdered by his stepmother to enable her own son, Aethelred, to become king in 978. No warrior, and unable to command the noblemen, he earned his name 'the Unready' or 'Unwise' in being unable to deal with the Danish invaders, and £10,000 was paid to buy them off. Naturally they returned for more, these payments of Danegeld bleeding the country white for many decades. Complaints about it here in Shrewsbury were still being made after the Conquest.

In 1006 it is recorded that being pursued by the Danes, King Aethelred 'went across the Thames into *Scrobbescire* [Shropshire] and there received his food rents and Christmas entertainment', it is believed in Shrewsbury. In the following year he resigned the government of Mercia to his son-in-law Aedric, who resided in the town from time to time.

Aethelred tried bribing the Danish nobles, with promises of land, to fight on his behalf. When the plan failed, he ordered every Dane in England to be killed. In revenge Sweyn, the king of Denmark, raided and plundered every year until, in 1013, the country finally surrendered. Sweyn 'Forkbeard' was crowned in London, but mysteriously died soon after. Sweyn's young son Canute then returned with an army and Aethelred fled to Normandy, leaving his son Edmund 'Ironside' to resist them. Edmund was victorious and agreed to share the kingdom as in Alfred's time. Mercia was to have been governed by Canute, but now Edmund also died suddenly, probably from poison.

Canute thus became king in 1016, and added Britain to his scattered empire. He married Aethelred's widow, Emma of Normandy, became a Christian, restored

A stone grave slab of traditional Saxon design which was found under the foundation of a Norman pier of St Mary's church in 1850. The wheel-headed cross combines pagan and Christian styles and beliefs. By legend, Odin fought a serpent, whilst the 'plaited strap' motif is seen in the 7th-century Lindisfarne Gospel illuminations and in the *c.*650-660 Sutton Hoo treasures, although the thick, four-stranded interlace suggests a later, 10th-century date.
(Stephen de Saulles)

14

Saxon customs and came to be well respected. When he died in 1035, his lands were divided between his sons but the English throne was left vacant for a few years. During this time, around 1039, Gruffyd ap Llewelyn, while endeavouring to unite Wales, caused devastation in some parts of Mercia, including Shrewsbury. The Welsh came to be regarded as a menace for the next quarter century.

Canute's son, Hardicanute, was the last Danish king of England, ruling only between 1040-42. The Witan, (normally summoned by Anglo-Saxon kings themselves), consisting of aldermen, thegns and bishops, had to approve the succession of kings. It now chose Edward (later 'the Confessor'), the son of Aethelred and Emma, and living in Normandy, to become king. He came to England, bringing a number of Norman followers with him, and reigned for 23 years. During these years the influence of the family headed by Earl Godwine grew. Godwine, the son of a Sussex thegn, had been one of Canute's chief counsellors, and when Edward the Confessor died he managed to have his own son crowned as King Harold in 1066.

During this period Shrewsbury's importance had increased and the number of permitted moneyers had been raised to three. The later Domesday survey shows that in the time of Edward the Confessor, the borough still included four churches, but also had three mills and 252 houses, each inhabited by a burgess. (If each burgess had on average a wife and three children, the population would have been 1,260.) There is reason to believe that the houses were probably clustered on the high ground, around the upper part of Wyle Cop, which lends some credence to the legend which places the palace of Brockwel Ysgythrog, prince of Powys, on the site of the collegiate church of St Chad. Each house would have been built with a timber frame, with wattle and daub infill and a thatched roof vulnerable to fire. The fire prevention measures of the time were simple, but probably effective. A burgess whose house caught fire, whether by negligence or accident, was obliged to pay 40 shillings to the king and two shillings to each of his next door neighbours.

Anglo-Saxon kings were peripatetic as this enabled them both to govern their kingdom and to receive the revenue due to them, which often consisted of payments in kind, notably of foodstuffs,

A possible prehistoric marker stone, now preserved on the town side of English Bridge, that would have marked the position of the ford before a bridge existed and that was still in use in Saxon times, when the river level was a few feet lower. It was later used to mark the parish boundary. (Stephen de Saulles)

which they could then consume. Royal visits to Shrewsbury are indeed implied by the duty that was imposed on 12 of the more respected burgesses to act as bodyguards to the king whenever he stayed in the burgh. They were also obliged to provide horses and to accompany him when he went out hunting.

Roman roads had bypassed the site of Shrewsbury, but Saxon routeways focussed on the centre of the city and made use of fords to cross the river, which was then much lower (it is the later weir that has raised levels within the town). There was probably a north to south route crossing the peninsula, linking Chester, Shrewsbury and Hereford, (as the present A49). Another, more minor way, from Siward's church, established a route up from the river crossing near the present English Bridge, then followed the line of Wyle Cop (then much steeper, as the lower part was raised many years later as an anti-flood measure), and Dogpole. On the north-west side of the town, from Wales, there was another ford, and a dry route to the centre along the slight ridge raised above the surrounding marshy land, following the road now called Mardol. There was a third route in from the north through the narrow isthmus created by the tightened river loop.

Thus Shrewsbury became a well-established Saxon burgh of some importance, although our knowledge of it is still hazy.

3 A NORMAN STRONGHOLD

'I was baptized on the sabbath of Easter, at Attingesham, a village of England, seated upon the great river Severn. There, by the ministry of Ordericus the priest, didst Thou, O my God, beget me anew, by water and the Holy Ghost, and gavest unto me the name of my godfather, the aforesaid priest. Thence, at the age of five years, was I sent to school in the city of Scrobesbury; and offered unto Thee the first services of my clergyhood in the church of St Peter and St Paul the apostles. There did Siguard, a famous priest, teach me for the space of five years, the rudiments of the Latin tongue, and instructed me in psalms and hymns, and other necessary parts of education. In the mean time, Thou didst exalt the aforesaid church which belonged to my father, and which was situate on the river Mole, and didst erect the venerable Abbey, through the pious devotion of Roger the Earl.'

Ordericus, b.1075 son of Odelerius Constantius of Orléans, a chief counsellor of Roger de Montgomery, writing *c.*1141 in his fifth book of history just before he died. He was the first Salopian author of whom we have any knowledge.

In just one day, in September 1066, the whole kingdom was lost, and won. From experience gained in Normandy, where he was already called 'the Conqueror' before his English expedition, William reorganised the administration. Despite the pope's blessing received beforehand, he rejected Rome's authority in all church matters. William appointed Lanfranc, who was abbot of Caen and a trained lawyer, to be his archbishop of Canterbury and adviser, thus controlling state and church, acting through the Curia Regis, the body of the king's advisers that replaced the Saxon Witan. Thus all land was to be held from the king by his tenants-in-chief, and their sub-tenants, in exchange for military service or 'burgage', a money payment made in lieu, in the case of some properties in towns.

Most Saxons were removed from positions of trust, at the same time as the Normans devastated large areas of the county. Like the succession of invading Romans, Saxons and Vikings before them, the Normans seemed to be in no hurry to conquer Wales. As each regime in turn before him, William's primary objective was to obtain the submission of the Welsh and prevent their raids on the more prosperous lands this side of the border.

To establish his authority and overawe his new subjects, William had a number of castles quickly erected, built with Saxon labour, to be garrisoned by Norman lords. But within a few months rebellion broke out in the west midlands, led by Edric Sylvaticus, or Edric the Wild, a Saxon thegn who owned large estates in south Shropshire, including one at Bayston in the parish of Condover, and in Herefordshire. In alliance with Owain Gwynedd, prince of north Wales, he harassed the new garrison at Hereford. Then, in 1069, with additional help from Wales and Chester, he besieged the newly constructed castle in Shrewsbury.

King William dispatched two earls to relieve the castle, and forced the attackers to disperse, burning an area of the town as they left. Eventually defeated and captured in a battle at Stafford, one story has it that Edric was leniently treated and subsequently favoured by William. Edric the Wild has always been regarded as a local folklore hero, and one legend lives on. According to this, Edric waits in the old lead mines of the Stiperstones and when war threatens his band of followers is seen riding over the hills, with Edric and his wife at its head.

Roger de Montgomery was a son of William's cousin and contributed some 60 ships, and large sums of money, to the invasion fleet. He had commanded the right wing at the battle of Hastings, been rewarded with the Rape of Arundel (an area roughly equivalent to the modern county of West Sussex), and then had returned to Normandy. William then granted him estates in Shropshire and created him earl of Shrewsbury, one of three powerful overlords entrusted with the duty of safeguarding the Welsh border. These nobles were given additional powers and also large holdings of land from which to raise revenues for funding their military needs. Special rights not shared by other earldoms included those of acquiring further lands in Wales by conquest, administering law and levying taxes. Due to this, the laws and customs of the Marches became different in certain respects, leading to various problems for the Shrewsbury merchants later on.

Roger de Montgomery became one of the largest landowners in England and set about making improvements to the castle. It is likely that he increased the height of the motte, probably cutting back the slope and facing it with stone to make attack more difficult. The Domesday record, a few years later, provides evidence for this work as it states that his castle occupied the space where 51 houses once stood and that 15 more were demolished to give clearance space against fire or attack. The inner bailey, roughly the area of the existing castle grounds, would have been delineated by an earth bank, surmounted by a timber stockade. The ground cleared of houses would have been taken to form the larger outer bailey, again of earth and timber. It apparently followed the line of the high ground from the motte, where Laura's Tower now stands, to half way up St Mary's Water Lane, then turning west to the top near Windsor Place, crossing Castle Street, returning behind the present library to reach the old Foregate (removed for road widening) and the castle.

Roger appears to have been kindly and well-liked. Ordericus Vitalis, the son of Roger's chaplain and adviser, Odelerius, who chronicled the history of the period, describes Roger as wise, moderate, a lover of justice, and one who enjoyed the society of intelligent and unassuming men. He was also a just man; he was evidently willing to improve the conditions of local people. He built a new mill for the townsfolk, and apparently imported stallions from Spain to improve the breed of warhorses in the borderland. He also leased out land in exchange for military service, as was the normal procedure. The western hilly district went to his friend Corbet, who came from Caux in Normandy. He built Caus Castle, and the Corbet name recurs in Shropshire's history through later centuries. Others who came with Roger and owned manors under him include Picot de Say near Clun and Reinauld de Bailleul near Oswestry.

In 1083, Roger's building work on the castle was finished and he sent for his wife to join him from Liseaux. He had left his first wife, Mabel de Belesme, in Normandy to manage his estates, and probably for other reasons as well. (She was murdered in 1072 by four men whose lands she had purloined – according to the confession of one of them dying on a Crusade some years later.) His second wife, Adeliza de Puiset, who seems to have been a very different character, gentle and well-liked, set out to join him. During a rough sea-crossing, Adeliza vowed that if she reached her husband safely, she would build a church in thanksgiving, wherever she found him. When she arrived, he was away hunting a few miles downstream at Quatford, so she was taken to meet him in the forest. There she found him, and the church she built in fulfillment of her vow still stands, two miles south-west of Bridgnorth on the cliff above the river. Under his wife's influence, Roger also re-founded Wenlock Priory, which had been destroyed by the Danes.

The Domesday survey of 1086 shows that there were only two boroughs in Shropshire – Shrewsbury and Quatford – and notes that there were fewer houses than in Edward the Confessor's time. The great grievance that the burgesses (freemen, or citizens) had was also recorded. They complained that, with 51 houses cleared to make space for the earl's enlarged castle and a further 50

The Domesday survey (from Old English 'dom' – 'assessment') shows that in Edward the Confessor's time there was a fort, four churches, three moneyers and 252 houses. Amongst the property owners were the bishop of Chester and 43 French-born burgesses.

demolished to provide clear space round it (a safety measure against surprise attack), together with 39 given in endowment to the abbey that the earl was building, and a further 43 houses occupied by French burgesses who were exempt from tax, the same amount of tax had to be paid as previously – but by only half the number of taxpayers. The outcome of the complaint is not known.

The Abbey

The suburb outside the loop of the river, to the east, had been owned by Siward, a rich Saxon thegn related to King Alfred. It included a 'monasterium', his own private foundation, which included a few monks and was based around a timber church dedicated to St Peter, that may have once been a hermitage. It also had parochial status, and held two manors. The monks claimed that it also had the rights to the tithes of Upton on Severn. Roger granted this monastic estate to his chaplain, Odelerius. In 1082 Odelerius went on a pilgrimage to Rome. He was impressed by the scale and splendour of the buildings there, also dedicated to St Peter, and resolved that if he returned home safely, he would rebuild his own church in stone. Odelerius may also have visited the monastery at Cluny in Burgundy on his return journey. Cluny was where the 'Cluniac Reform' of the Benedictine Rule began, the rule having strayed from its original precepts. St Odo (878-942) had founded an abbey there in 910 that was to be subject only to the pope and thus established the principle of self-governing independence for all Benedictine houses. Its abbot at the time was Hugh (1024-1109) who was said to be the perfect example of the monastic ideal. Any such visit is likely to have inspired Odelerius with confidence in undertaking such a project in Shrewsbury.

On his return, Odelerius inspired Earl Roger (who had founded a private abbey in his home town of Séez, about 20 miles north of Alençon, in France) to found an abbey in Shrewsbury. Odelerius further proposed his own newly acquired property, apart from his own family residence, as its nucleus, exchanging it for the manor at the village now known as Cheney Longville. (At his death, he bequeathed the manor to the abbey.)

On 3 March 1083, the project was approved at a meeting Roger de Montgomery convened at the castle with the sheriff, Warin, Picot de Say and others of his vassals. At the end of the meeting, they walked to the church and, as a token of his vow to found the proposed abbey, he placed his gauntlet on the altar. (At a time when drawing up a written document was a lengthy process, providing a witnessed token of this sort was a common procedure for confirming a contract.) The abbey was to be a house of the Benedictine order, dedicated to saints Peter and Paul. It was still a private foundation and so entirely independent of any religious house, but under the supervision of the diocese of Lichfield.

It was an ambitious development, including the great abbey over 300 feet (nearly 100 metres) long, (only part of which remains, as a church), also various monastic buildings such as cloisters, chapter house, refectory and dormitory. Knowing the building work to be beyond local capabilities, Earl Roger brought two experienced French architect monks over from his own earlier foundation in Normandy to design and direct the work.

For such a project, the site, although restricted, had several advantages. Most importantly, it was on the main entry route into the town. It was also close to the river which would be used for transporting building materials, and to the town for other supplies and services. The town could also supply labour, and temporary accommodation for workpeople from elsewhere. Another major consideration was its potential for milling, the site having control over the Rea brook, an excellent milling stream. Moreover there was also fertile land adjoining for necessary grazing, cultivation and fruit-growing. Significantly, the site was also on the side of the town furthest from Welsh livestock rustlers and other raiders. Its only immediate disadvantage was the liability to occasional flooding. Politically, a stone abbey building together with the commanding castle site, close by on the other side of the river, would not only enhance the status of the town but also emphasise the Norman dominance of the area.

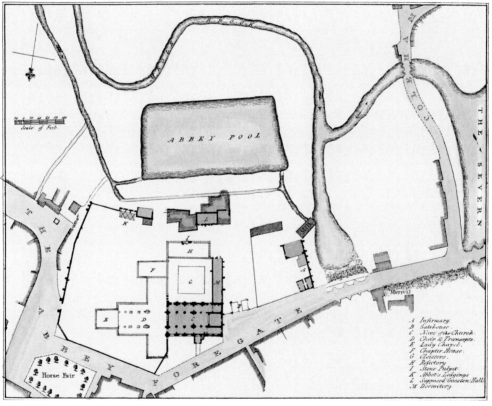

The abbey precinct was bounded on the south and west by the Meole (now Rea) Brook just before it joins the Severn, and on the north by a high, embattled wall of which considerable parts were still standing in the early 19th century when John Carline Jnr drew the plan. Telford's A5 road, constructed in 1836 (after his death), covered the foundations of the chapter house, cloisters and refectory, leaving the reader's pulpit isolated (see p.50). The abbot's fish pond was probably part of the abbey pool which had been two separate pools in 1825.

The abbey mill shown on the previous site plan. Under the founder's grant, confirmed by Henry I, the monks claimed exclusive right to grind all the town's corn. During the next two centuries the townsfolk, resenting this, erected six horse mills and a windmill. The monks appealed to Henry III when he visited Shrewsbury in 1267, and it was agreed that the three mills in the suburbs were to be destroyed while those within the walls and two water mills on the river were to be jointly owned and the profits shared. (SA PR-1-416)

This was a major project for its time, and in this country. It was to be funded by rentals from the Abbey Foregate suburb, and many other properties gifted or bequeathed by landowners. It was to have milling rights over the town and various other sources of income, such as the profits and tolls from the right to hold an annual three day fair. It was also exempted from various tithes, tolls and obligations by charters granted by the king. Nevertheless, funding proved barely adequate at first. It is recorded that the early monks suffered considerable hardships but gradually, as the construction progressed, the religious beliefs of the time prompted increased generosity.

By 1086 the building work was in hand. The intended abbey was to be a 'conventional Norman design', a cruciform, high-roofed structure, having substantial transepts, and with central and west towers. It was to have an apsidal choir, with a rectangular lady chapel beyond. Being in the Norman, or Romanesque style, the typical sturdy drum nave columns, 5ft (nearly 1.5m) in diameter, were necessary to support the heavy clerestorey walls above, only being pierced with small windows, carried on round-headed arches. This was the form developed in continental Europe – where the need was to protect the interior of the building from the heat and strong light of the sun. Further north, this did not apply, but this was not realised until a few years, and a few cathedrals, later. (Here in Shrewsbury, alterations, incorporating larger window openings, were made as soon as circumstances allowed. In a new idiom, involving a less weighty form of construction, columns could be more slender at ground level.)

When building work was sufficiently far advanced to house a nucleus community, the first abbot, Fulchred, was appointed from the founding group of monks, ruling from about 1087-1115. Thus monastic life, with a few French monks, was able to begin.

The Benedictine Rule was the earliest, and most influential, of the monastic 'orders'. It was based on a set of rules compiled by St Benedict of Nursia in about 550. Its purpose was for the monks to devote themselves to God through meditation, prayer and the mass, and to do God's work, Roger de Montgomery introducing a stricter version of the reformed 'Order'. A Benedictine abbey was a close, but not a 'closed' community. Monastic life was devoted to a routine of prayer, worship and manual work, with a sense of balance which was its strength. In addition, Benedictines were obligated to care for the poor and needy and, in particular, to include study. The manual work for Benedictines was not intended to be of the heavy type, which Benedict regarded as discriminating against the weak, but rather it required more specialised 'workshop' and craft work. Monastic communities were not large, even in the major establishments, and in Shrewsbury there were never more than 20 monks.

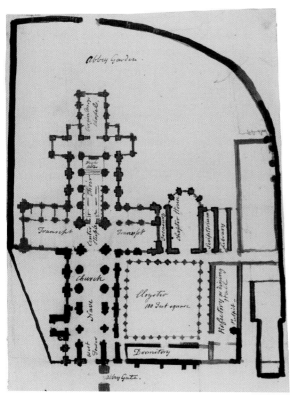

Plan showing the extent of the original Norman abbey started soon after 1083 under the direction of two monks selected for their skills in building, and brought over from France by Roger de Montgomery from the work they had in hand at Séez in Normandy. It was the venue for the historic parliamentary sittings of 1283 and 1397. Doors in the south walls gave access from the dormitories for 1.30am Matins and from the refectory for processing and chanting grace after meals, and to the chapter house for the 5am assembly through the opening, now blocked, behind the founder's tomb. The parts outlined in black were spared at the Dissolution. (SA 6001-198-399)

Monasteries aimed at self-sufficiency through their own agricultural, horticultural, piscatorial, brewing and other activities. In Shrewsbury, their manual work would have included extensive building work and farming, as well as milling and various indoor crafts and skills. The emphasis on study is indicated by their sending monks to university, and they built up a significant library.

Both Fulchred and his successor were French, coming from Roger de Montgomery's abbey in Séez. Subsequent abbots were elected for life by the monks, usually from their own number. Their choice was based partly on seniority, but also on the basis of abilities and leadership qualities. Being under crown patronage from 1102, their choice had to be approved by the king. Reputedly a powerful speaker, Abbot Fulchred spoke out against the unpopular William II. Preaching in Gloucester in August 1100, he allegedly predicted the king's death as a godly punishment, saying 'The bow of celestial anger is bent against the reprobate; and an arrow, swift to wound, is drawn from the quiver'. Next day, while out hunting in the New Forest William was killed by a companion's arrow. When Earl Roger died, Fulchred probably conducted his burial 'between the two altars'.

Death of Earl Roger, and revolt

By 1094, Earl Roger had been ailing, and a few days before his death he entered the monastery, allegedly with his wife Adeliza's permission, and with a shaven head, as a monk. Entitled as a lay associate of a Benedictine House to wear the 'kirtle (or tunic) of

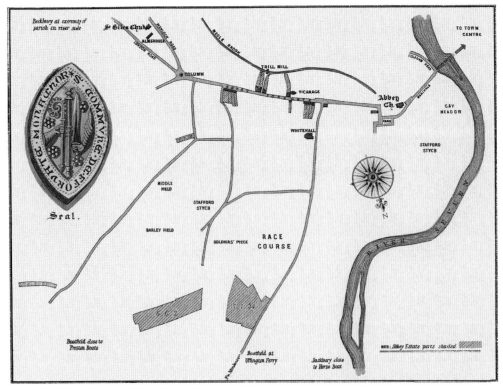

An account of Edward III's time, partially confirmed by Domesday, indicates the local estates granted to the abbey as shown on this later map.

St Hugh' he had received from Cluny, (again suggesting the link with that centre), and to be buried within the abbey, Earl Roger took the first vows of a monk a few days before he died, and was buried between the two altars in the choir and the lady chapel. His body may have been removed to a more imposing tomb in the newly completed lady chapel at the same time as the later building of St Winefride's shrine, a shrine built to house the saint's bones with their legendary powers of healing, brought from Wales to encourage pilgrims (see below). This could account for the style of the armour on what is now believed to be Roger de Montgomery's effigy being about a hundred years later than the armour he would have worn. After the Dissolution, when the lady chapel was destroyed, the tomb was moved into the nave and was ascribed to Roger when the Heralds of the College of Arms made their inspection in 1623. (There is also a story that a possible grave was found during some early excavations, but this has never been confirmed.)

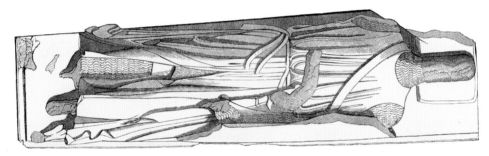

A Victorian illustration of a damaged effigy from the part of the abbey destroyed by Henry VIII ascribed to Roger de Montgomery during the Heralds' visit of 1623 to authenticate pedigrees and coats of arms in use. The armour, however, is of a later period. His tomb is now in the south aisle of the abbey church, as in the lower photograph. (Stephen de Saulles)

On Earl Roger's death, his possessions were divided between his two sons. Hugh, the son of Adeliza, inherited the Shropshire lands, while Robert de Belesme received the estates in Normandy. Within four years, Earl Hugh was killed on Anglesey fighting Viking raids, allegedly by an arrow fired by Magnus, king of Norway. By paying a large sum of money to the king for the privilege, his brother Robert gained possession of the Shropshire estates.

On William II's death, his younger brother Henry seized the throne. His elder brother, also named Robert, who had been granted Normandy when William the Conqueror died, now sought to take the throne and landed in southern England. One of the nobles to support him was Robert de Belesme, who had strengthened the castles at Shrewsbury, Montgomery and Ludlow, and built a new castle at Bridgnorth. Part of the castle at Shrewsbury was allegedly still in timber, but included a barrier wall across the isthmus. King Henry quickly captured Bridgnorth and then, cutting a new route over Wenlock Edge, perhaps that still used today, reached Shrewsbury, where Robert de Belesme had retired so as to be closer to his Welsh allies.

By tradition it was through this still existing Norman gateway that the leader of the barons' revolt, Robert de Belesme, came out 'bearing himself the keys' to surrender his possessions to King Henry I in 1102.
(Stephen de Saulles)

Surprised by Henry's speed of action, Robert de Belesme met the king at the gates, confessed his treason and relinquished the keys of the castle. He was banished from the country, to the great relief of the townspeople he had oppressed, and his property was forfeited to the Crown. Shrewsbury Castle thus became a royal fortress, under the custody of a constable.

From later references in a charter of King John's reign, which referred to rights and privileges gained in his great-grandfather's time, it seems that Henry I helped the city's recovery in various ways, and probably visited from time to time. At the beginning of his reign in 1100, he had issued a Charter of Liberties in which he agreed that the Saxons should be governed by the laws in force during the reign of Edward the Confessor. He also lifted various irksome restrictions which had been imposed, such as the curfew which kept citizens indoors during hours of darkness. During Henry I's reign (1100-35) trade increased, towns grew, Oxford University was founded, and Cistercian monks arrived and began the sheep-farming in the more desolate parts of the kingdom on which later prosperity, including Shrewsbury's, was to be founded. Administrative systems were improved, and the Exchequer was introduced, taking its name from the chequered boards used to calculate the taxes. A merchant guild is also thought to have been formed as early as 1128.

In Shrewsbury, both bridges had been built before 1100, and one of them, now English Bridge, in stone, probably by the monks while they built the abbey. (When new water mains were laid in 1999, remains of the early bridge were found beneath the Abbey Foregate roadway outside the Wakeman school, showing that the monks constructed not simply a bridge across the Severn, but a bridge and causeway which spanned two minor streams near the abbey, an island [now Coleham Head], and then presumably more flood-plain to reach Wyle Cop. ['Wyle', from the Welsh *hwylfa* – a road leading up a hillside, and *coppa* – top or head.] The total length of the combined bridges and causeway would have been over a fifth of a mile long.)

Abbot Godfrey, the second of the French abbots, ruling from about 1115 to 1128, equalled Fulchred's reputation for preaching. It is reported that he died suddenly, 'worn out by age'. He was followed by Abbot Herbert (1128-38), who was evidently not a success. Historian Orderic Vitalis recorded that 'he usurped the rudder of the infant establishment'. However, his period of office was distinguished (until he was deposed by the papal legate's council in Westminster) by a remarkable event: the acquisition by the abbey of the bones of a saint.

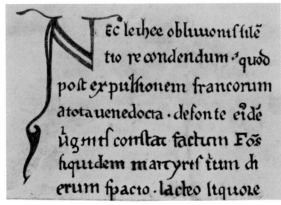

The legends of St Winefride's bones as recorded in the Latin Cotton MS in the 11th century.
In 1137 Abbot Herbert sent his prior to negotiate with the Welsh for the acquisition of the remains of St Winefride. She is still celebrated in the abbey church, and present-day pilgrims still visit her well, at Holywell, Flintshire, referring to it as the Lourdes of Wales.
(SA 6001-198-403)

St Winefride

By the 1130s, the monks had evidently been expressing concern over the lack of holy relics in their church. Prior Robert wrote, 'the monks very much lamented amongst themselves that they were very deficient in the relics of saints'. The monks began a search and found the remains of St Winefride in Wales. Winefride was the daughter of a 7th-century Welsh prince who had taken a vow of celibacy. A young nobleman, Caradoc, fell in love with her, but angered by her rejection of his passionate advances, he cut off her head as she ran. According to legend, her head rolled to where her uncle, St Bueno was praying nearby.

Cursing Caradoc, he replaced it on her body, and she lived whilst Caradoc 'melted away as wax before the fire', or some say that 'the ground swallowed him up' – and at the spot, a well sprang up, which became an object of local pilgrimage and alleged miracles.

In 1137, Abbot Herbert sent a deputation to Basingwerk Abbey in Wales, where the bones currently rested, to negotiate to acquire the relics. Prior Robert duly led a party of monks to the village of Gwytherin, near Basingwerk Abbey. They were well received by everyone except one Welshman who vowed he would not let them take the relics. That night, the monks had a vision of the Virgin Mary, assuring them of success. Prior Robert reported that he saw the ghost of Abbot Godfrey, and that the ghost had also encouraged them. Consequently, the next day, the priest who cared for the graves, and had also had a supportive dream, allowed the bones to be exhumed. Robert and the priest reported the visions and dream to the villagers, and gained their approval. (The objector was persuaded by a suitable bribe.) The bones, carefully wrapped in a linen cloth, were carried to Shrewsbury, and taken overnight to St Giles church on the way into the town.

Next morning, while preparations were being made at the abbey, and the arrival of the bishop awaited, there occurred the miraculous cure of a youth of the town who had lost the use of his limbs. He came to St Giles on horseback, held up on each side; but he returned home on foot. In due course the procession set off for the abbey, and as rain fell, the procession of precious ornaments from the abbey that was accompanying St Winefride's bones on this final stage of the journey remained dry, the rain 'restrained by a celestial power'. The bones were re-interred in a shrine at the west end of the abbey, and the news of the miracles spread across the county, attracting many pilgrims and bringing great wealth and a powerful reputation to the abbey.

The Anarchy

On Henry I's death in 1135, a Civil War ensued between the supporters of two rival claimants to the throne. Henry's only legitimate son, Prince William, had been drowned, with many others, when the *White Ship* sank in 1120 off the coast of France. This left his widowed daughter, Matilda, as his heir. Matilda had subsequently been married to Geoffrey of Anjou; his badge was a sprig of broom, the *planta genista* that later gave the name Plantagenet to her heirs. Henry made his illegitimate son, Robert Fitzroy, Lord of Gloucester and Glamorgan. However, although Henry had made the barons swear that they would accept his daughter Matilda as his heir, when it came to the actual succession, there was some reluctance to accept a female monarch.

When King Henry I died in 1135, Stephen, the king's nephew, and grandson of William the Conqueror, (being the son of William the Conqueror's youngest daughter), immediately crossed from France to claim the throne, and was crowned in Matilda's place. Despite earlier assurances to Henry, Stephen was quickly accepted by the Church, the city of London and high officials, because he was male, well-known and popular. By contrast, Matilda had only spent two years in England and was female, and her new husband, Geoffrey, was hated by the Normans for his cruelty.

Robert Fitzroy initially supported Stephen, but then changed allegiance and became the head of Matilda's cause in England. Much of Shropshire, Herefordshire and Gloucestershire followed suit in declaring for Matilda, and the then governor of Shrewsbury, William Fitzalan, garrisoned the castle in her cause. In 1138 King Stephen with his army besieged the castle for four weeks. Eventually Fitzalan fled and Stephen, 'exasperated by their obstinacy', put 93 of the defenders to death. Following this, other castles were forced to surrender.

Empress Matilda herself eventually landed in England, and warfare between the opposing factions became general on the frontiers of the country. Unlicensed castles were built, mercenaries plundered, 'unspeakable torture' took place and no man's castle was safe. Crops rotted because there was no one to harvest them; reapers had taken sanctuary or died of hunger. Barbarism was not confined to any one side, and often the damage was caused by foreign mercenaries. When Robert died, Matilda, although still considered the rightful heir by some, retired to Normandy, but during this period of anarchy, Matilda's son Henry reached maturity. After something of a military stand-off, it was agreed that Stephen would remain king during his lifetime, that Matilda's son, Henry would succeed him, and that in the meantime they would 'share in the government' and work to rectify the damage done. This agreement was confirmed by the Treaty of Winchester in 1153, and on Stephen's death the following year, Henry succeeded him. Fitzalan returned to the castle, and 'normal service was resumed'.

In barely a century, a comparatively small number of Norman lords, together with their immediate followers, had transformed the country. They had created a united and strong

King Stephen as depicted on a coin dating from his reign (1135-54).

29

system of government in place of Saxon states, replaced the Witan with the more centralised Curia Regis, and established a feudal system that made military service an obligation on all landowners. It had introduced a new ruling aristocracy with French manners, customs and language, which all developed in parallel with the native Anglo-Saxon. All these fused into the beginnings of a new culture, and a new association with France that has been reinforced in Shrewsbury in various ways in later periods.

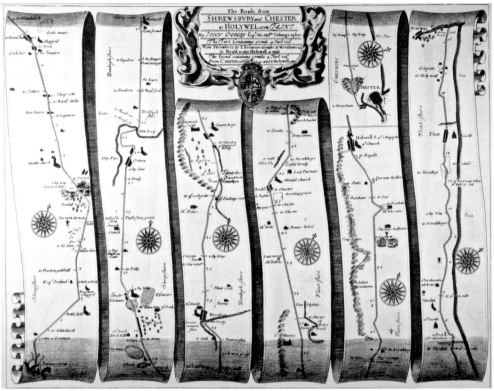

John Ogilby's strip road map of the roads from Shrewsbury and Chester to Holywell, site of St Winefride's Well, published in his *Britannia* atlas of 1675. (SA CM/2/35)

4 PLANTAGENET SHREWSBURY AND THE WELSH CONFLICT

'We then came to Slopesbury, a town almost surrounded by the river Severn: here we spent a few days to recruit, after the fatigues of our journey, and here too, thanks to the admonitions of the Archbishop and the gracious sermons of the Archdeacon of Minevia [St David's], we persuaded many to follow the cross. We also excommunicated Owain de Keveiliauc [Owen Cyfeiliog] because he was the only Welsh prince who had refused to come with his people to meet the Archbishop.'

Giraldus Cambrensis, Archdeacon of Minevia, writing of his journey through Wales in 1188 with the archbishop of Canterbury preaching the Crusade.

When Henry II came to the throne in 1154 he was the head of an Anglo-French empire, and the most powerful man in Europe. Clever, well-educated, speaking several languages, he was an expert in law and tirelessly energetic. He travelled widely through his dominions with all the trappings of a medieval court. In England, he set about repairing the damage of the previous 20 years. The castles erected without the king's permission during the Anarchy were destroyed, and the countryside returned to cultivation. Travelling judges heard cases in the shire courts, and the common law of England evolved above the justice of the barons' courts and, alongside it statute law, made and written down by Parliament. Early in his reign, Henry with his army passed through Shrewsbury in 1158, on an expedition into Wales.

By 1150 Shrewsbury was the foremost market town in the Marches, and the king had forbidden wool merchants to buy any wool in the county other than in the market towns – which gave Shrewsbury a valuable commercial advantage. Also at this time there was another, possibly even more important trade. There was not only a thriving leather industry in Frankwell and probably also near the quay by the old Stone Bridge, but leather was also being imported from Cordova for making-up and tooling in the town.

By 1164 Henry was evidently beginning to rebuild the castle, using stone. Evidence of probable increased height was found in 2008 by archaeologists using ground-penetrating radar. It revealed the buried foundations of stone buildings, and showed that the existing parapet walls are built up on medieval walls that were over six feet (2 metres) thick. The royal accounts, called Pipe Rolls from the way in which they were stored, record frequent expenditure between 1166-87 on the defences, and 'the king's house in the castle'. Thus it can be said that it was Henry II, who reigned till 1189, who built the first main hall, added a tower, incorporated a chamber of some kind, and built the inner bailey wall in stone.

The abbey was developing its own spirit of enterprise. By the reign of Henry II, the monks had contrived to enhance the attractiveness of the original shrine of St Winefride by adding relics of Thomas à Becket, including fragments of his attire such as his hair shirt, his collar, girdle, cowl, woollen shirt, a glove and some cloth stained with his blood and brains. These were all allegedly brought from Canterbury by Adam, abbot of Shrewsbury at the time of the prelate's death. Adam had made a pilgrimage to Canterbury not simply to expiate his owns sins, but also probably to enrich 'the sacristy of his abbey with relics which would be as efficacious as those of the Cambrian virgin, for the cure of diseases'.

The history of Shrewsbury at this time shows a town gradually gaining independence from the Crown – by charters purchased from, or granted by, the king. Kings used

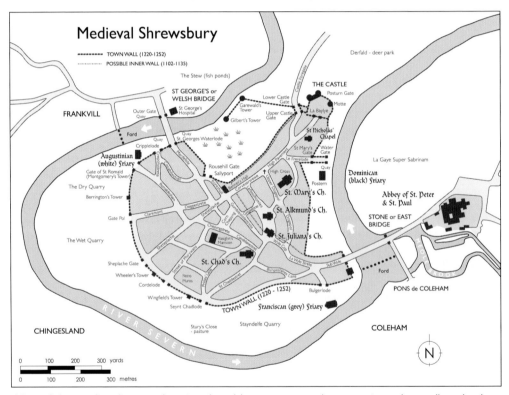

Map of the medieval town, showing the old street names (not consistently used) and other features. Shrewsbury has one of the best-preserved street layouts of the period in the UK with many of the property boundaries remaining unchanged. The map shows the main stone buildings of the time, and the approximate lines of the old town walls. At intervals along these walls were watch towers, postern gates that gave access to pasture and arable land used by the town dwellers and openings giving access to the friars whose houses lay outside the walls. The openings, known as lodes, also provided drainage outlets for surface water and sewage, the lanes leading to them being known as waterlodes. (Stephen de Saulles)

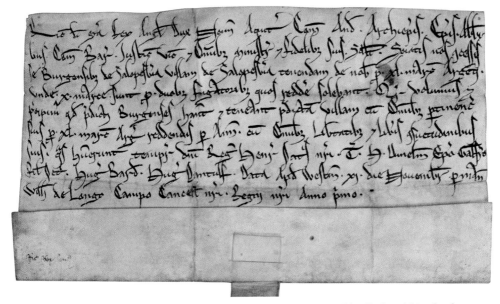

The earliest charter for Shrewsbury, still preserved, was granted by Richard I in the first year of his reign and within three months of returning from the Crusades where he had heard of the death of his father, Henry II. An earlier charter of Henry II had been lost by the time of Elizabeth. (SA 3365-1)

charters as instruments of government and control, and also as a way of gaining favours, or of raising money for national and royal household expenditure. Charters could give a town the right to collect dues, establish its own court, elect officials, form a merchant guild or hold markets. Of Shrewsbury's remarkable set of more than 40, the earliest may have been granted by Henry I. In 1170 the town paid two marks to Henry II for the right to collect its own rents and, five years later, agreed to pay £20 a year plus two hunting dogs for further privileges. The earliest charter that is still preserved was obtained in 1189.

Richard I (1189-99) and King John (1199-1216) were especially cooperative in the matter of grants. By the end of Richard's reign, the burgesses had been granted a charter by which they held the town in return for 40 marks of silver every year. (A mark was 8-10 ozs, or 230-280 gm of silver. Ten marks would have been about the value of a pair of hunters or 50 oxen.) In 1199, a charter from King John allowed them to appoint two of their number to rule the town as provosts. Two further charters in 1205 and 1209, achieved largely through the strength and vigour of the town's Merchant Guild, provided a major breakthrough in obtaining full autonomy.

The Guild then included all the trades and crafts, probably a hundred or more, and anyone trading in the town had to be a member. The skills would have covered various types of leather workers such as tanners, skinners, shoemakers, glovers, 'boulgers' (purse or pouch makers) and parchment dealers; craftsmen in metal, stone, wood and horn; and workers in the cloth trade such as drapers (cloth makers), shearmen (cloth finishers), tailors and mercers (textile dealers). In addition, there were all the trades associated with an important fortress town, such as armourers, bowyers, fletchers (arrow makers) and farriers (smiths); and also those connected with the river, including boat building, sail making and chandling, (candle and lamp makers); the various building crafts, and those involved in the production of food. As time went on, others were permitted to practise a craft by paying an annual fine, but they did not share in the same immunity from external taxes or other privileges.

Burgess numbers were restricted, and their rights jealously guarded. They obtained the rights by birth, or by serving a seven-year apprenticeship within the borough to a freeman of an incorporated company. By 1209 only burgesses were allowed to buy the all-important hides or undressed cloth in the Shrewsbury market. Goods had to be processed in Shrewsbury before resale to others, and this gave an advantage over traders from outside the town.

Richard Coeur de Lion, away at the Crusades, spent only a few months in the kingdom during his ten year reign. In 1199 his brother John succeeded him. John is remembered for his quarrels with his barons, the loss of the lands in France and his oppression of the people resulting in the issuing of Magna Carta – the Great Charter. In the meantime, the Marcher lordships in the west of his remaining kingdom had consolidated as independent buffer states between the Welsh and the central royal authority exercised by succeeding kings. Wales was divided into three main kingdoms. They were frequently at war between themselves, occasionally making alliances with rebels, making independent attacks on lands this side of the border, or resisting the encroachments of the marcher lords.

Owain Gwynedd, ruler of Gwynedd (1137-69) had resisted the English under Henry II. His grandson, Llewelyn ap Iorwerth (the Great), ruling the princedom from 1192 to 1240, was dedicated to relieving the injustices which his people felt had been done towards the original British who had been driven west by successive invaders into the mountain areas west of Offa's Dyke.

In 1192 Llewelyn called a meeting of all the Welsh lords at which they resolved to restore Wales to its old boundaries, and swore homage to him. Later, he sent a deputation to Rome, requesting the pope to release him and other Welsh lords from their oaths of fealty (loyalty or homage) to the English king. The pope, having little regard for John, granted the request. The king endeavoured to gain Llewelyn's favour by giving him his daughter in marriage with the lordship of Ellesmere as a dowry. However, in 1211 Llewelyn began open warfare against his father-in-law. John's response included seeking the favour and support of Shrewsbury by granting further charters. The privileges then given included the right to take tolls on all merchandise brought into the town by the Welsh. (The Welsh woollen trade was considerable by this time.) John assembled an army and pursued Llewelyn around the north Wales coastlands, but Llewelyn cut off his retreat and inflicted heavy losses. John returned in the following year with larger and better equipped forces, and this time Llewelyn sued for peace through his wife Joan. Satisfied with this humiliation, John retired, taking nearly 30 high-born hostages, and valuable spoils in the way of cattle and horses.

Sore at this defeat, Llewelyn called another council in 1213, and raised an army of many thousands, capturing several castles garrisoned by the English. They next attacked the marcher lords. King John reacted by ordering that the hostages be put to death. This exacerbated the situation, and caused some of the English barons to support Llewelyn, fearful for the safety of their own offspring at John's hands. In 1215 Llewelyn advanced on Shrewsbury and the town and castle were handed to him without a fight.

When John died in 1216, his son Henry III was still a child. The elderly William the Marshall, earl of Pembroke, was chosen as regent by the peers. Disregarding the Welsh grievances, he seized a castle in south Wales. Llewelyn retaliated by devastating the earl's lands while he was away in Ireland. When Hubert de Burgh, who had been prominent in the Magna Carta negotiations, was appointed regent in 1218 on Marshall's death, one of his first acts was to issue an instruction to the townspeople of Shrewsbury to 'enclose the town strongly'. Shrewsbury was now in the front line, and the bailiffs (king's or lord's representatives) were charged with the responsibility for the construction of the walls and their upkeep. To finance the work the town was granted the right to collect a murage toll on all goods brought into the town. Records show that the fortifications took over 30 years to build.

Although a treaty was signed with the Welsh in Shrewsbury in 1221, work on the walls must have been put in hand fairly quickly because only four years later King Henry III issued a writ commanding the sheriff to allow the preaching friars (the Dominican friars who had come from Normandy in the previous year) to have the stone which 'lay in the Severn under the bailey of the castle' for the building of their church, which was to be outside 'the walls newly built of stone', near St Mary's Water Lane. While this tells us that at least that section of the walls had been completed, it raises the query as to how the stone came to be in the river for the friars to salvage. It is thought that

Remains of the outer towns walls, built when trouble on the border prompted Henry III to order the townspeople in 1218 'to enclose the town strongly'. (Stephen de Saulles)

stone for the walls was brought upstream from a quarry near Haughmond Hill, probably being unloaded at a landing by the Watergate, later Union Wharf. Was too much delivered there instead of being taken further round the loop for later sections of the work? Was there a series of mishaps, or had the old facing on the motte been eroded and fallen in the river?

The new 13th-century walls were built outside a conjectured earlier inner ring of walls in places (see map on p.32). They took a wider sweep from Wyle Cop, round the line of the roadway called, appropriately, Town Walls enclosing the various properties that had been developed outside the possible line of an earlier wall, and included the 'second hill' within the fortified area. The 'second hill' was the higher land on which old St Chad's collegiate church was built, the site of the legendary Welsh palace. A debate continues as to whether the various retaining walls and terracing evident in many undercrofts and cellars in the town first formed part of an earlier defensive wall. These walls have generally been roughly built in irregular courses in friable red sandstone from the Dingle area in the Quarry (now part of the town's parks), up to c.3ft (nearly 1m) thick, and were erected between about 1100 and 1135.

The stone arch at the bottom of St Mary's Water Lane, known as the Watergate or sometimes as the 'Traitors Gate' for the part it played in the town's later history, is the only 13th-century gateway still standing. Other parts of existing fortifications were strengthened, and St George's Bridge fortified with round towers on the town side. The

Wheeler's Tower is the sole surviving 14th-century watchtower on the town walls. Watchtowers were spaced c.500ft (155m) apart and linked by a raised walkway indicated by the high doorway. (Stephen de Saulles)

In 1252 a law was passed ordering all men between the ages of 15 and 60 to equip themselves with bows and arrows to fend off Welsh attacks. Further legislation in 1363, in the reign of Edward III, made it obligatory for men to practise archery every Sunday. This would have been after church at nearby 'butts' as evidenced by the depth of the grooves scored into the stonework of St Mary's church where men evidently sharpened their arrows.
(Stephen de Saulles)

massive defensive ditch north of the castle, now occupied by the railway, was reinforced with a huge drawbridge and chevaux de fuisse (a palisade of sharpened stakes set close and pointed outward to deter charging horses and hinder scaling). The landward entrance to the town below the castle was fortified with two sets of round towers with portcullis in 1234, and remained in place until removed for road widening in comparatively recent times.

Henry III, while still young, came to his Shrewsbury base several times in his attempts to subdue the Welsh, or make peace with them. (On one subsequent occasion, the king, known for his love of pomp, is alleged to have arrived and departed in a highly ornamental royal barge.) In 1232 the pope intervened in the dispute and, on his orders, peace negotiations were due to be held in St Mary's church. However, in 1234 Llewelyn, now allied with Richard Marshal, took Powis Castle and advanced on Shrewsbury a second time, devastating part of the town (perhaps Frankwell outside the walls), and also laying waste large areas of land between Shrewsbury and Oswestry.

By 1237 Joan had died and Llewelyn, getting old himself, called his lords together, exhorted them to remain faithful to the cause, and appointed his son David as his successor. David, however, was not as resolute as his father, and he paid homage to Henry. Henry evidently decided to press the advantage gained. In 1241 he marched to Shrewsbury with his army, staying a fortnight. Prince David relinquished all the land his father had regained during the wars with King John. Five years later, David and the Welsh lords chose two of Llewelyn's grandsons to succeed him, Owain and Llewelyn ap Gruffydd but, after a few years, the brothers disagreed and Llewelyn became the sole ruler. Soon he was being urged by Simon de Montfort, earl of Leicester, who had his own quarrels with the king, to resist the oppression of the Marcher lords, as his illustrious predecessor had done. The two men combined to fight Henry III and his supporters. However, Henry's son, Edward, was well supported by the Marcher lord Roger Mortimer, amongst others, and in due course crushed de Montfort at the battle of Evesham, and the Marchers soon turned their attentions to Llewellyn, seeking to

Between 1220 and 1250 the landward entrance to the town below the castle was fortified with two sets of round towers and portcullis gates. They were completed at about the time of the attack by Llewelyn the Great in 1234. The lower set opposite Meadow Place were demolished piecemeal, 1773-1825; the upper set on the corner by the library, referred to as the Burgess Gate and used as a prison, was demolished c.1780 and the road level lowered in 1825 to ease the gradient.
(Shropshire Archives)

regain lands lost to him in the previous years. In 1272 Henry III died and Edward was crowned King Edward I.

Llewelyn ap Gruffydd had been affianced to Eleanor, a daughter of Simon de Montfort. She had sought safety in France, and on her way back to marry Llewelyn she was captured by King Edward's men and taken to London. Infuriated, Llewelyn raided the borderlands, but offered to meet the king at Oswestry or Shrewsbury to give his oath of fealty in exchange for Eleanor's release. Edward refused and declared Llewelyn a rebel. He set out for Wales with the archbishop of Canterbury, intending to subdue the Welsh by diplomacy if possible, and ultimately Llewelyn made peace. In 1280 Edward held a court at Chester to hear the Welsh complaints, which it seems were not all against the English; some were against Llewelyn himself.

After the hearing, the king summoned Llewelyn to attend his court. Offended by the manner of the command, Llewelyn refused, and again resorted to arms to defend his countrymen's rights. Leaving his brother David in command in north Wales, Llewelyn went south, where he was killed in a skirmish near Builth Wells soon after, probably as a result of treachery, and his head was put on display in London. David continued the struggle for a time but was finally defeated, taken prisoner and brought in chains to Shrewsbury. Determined to settle the Welsh trouble for good, in 1283 Edward summoned Parliament to meet in the abbey's chapter house to try the captured Prince David for treason.

This was the first (constitutional) Parliament at which commoners were represented, building upon a process begun by Simon de Montfort when he was essentially in control of the government, while holding Henry III as a prisoner in all but name. (The abbots had been obliged to sit in Parliament from about 1250 and Shrewsbury was one of the first boroughs to be represented in 1268.) Now, 20 principal towns, including Shrewsbury, were instructed to send two deputies, and each sheriff of the shire to send two knights. They met at the abbey, and David was condemned on five charges, ranging from being a traitor to committing murders on Palm Sunday. As a traitor knight, he was to be dragged through the town at the tail of a horse, and then to be hanged and quartered, his quarters being sent to York, Bristol, Northampton and Winchester. As evidence of the final outcome, his head was displayed alongside his brother's at the

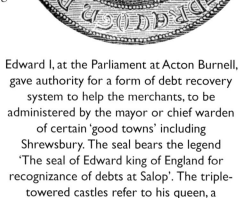

Edward I, at the Parliament at Acton Burnell, gave authority for a form of debt recovery system to help the merchants, to be administered by the mayor or chief warden of certain 'good towns' including Shrewsbury. The seal bears the legend 'The seal of Edward king of England for recognizance of debts at Salop'. The triple-towered castles refer to his queen, a princess of Castille. (Shropshire Archives)

The finely gilded and illuminated initial letter of a charter from King Edward I granted in 1291 to the Austin Friars. It shows him holding an orb and sceptre, receiving a supplication from the friars in connection with an embattled building overlooking the river, which was to be available to the bailiffs in time of war, reverting to the friars in times of peace. (SA 6001-115)

Tower of London. The gruesome execution took place near the High Cross, and is commemorated on a plaque nearby.

Edward's Chancellor of England was Robert Burnell of Shropshire, and after sentencing David, the Parliament adjourned to his castle at Acton Burnell. The lords' sitting was in the castle's hall, while the commons sat in the stone barn close by – whose gable end walls can still be seen. There, they passed legislation in connection with local commerce, and in particular, the extensive woollen trade based on two main centres at the time, Oswestry and Shrewsbury.

To enforce the peace with Wales, Edward I initiated a programme of stone castle building, not only on the borders but also deep in Wales itself, at Conway, Harlech, Caernarvon and elsewhere, each castle to be strongly garrisoned to prevent further trouble.

More work was also carried out at Shrewsbury Castle, completing it almost in its present form. The long period of border wars thus came to an end. Thereafter the hostilities were on a lesser scale, with the exception of the Glyn Dwr rising, and Shrewsbury's military importance was much reduced. Peace allowed trade and commerce to flourish.

The Wool Trade

During the 1200s the wool merchants were establishing family businesses that became élite merchant dynasties, and these years saw the formation of a loose association that gradually developed into a merchant guild. Members of the families who formed the different trade guilds started to fill the various public offices, and the guilds were set to become a dominant element in the town, by the 14th century administering all the trade in the town.

John is the first recorded member of the 'de Ludlow' family living in Shrewsbury, presumably descended from a Ludlow family whose head might have been steward to the Norman de Lacy family. The stewardship would have given him an opportunity to accumulate wealth, and then make a move to Shrewsbury – a more developed and advanced town than Ludlow. With his administrative experience (and contacts), he became a successful entrepreneur in the wool trade, supplying high quality wool to the cloth-making cities in Flanders and France.

In 1250 Nicholas de Ludlow (*c.*1200-78) emerges in Shrewsbury as 'wool merchant to Edward', the future Edward I. He was mentioned frequently and acknowledged to be the richest wool merchant in England. Recent research now considers that he built the impressive stone hall, later known as Bennet's Hall (at the back of No.2 Pride Hill), and that he traded from there. (Parts of the hall are preserved, and can be seen at the rear of the present retail shop.) In 1261 the bailiffs' toll records show that Nicholas de Ludlow sent a total of 37 sacks of wool out through the Castle Gates, and 118 through the Abbey Gate – reckoned to be a total of nearly 40,000 fleeces. He also traded in cloth and skins. Nicholas became the equivalent of a multi-millionaire and when he died in 1279, continental merchants referred to him as a 'King's merchant'.

The Friaries

Shrewsbury must have been one of the first towns chosen by the Dominican Friars in which to establish a base. A mendicant order approved by Pope Honorius III in 1216, who had associations with the universities in Toulouse and Bologna, the Dominicans were dedicated to preaching and education and so normally selected university towns, first settling in England at Oxford in 1221. A year later, the king gave them a site outside Shrewsbury's newly constructed walls, alongside St Mary's Water Lane, near St Mary's

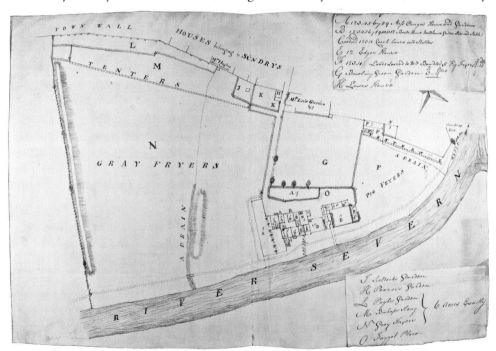

Plan of the area, a short way upstream of the Dominican friary, given to the Franciscan or Grey Friars, who came to Shrewsbury c.1245. In the 14th century Hawise, heir to the ancient princes of Powys, and wife of Lord Charlton, may have funded the building of their church, thought to be the original location of the Jesse window now in St Mary's (see p.47). Her father and grandfather had been interred there. (SA 6001-198-145)

Well, which was alleged to have holy properties. With gifts from the king and town, the friars constructed their buildings below the town wall, forming an embankment projecting into the river to strengthen the riverside foundations. The monks at the abbey feared that it would interfere with the river flow, and also their fishery tolls if river traffic was affected. They went to law, and some of the monks also destroyed part of a ditch built by the friars. In 1269 the case ended with the friars being allowed to occupy some neighbouring land as well.

The Franciscans were granted a site a little further upstream in 1245. They ministered especially to the poor, and those not eligible to be members of the protected trade guild. One burgess built them a church. According to tradition, it was large enough to house the famous stained glass Jesse window now in St Mary's church. Another burgess built their domestic quarters. The king again provided materials, including 50 loads of lime and 40 quarters of chalk, presumably for the protective lime washing of their stonework. In their excessive zeal for poverty, it is related that the friars requested clay mud in lieu of stone walls in their dormitory. The benefactor evidently preferred to meet the additional cost involved in using a more permanent material, and probably had little sympathy with their extreme and unwise desire for 'sackcloth and ashes'.

The Austin Friars arrived in 1250. They were given a site near Welsh Bridge on marshy ground that had been used as a burial ground during the papal interdict of King John's reign – the national equivalent to 'excommunication'. Their church possessed the right of sanctuary, by which even a murderer could claim 40 days' immunity from the law.

The friars represented a new religious movement in reaction to the property-owning monastic orders of the time, and re-established their earlier more strict rules. The Black Friars founded by the Castilian, St Dominic, based themselves on the teachings of St Augustine and were dedicated to learning. (The prior of Shrewsbury's Dominican Friars preached before Richard II in the 1380s and 1390s, but not, as far as we know, in the town itself.) The Franciscans, known as Grey Friars from the colour of their habits, followed the teachings of St Francis of Assisi. Friars were educated and dedicated men living by Christian principles, but entirely independent of church and state. Nationally, and surely locally, they made a fundamental contribution to social welfare and education. They were certainly welcomed and much respected in the town.

Affairs at the Abbey
Henry, a monk from Evesham Abbey, was elected by the community as its abbot between the years 1251 and 1258. While he had been a cardinal's chaplain in Rome, he took the opportunity to meet the pope, who later granted him the right to wear the ring generally only given to bishops and cardinals. Although this annoyed the king, he still entrusted Abbot Henry with a personal mission to the king of Castile, whose daughter Eleanor was to marry Henry III's son, the future Edward I. He completed his mission, but became ill, and resigned the abbacy on his return in 1258. He later left the abbey and the Benedictine Order, so he was listed surprisingly as a 'fugitive monk' by the Benedictine General Chapter.

Following him was another troubled abbacy. Abbot Thomas (1259-66) supported Simon de Montfort in his quarrels with the king, and as a result had his own troubles with John Fitzalan, a loyal baron and lord of Oswestry, who was depriving the abbey of profits due to them from Oswestry church. Thomas wrote to the archbishop of Canterbury complaining about Fitzalan's actions. At the same time the abbey was quarrelling with the royalist town which was ignoring the abbey's milling rights. Thomas may have been the first Shrewsbury abbot to sit in Parliament when de Montfort, in 1261, held his assemblies of barons, senior clergy and citizens. He died shortly after de Montfort was killed and Henry had regained absolute power.

The Defences

Meanwhile, by 1255, part of the motte had slipped into the river due to erosion on the inner curve. This probably drew attention to necessary repair work on the defences

Leland, Henry VIII's antiquary, described the old Welsh Bridge in the 1530s as 'the greatest, fairest and highest upon the stream'. The western bridge was originally known as St George's, a name also given to a hospital that stood alongside on land now occupied by the new theatre. (This hospital closed in the 13th century, its chapel becoming part of the adjacent hospital of St John the Baptist. By the late Middle Ages the latter was no more than an almshouse.) Possibly originally built of timber, it was built or rebuilt in Keel bed sandstone quarried locally sometime between the late 11th and mid 13th century. The main gate tower, Mardol Gate, was at the town end; the smaller Welsh Gate at the Frankwell end. Mardol Gate was taken down in 1773; the Welsh Gate in 1775. The present replacement bridge was built a little way downstream in 1796. (Courtesy of Shropshire Museums SHYMS FA-1991-054-3)

elsewhere. Trouble between Henry III and his barons led to strengthening of the defences by royal orders in the mid 1260s. Besides work on completing the town walls, strengthening existing gates and bridges, creating a new gate on the west bridge (the old Welsh Bridge) with two towers at the landward entry to the town, it also included work to the defensive equipment. This included repairs to the large siege engine and great crossbow, complete with the provision of a plentiful stock of new bolts. Records of expenditure even include the costs of overhauling the winding gear and providing new ropes for the two main drawbridges.

Fortunately, the town avoided any siege in the wars with Llewelyn, but further defensive work was carried out in the late 1260s. This part of the work included the addition of wooden firing platforms to the town walls, and creating further ditches, embankments and wooden palisades along riversides. All this was in connection with the final phase of the Welsh conflicts. The great wooden tower had been abandoned, and it finally collapsed in about 1270.

The main castle structure as it now stands is the work of Edward I. He enlarged Henry II's hall, the height of which can be seen by the weathering above the arch of the door of his main entrance in the east tower. The rougher, weathered work of the middle storey dates from Edward's time. It is visibly different from the earlier, harder, smoother stonework. The deep embrasures of the windows, with splayed reveals to let more light

The medieval stone English Bridge, probably built by the monks before 1100, carried across a small island, and with 17 arches it reached almost to the abbey before the level of the ground was raised. It included a drawbridge and fortified gateway and, like London Bridge, houses and shops were built up on either side, leading to various calamities in times of flood. When the bridge was replaced in the 1760s, the workmen discovered a large reversed, carved stone used in repair work after floods in 1545. As it was from the original shrine to St Winefride in the abbey, it was returned there. (SA 6001-198-369)

The Norman castle, sited on the narrow neck of land guarding the landward entrance to the town, replaced earlier timber forts. The original castle, built by Roger de Montgomery in 1071, was confiscated in 1102 by Henry I, who gave orders to strengthen it and build a wall around the town. Henry III, who ordered the building of the town's outer wall in 1218, made his son, later Edward I, governor of the castle. He rebuilt the castle, largely in the form as seen today, apart from the great hall whose upper floor was added in Elizabethan times.
(SA 6001-198-269)

in, are still obvious inside the hall, with narrow external openings. He added the great round towers at the east and west corners of the hall in about 1300, incorporating, within the wall thickness of each tower, a stone staircase leading to the upper storeys. (Foundations of the late 13th-century turret can be seen protruding from the present parapet wall of the base of Laura's Tower.) Crenellation to the inner bailey wall was probably added later.

Relations between the Abbey and the Town

The relationship between the abbey and town was an uneasy one. They were mutually dependent for enhanced prestige and commercial benefits, yet these factors were a source of underlying tension. This could lead at times to conflict between them, at others to considerable cooperation, and even occasional generosity. There were three main subjects of contention: the 'Liberty of Foregate', a tannery on the town's side of the river, and, most importantly, rights to operating mills.

The town's jurisdiction only extended up to a boundary point on the pair of bridges that stretched across the river and marshland between the town's and the abbey's lands. The abbot of Shrewsbury therefore had civic jurisdiction over Monks Foregate (now named Abbey Foregate), which was thus independent of the governance of the town. This was an area of privilege the abbey claimed from the date of its foundation by Roger de Montgomery and was a source of constant irritation between abbey and town. The exact extent of the limit of their jurisdiction was only finally agreed with the burgesses of the town in the early 1500s.

The Dominican friars appear to have created a tannery on the town side of the river, below the monks' south-east facing vineyard. The monks objected to it on the grounds that it interfered with the river flow, but the smell would have also interfered with their pleasure in tending their vines on warm sunny days – away from the abbot's supervision.

The rights of milling, known as 'soke', had been a subject of friction between the town and abbey authorities since the latter's establishment in 1087. The abbey lands included the four or more water mills along the Rea Brook. This obliged the town dwellers to take their grain to the abbey mills for grinding, and to accept the charges made. They naturally resented this, and as soon as a new technology, windmills, reached this part of the country in the 12th century, entrepreneurs set up the new devices on the high land of the town centre, taking business from the abbey. Abbot Thomas took the matter to court but, being currently out of favour as he was supporting Simon de Montfort, he lost the case, and had to pay a large fine to the king, Henry III. However, a few years later when Henry III was visiting the town to agree a treaty with the Welsh, he pardoned the abbey and allowed the town to retain four mills, provided that profits were shared with the abbey, which was also permitted to build two new watermills. Other mills in the town were to be demolished.

However, the bones of St Winefride created a common interest, as the presence of the saint was commercially valuable to both parties. The shrine of St Winefride, with its reputed healing miracles, brought many pilgrims to visit the abbey and thus much indirect prosperity to the adjacent town. Cooperation was therefore mutually beneficial. The town also benefited from the official visits made to the abbey by royalty, leaders of the church and many of the rich merchants of the day, and town and abbey both benefited from the additional status created by the two Parliaments called to meet here by the king, in 1283 and 1398.

More activity at the Abbey
Through the efforts of Abbot William de Upton (1266-71) the monks won back the valuable right to hold custody of the abbey during vacancies in the abbacy, otherwise the king would have retained the right that he had gained in 1102 to impose his own choice, as opposed to approving that of the monks.

The abbey accounts show income from a range of sources. The abbey owned lands and churches in six other counties besides the mills and houses in Shrewsbury, including salt pans in Droitwich and Cheshire, fisheries in Shropshire and Lancashire, and the small beginnings of coal mining and iron working – not worked directly by the monks, but granted to lessees.

Abbot Luke de Wenlock (1272-78) was elected in the year Henry III died. He appears to have enjoyed good relations with the new king, Edward I, and attended a papal Council in 1274. With recurring business in London, he purchased a property in Bishopsgate which became the official London residence of future abbots. The abbey's estates, seized by the crown for contempt of court, probably due to supporting Simon de Montfort, were fully released from royal hands in 1278, on payment of a £26 fine, and the relationship between the abbey and town improved. The king pardoned the abbey 'all indignation and rancour of soul'.

The 40-year-long abbacy (1292-1333) of William de Moleleye, who probably came from Muckley (south-east of Much Wenlock), saw a fall and then rise in economic circumstances. A succession of poor harvests and epidemics of animal diseases, referred to as 'the Pestilence', was followed by famines and plagues. The abbot complained that food resources were insufficient to provide hospitality for visitors, whilst the abbey's income from property was reduced through damage to tenements and lack of maintenance. Mills were being misused or plundered by the Welsh, and also by the English Marcher lords. However, the abbey obtained the bailiffs' agreement in 1298 to close the town shops during abbey fair times, although still allowing the townspeople to sell drinks to fair goers. Fortunes, at least for the abbey, improved and by 1313 they were able to lend the king £71 to help finance the war against Scotland.

The Monastery
It was in Edward II's time (1307-27) that the three west bays of the abbey's Norman church nave were taken down and replaced by two Gothic bays and a west tower 104ft (nearly 32m) high. The Norman and Gothic styles join in massive rectangular piers designed to carry the weight of the tower.

Vaughan's Mansion, built c.1375, was not embattled, suggesting a greater sense of security behind the new defences. The remains were incorporated in the bar to the Music Hall, and are being included in current alterations. (SA 6001-200-282)

The great Hall of Sir John de Charlton. It was one of the early stone mansions, built c.1325 on a site bounded by St John's Hill, Cross Hill, Swan Hill and Market Street beyond the line of the possible inner wall and probably before the new defences were completed. Door openings show that access was at first-floor level. (SA 6001-5326-9)

Sir John de Charlton, Lord of Powys by marriage to the heiress Hawise, born in 1291, depicted in the Jesse window now in St Mary's church (the text was wrongly assigned to each image during restoration of the window). (Stephen de Saulles)

However, when the bishop of Lichfield visited in 1322, he had a number of criticisms. Accounts were badly kept, he reported, and corrodies (allowances of food and clothing) were wrongfully being sold. Rules were not being read to the monks twice a year as they should be. Monks were not attending communal meals, so were not hearing readings. Novices were playing truant. The bishop issued various instructions to remedy affairs, and all novices were confined to the abbey until they became proficient monks. Things evidently improved. When Abbot William died ten years later, it was recorded that he ruled 'with diligent foresight, that he not only recovered what had been lost, collected together what had been dispersed, and attentively preserved what was collected together, but also increased their rents and possessions, and moreover acquired new ones, and ... nourished them happily and instructed [the monks] as well by the example of good works, as by spiritual food'.

Bear Steps Hall, St Alkmund's Square, (late 14th century) restored by the Civic Society in 1970s, is now their headquarters and houses changing exhibitions. It shows an early roofing system where the load is carried to a 'king', or single post, supported on the substantial tie-beam, with no truss or purlins as in later roofs. An interesting feature is the interrupted ogee bracing to the roof, reflecting the fashion for double curves at that time, as in the stonework of the west window of the abbey. (Shrewsbury Civic Society)

In 1333, the abbey had two monks studying theology at university, although a few years later they could only afford one. Using revenues of Wrockwardine church to support them, the abbey's scholastic reputation was being enhanced, and in 1343 Prior Thomas de Calton was appointed Regent (governor) of Oxford University.

The Black Death

Recovery from the earlier pestilence and famine was short-lived. Only a few years later the Black Death, as the plague was called, reached England. Its far more serious effect, both nationally and locally, was described by Owen & Blakeway in their *A History of Shrewsbury* in the following extracts: 'On the first of January 1349 ... parliament was to have met on Monday ... is postponed on account of a plague ... to Easter' ... and in

March, 'adjourned sine die on the same account'. 'The contagion raged through the whole of that year', and there was a command to 'shut all the ports in the kingdom'. 'In Shrewsbury ... the wealthier burgesses, who had somewhat more to lose and therefore were loth to risk it, would absent themselves from the public assemblies of the town, perhaps retire from its infected walls; and leave their inferiors who valued their lives at lower estimate, to assume that ascendency for which they were little qualified, either by their stake in the welfare of the town, or by their knowledge of its interests.' It has been estimated that between 30 and 60% of the country's population died from this outbreak of the plague.

Labourers who survived the Black Death were able to demand higher wages and for a while their standard of living rose. With the closure of the ports and decline in the population, there was also a marked shift in the economy, from the international export of raw wool, which continued to service the home market, to its use by cloth-making manufacturers elsewhere in England. Another consequence of the Black Death was that due to the death of large numbers of the clergy, who had been taught French and Latin, much of the education given to the sons of the nobility and gentry now had to be undertaken by people whose only language was English.

Recovery: Abbey, Town and Parliament
Abbot Nicholas Stevens (1361-99) was able to improve the abbey buildings due to the interest of Edward III and, from 1377, Richard II (1377-99), who sympathised with the monks' complaints, and took forceful action on the abbey's behalf. He remedied the mills problem by ordering that the abbey's three mills that were still functioning were to be repaired at the town's expense, that 12 mills built without requisite permission be demolished, and that in future the cost of maintaining the legal mills should be jointly shared.

The abbey's great west window and the ornate refectory pulpit all date from this time. St Winefride's shrine was also rebuilt. It was known that St Bueno had been Winefride's uncle and confessor, and to increase the abbey's attractiveness to pilgrims, Abbot Nicholas sent his monks to 'acquire' the saint's bones from a chapel at Rhewl, near Ruthin. The abbey was fined for this irregular act, but allowed to retain the trophy. Richard II himself may have visited as a pilgrim, because he referred to the special devotion he bore to St Winefride in a charter he issued in 1389.

The west window was installed in 1387. It was 46ft high by 23ft wide (14m x 7m), in the Decorated style, divided by horizontal stone transoms and six perpendicular mullions. It was described by Henry Pidgeon in his 1837 *Memorials of Shrewsbury* as 'one of the most magnificent windows in the kingdom'.

The relationship between the abbey and the town had clearly improved, for it appears that in 1389, the earl of Arundel (now the primary noble in Shropshire), the abbot and Shrewsbury corporation met at the abbey to draw up a 'composition for the government of the town'.

In 1397, Nicholas was the first Shrewsbury abbot to wear, by papal licence, the mitre and other 'pontificals' appropriate to bishops. (The point is made in Owen & Blakeway that it was the abbey that was 'mitred' by its right to be represented in Parliament, but as yet no record has been found of the separate grant to the abbot personally.) In 1398, Richard summoned Parliament, subsequently called 'the Great Parliament' due to the large entourage at the abbey, where he also stayed. The Lords met in the chapter house and afterwards feasted in the refectory 'in great splendour', but change was to come.

Perhaps fortunately for Nicholas, he died just before Henry of Lancaster seized the throne as Henry IV from Richard in 1399 and so escaped any troublesome accusations of undue loyalty to Richard.

The abbey's refectory reading pulpit, built 1361-99, is a remarkable survival from the Dissolution of 1536-41. Originally it was part of the refectory wall, and the monks read aloud from it during their otherwise silent meals. (Stephen de Saulles)

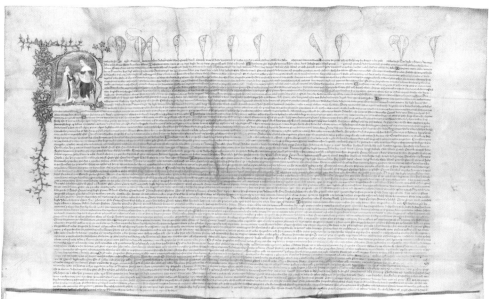

The charter issued by Richard II in 1389 confirmed the rights granted to Shrewsbury by his grandfather, Edward III. The illuminated initial R shows his wife Anne of Bohemia interceding on behalf of the people of Shrewsbury. Richard summoned his Parliament, later called 'Great Parliament', to meet in Shrewsbury in 1398. (SA 48093-3365-24)

5   BATTLE, GUILDS AND PRINCES

'Such was the end of this horrible day, one of the wyrst batayles that ever came to Inglonde, and unkyndyst; a day rather to be celebrated with tears than triumphs fought out between Englishmen, with a fierceness hitherto unequalled, and a slaughter hitherto unknown.'

Wylie's *England under Henry IV.*

Shortly after Henry IV (1399-1413), grandson of Edward III, was crowned king, he was faced with his own rebellions. Henry had usurped the throne from Richard II with the help of the Percy family of Northumberland, but they soon felt insufficiently rewarded for their service in this act, and also for their long-standing defence of the Scottish border, done largely at their own expense. When Henry claimed for himself the ransom monies arising out of their latest defeat of the Scots near Berwick, they finally rebelled against him. Meanwhile, Owain Glyn Dwr, who had served in Richard's army in Scotland and had married Margaret, the daughter of Marcher knight Sir David Hanmer, became involved in a squabble with Lord Grey of Ruthin that provided the catalyst for Welsh anger at their treatment by the English to explode into open conflict. It wasn't long before Owain was proclaimed 'Prince of Wales' by his followers and was in open rebellion against the king. In an early phase of the resultant war, Prince Henry (later Henry V), only 15 years old at the time, had destroyed Glyn Dwr's properties in Sycharth and Glyn Dyfrdwy and returned to Shrewsbury.

The Battle of Shrewsbury
In an alliance that was to prove disastrous, the rebels agreed to make a joint attack on Shrewsbury. The men from Northumberland, led by the duke's son Henry Percy, known as 'Hotspur' for his battle prowess in the north, marched south to Cheshire. Here he gathered an army of archers, and was joined by his uncle, Thomas Percy, earl of Worcester. The king, originally on his way north to support the Percys against the Scots, hearing of the Percy rebellion and their intention to link up with Glyn Dwr, was anxious to quell the revolt before the jointure could occur or be reinforced from Northumberland. Hastily changing plans, he marched to Shrewsbury to join his son, summoning further troops to give support. The king arrived at Shrewsbury only a few hours before the rebels, and raised his banner to indicate his presence. Finding this signal, and the gates shut against

them, Hotspur's troops retired to a nearby village to set up camp. Next morning, the armies marched towards each other, and battle lines were formed.

Abbot Thomas de Prestbury of Shrewsbury offered peace terms on behalf of the king. Hotspur was inclined to accept them, but the earl of Worcester's responses made further diplomacy impossible, and by afternoon the king ordered the advance. The battle

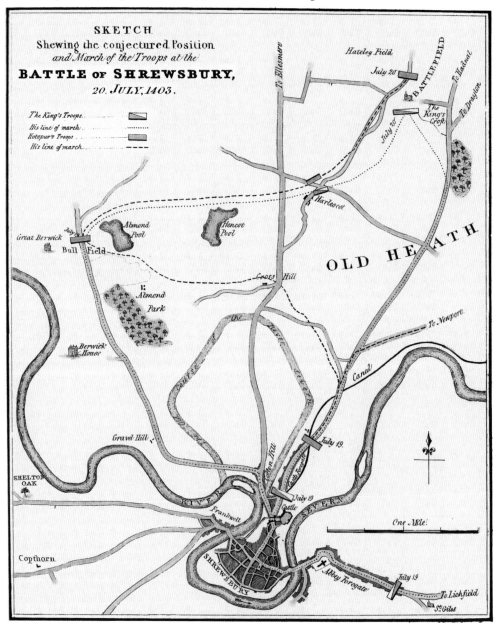

Map showing the conjectured position and march of the troops at the battle of Shrewsbury, 1403. Hotspur's troops had spent the night encamped at the village of Berwick.

opened with a great discharge of arrows on both sides, in which the Cheshire archers were superior. In the mêlée of fierce personal combat that followed, the king was the centre of the rebels' attack, but managed to survive. The young Prince Henry, although wounded by an arrow, refused to retire; allegedly he attributed his survival to his earlier visit to St Winefride's shrine. By sunset it was a decisive victory for the king; Hotspur had been killed, and the remnants of his army fled.

In one afternoon, some 2,000 of the high-born in the land – nobles, knights and gentlemen – were slaughtered, together with another 6,000 soldiers, who were buried in mass graves at the site, still known as Battlefield. One account says 'the dead lay thick as leaves and passage over them was difficult'. The moon, rising over the field of battle, is said to have been 'eclipsed that night, symbolic of the eclipse of the chivalry of England'. Many of the nobility were brought back into the town for burial, in sanctified ground, at the friaries. There were executions at the High Cross and, ironically, the earl of Worcester was later buried, headless, by the abbot whose mediation he had spurned.

Battlefield church, founded as a chantry by Henry IV, stands as a local memorial to this battle, and for the 500th anniversary, in 2003, a visitor centre was created at the site (see p.246). This momentous battle secured the succession, and prevented the division of the kingdom proposed by Hotspur, Northumberland, Glyn Dwr and Edmund Mortimer. (The latter had been captured in a battle the previous year, but now supported Glyn Dwr, marrying one of his daughters.) The battle was also to hasten the end of feudalism, due to the numbers of feudal lords who perished.

According to legend, Hotspur had been warned by a soothsayer that he would 'meet his fate at Berwick', which he took to mean the northern town. Thinking the prediction could be discounted in view of his recent victory there, he was dismayed before the battle to be told, when calling for his sword, that it had been left behind at camp 'at Berwick' where they spent the night. It was an age of superstition, and perhaps this was the reason for his willingness to accept the peace terms offered by the king. Another less likely story tells how Glyn Dwr, unable to cross the swollen Severn, watched the progress of the battle from 'high in the branches of the Glendower's Oak' at Shelton. In fact Glyn Dwr was in south Wales at the time.

Some more of the Abbots

Abbot Thomas de Prestbury spent much of his time away from the abbey, involved in academic affairs at Oxford. After studying there, he was appointed 'elector of university visitors' by the Benedictine General Chapter in 1393. He was chancellor of the university from 1409 to 1412, following in the footsteps of an earlier Shrewsbury monk, Ralph, who later became bishop of Bath and Wells. During his chancellorship, Abbot Thomas presided over the public burning of books by John Wycliff that were deemed heretical, and in 1413 he arranged for two rooms at Gloucester College priory in Oxford for the use of Shrewsbury monk students.

Abbot Thomas Mynde (1460-98) studied at Cambridge, where he became a Bachelor of Theology. His learning and reputation for good moral character resulted in his being elected abbot despite being the second youngest monk in the community. He was much concerned with the development and promotion of St Winefride's shrine. The abbey's property-based income was depressed, so supplementary funds were needed from pilgrims. The saint's reputation had probably been enhanced when it was alleged that Henry V had walked from Shrewsbury to St Winefride's Holywell in Wales, a distance of nearly 30 miles, to give thanks for his victory over the French at Agincourt in 1415, but that was now a few decades in the past and France had since been lost. Anxious to promote the shrine, Thomas Mynde used the revenues from Great Ness church to fund a monk chaplain to celebrate a chantry at the shrine in memory of King Henry, who had died without fulfilling his promise to endow a chantry.

The Abbey site

Recent excavations have shown that there were monastic buildings to the west of the cloisters, near the river. At the end of the range there was a hall, (probably with an upper, private floor level), and what appears to have been a watergate and probably a small dock or slipway, perhaps with a timber landing stage. In the 1400s, a long range of buildings had been constructed next to it. This had a series of arched openings along what had been the waterfront. It may have served as warehousing in connection with movement of goods along the river, as well as in connection with milling, leather working, building materials and other provisioning. The archaeologists also found that landfill had been used to reclaim a considerable area of the riverside floodplain to provide extra land in medieval times. The Rea Brook's meandering junction with the Severn had been silting up over time and some land was reclaimed as early as the 14th century, enabling the abbey's inner court to be extended by a few feet. In the following century more extensive areas were reclaimed, probably enlarging the site by some 10 per cent, thus allowing the monks to build additional accommodation, including guest rooms, alongside the river.

This area has provided a rich source of 'finds', revealing the prosperous lifestyle enjoyed by the abbey's guests. One of the most significant, made in 1986, was a silver bowl, dated to around 1424, likely to have been used for serving sauces or condiments at high status meals. It was stamped with a leopard's head, thought to be one of the earliest hallmarks ever discovered. Amongst the more unusual of the artefacts found was a very fashionable lady's shoe of the same period.

Shrewsbury Corporation seal, dated 1425, shows the fortified gates and walls, and the bailiffs' arms (similar to the early royal arms of Richard I) over the main gate. The shields at the side of the gate are those of the borough, charged with the 'loggerheads', 3 leopards' heads, their use believed by some to have been permitted from the royal arms. The design shows an early attempt at perspective.

The Merchant Guild

At the beginning of the 15th century, Shrewsbury was still suffering from the effects of the plague, and the continued disruption and expense of the Welsh attacks under Owain Glyn Dwr. It had been forced to petition for a reduction in taxes. But with the tide turning against Glyn Dwr from 1405, and his cause being lost by 1408, the town gradually recovered.

As trade increased again, it was natural for the single merchant guild to be replaced by separate companies representing various individual or groups of crafts. These were associations of 'masters' and 'journeymen' (the itinerant qualified and experienced craftsmen), and in the medieval period their objectives were almost entirely altruistic. They sought to safeguard high standards of materials and craftsmanship, and to uphold a reputation for good quality and fair dealing. Their rules, and all the 'mysteries' (methods, calculations and techniques) of their crafts, were based on long apprenticeship and strong religious principles. Each guild had its patron saint, and some had special altars for religious services and at which to make offerings in one of the parish churches, such as the Drapers in St Mary's church opposite their hall in St Mary Place, and the Shearmen in St Julian's, close to their hall. Besides ensuring proper systems of apprenticeship for the training of their sons (as they tended to follow their father's trade), they established charities to provide care and accommodation for their sick and aged members and their families.

Single cell almshouses, with open hearths, were built by the Guild of Drapers in 1444, very soon after they were incorporated, alongside the west side of St Mary's churchyard.
In 1647 fireplaces with tall chimneys were added, as shown here. They were demolished in 1825 and rebuilt on the opposite side of the road to a design by John Carline.
They too have since been demolished. (SA PR-2-436)

By 1444 the Shrewsbury Drapers had emerged as an organised body. The Welsh wool trade was well established, but gradually the trade in cloth was becoming more important. The Drapers became more prominent in the town when they founded almshouses for their widows and spinsters. The first group of 13 timber-framed cottages, a common hall and a warden's house, were built in the churchyard of St Mary's church facing Ox Lane (now called St Mary's Street). They were simple, single-cell dwellings, including a Welsh style 'sleeping shelf' and an open hearth, vented through the roof. They were demolished in the 19th century. This was the beginning of the Drapers' charity work, which still continues in the town with their funding of almshouses in Longden Coleham and plans to build a further 21.

Edward IV (1461-83), formerly the earl of March, brought up in the Marches, knew the area and its commercial needs. He seemed to regard the town as his second capital, injecting it at times with the excitement and extravagance of court life. He was greatly interested in trade and its promotion and by incorporating the fraternity of Drapers, he helped create a period of sustained opulence.
(The Drapers Company and Stephen de Saulles)

In 1462 Edward IV gave the Shrewsbury Drapers their Royal Charter, in which they were described as 'A Fraternity or Gild of the Holy Trinity of the Men of the Mystery of Drapers in the town of Salop'. The title had religious implications, and the charter required the guild to appoint a chantry priest to say mass for the guild, and to pray for the souls of Richard, duke of York, and his son, Edmund, earl of Rutland (father and brother to Edward IV), both of whom were killed at the battle of Wakefield in 1460 during the Wars of the Roses (see below). They built their first Guildhall in 1485.

The guilds gathered together at the Church's Feast of Corpus Christi on the Thursday after Whitsun, in an annual celebration which has led on, through various changes, to become the Shrewsbury Flower Show of today. The ceremonies were already being referred to in 1449 as going back as far as 'tyme owt of mynde', perhaps dating back to a pope's instruction in the 13th century.

A grand and solemn procession would assemble in the town, led by the priests carrying the Holy Sacrament under a rich velvet canopy. It would be followed by the parochial clergy and friars, and the bailiffs with the members of the corporation in their robes. Finally would come the guilds, each in their own colours and set order of precedence, and carrying their decorated banners. The whole colourful procession, accompanied by minstrels and candle-bearers, would make its way out of the town to Weeping Cross, 'there to bewail their sins', returning to celebrate High Mass in old St Chad's. Only after the completion of these religious ceremonies did the companies divide, each going to their own Hall, or rooms, to devote the remainder of the day to feasting, drinking and other forms of medieval entertainment.

There was a degree of cooperation between the guilds, and they expected to settle their own disputes, and regulate their own affairs, including the matter of training and controlling the numbers involved in any trade. By the 1480s the Drapers already owned considerable property, and gradually they were to become the wealthiest of the guilds.

Town Government

Shrewsbury was already an established royal borough by the end of the 11th century, and thus was directly ruled by a county 'reeve', or sheriff, as the king's representative.

Release from rigid Norman control, and achieving a certain independence from central control, was only slowly gained during the following half a millennium of negotiating successive royal charters. These granted certain rights in exchange for payment. Willingness or reluctance to permit rights could depend on the desire to gain local goodwill or the needs of the royal budget at the time, such as for waging war.

Degory Watur, founder of the Drapers' Almshouses and an early Company Warden, with his wife. The almshouses provided for 13 'poor persons of both sexes'. (The Drapers Company)

Over 30 royal charters were granted to the town. Apart from controlling civil and economic aspects, such as the exaction of tolls, they also dictated matters concerning the weekly market, the times and days for seasonal fairs, laid down rules regarding weights and measures, and also made provision for punishments for transgression for all but major offences through its own courts. The town gradually acquired rights to have its own coroners, a gaol and gallows.

The two earliest surviving charters, the first from Richard I in 1189 (which referred to a previous 'corporation') and then from King John in 1199, both confirmed that the town could retain the customs previously enjoyed under Henry I and Henry II, 'customs' that are thought to refer to the Norman 'Laws of Breteuil'. The charters also included a particularly important right, that of local control over trade in the town through the existing local guild merchant, believed to have been established some decades before.

The 'Laws of Breteuil' refer to a model of local governance already established at Breteuil, in France, and mentioned in Domesday. Breteuil lay in the lordship of William fitzOsbern, who became earl of Hereford after the Conquest, and the 'Laws' were subsequently adopted by other Marcher lords. Although no specific records survive, the administrative structure appeared to create stability and to be intended to encourage economic prosperity. It also gave special privileges to local burgesses including, for example, lighter fines for misdemeanours, larger plots of land, and rights to take wood from royal forests.

In 1170 Henry II had permitted the town to collect its own rents, giving it a limited amount of responsibility and autonomy, and in 1199 King John placed the governance of the town directly under two elected 'provosts', to be responsible to the king for the town's civil and economic affairs, and presiding over the town's courts.

After the disruptive effects caused by the Black Death in 1349, disorders arose in the town in 1351, 1361 and 1380 in connection with the election of bailiffs (previously the king's provosts). The abbot and Richard Fitzalan, earl of Arundel, a major landowner in Shropshire, therefore made proposals for enlarging the franchise for the election of the town's own bailiffs and other offices. These measures were approved by the king in 1381 and adopted, but further disorders broke out within a decade. Further adjustments were negotiated, resulting in an 'electoral college' being set up, to replace popular elections. The electoral college stipulated qualifications for office which soon created a self-perpetuating oligarchy.

In the meantime, Quarter Sessions were established. These were the meetings of the county Justices, the keepers of the peace, empowered to consider and determine cases, held four times a year.

The corporation established and confirmed by the charters included a mayor (from the charter of 1638) and other offices (over time varied to include such as a recorder, a steward, a common clerk, chamberlains, a sword-bearer and a mace-bearer). The corporation's councillors were to be elected by the burgesses of the town, the aldermen (when the corporation's rules were changed to allow their creation) were elected by the councillors, and the mayor was elected annually by the councillors. Burgesses were free citizens by descent or birth, or later qualified as such by serving a recognised 7-year apprenticeship in an incorporated company of craftsmen or traders.

Town Development

At this time wealthy merchants began building in timber. The earlier town houses were set parallel to the street, but as space diminished, they were later set gable-end-on to the street, with a side access passage. In plan they comprised a simple open hall, sometimes with a solar, (the private upper room at one end for the owners, usually overlooking the street), and with service rooms at the other end on the ground floor. Any shop would be at the front, with workshops, storage and provision for apprentices at the rear.

The system of jettying each floor out beyond the one below was soon developed. This method of construction may have been introduced by French carpenters who were already familiar with the system. It had great practical advantages. Floor joists were less likely to bend and sag, and so could be reduced in size, because the weight of the upper structure was carried on the projecting ends of the joists. Overhanging walls and roof helped protect the lower infill panels of wattle and plaster from the effects of rain and frost. A further advantage was in the increased floor areas obtained. Outside circulation space was valuable at ground level, but considered less important higher up, when scant regard was given to light and air. Surface water and general drainage would have been down the centre of the neighbouring streets and passageways, and the overhanging buildings would have provided sheltered walkways, protected from both rain and other less pure precipitation, ranging from the contents of chamber pots to food scraps.

There were no chimneys at this time. Smoke escaped through openings in the stone or clay tiled roofs. Straw was forbidden as a roof covering in the town because of fire risk. Windows were simple unglazed openings, closed by shutters, or sometimes timber-mullioned oriel windows, with traceried heads on more expensive properties. There was a fondness for curves, seen in the cusped bracing members and ogee (double-curve) timber door heads still surviving, especially in Frankwell. A simpler form of construction was the 'cruck', where pairs of curved timber 'blades' (specially cut, forming matching pairs of sections from a tree-trunk and curving branch), were used to form the frame for the

The Abbot's House (c.1450), believed to have been the town house of the abbots of Lilleshall as the land itself belonged to the abbey, stood at the corner of Butcher Row. The massive corner trunks of oak, using the natural springing of the roots or branches as supports. The timbers in the projecting upper floors, more exposed to weather, were repaired or replaced in the 18th century, when the alternate uprights were omitted on the second floor, so altering the building's appearance. Butcher Row was known as Le fflesshomeles in 1282 and there were still 16 butchers there in 1828. The remains of the typical medieval open shopfronts, with wide cills and shutters that could be let down to form counters, can still be seen. (SA 6001-200-372)

According to tradition St Mary's church was founded as a collegiate church by King Edgar (958-975), but its origin is now thought to be even earlier. Placed on the highest point of the near-island site, it was recorded in Domesday, with considerable possessions held in the time of Edward the Confessor. Its spire was added in the 15th century. Struck by lightning, the top fell once, but it survived the 1996 and 2008 earthquakes. (SA 6001-199-214)

roof and wall together. A few of these can still be seen. (A good exposed example is close to the Frankwell roundabout.)

Stone, however, was used to build spires for the churches of St Mary's and St Alkmund's in the Perpendicular style of the 15th century. That on St Mary's is one of the three tallest in the country, and it creates a major feature in the Shrewsbury skyline.

Wars of the Roses

Henry V had married the daughter of the French king, and was declared his heir. Henry died young, and his infant son succeeded him in 1422. Henry V had been loved and respected, not only for his famous victories in France, but also for his peace-making and strong government at home. His death was unfortunate, and Shrewsbury was soon drawn into national affairs once more.

Young Henry VI (1422-1461) was not healthy and, although he married the French princess Margaret of Anjou, they had no son for some time, and there was rivalry about the possible succession. One of the prominent figures of the time was Richard, duke of York, who acted as Protector of the Realm during Henry's spells of insanity. He clashed with the queen, and a rivalry between the two branches of the family, the Yorkists and

This 1920s postcard shows Mytton's Mansion on the left, a palatial timber-framed mansion built on Wyle Cop c.1460 by Thomas Mytton, the bailiff who initially refused the entry of Henry Tudor after he had landed at Pembroke and was en route to seek battle with Richard III. As in many other jettied timber-framed buildings, the ground level has been filled by newer shopfronts, set in front of the original timbers, as indicated by the inset position of many entrance doors. (Courtesy of Rob Oakley)

the Lancastrians, developed into the bitter civil war struggles between the two Houses which lasted on and off for 30 years – from the first victory by the Yorkists at St Alban's in 1455 to the final Lancastrian success in 1485 at Bosworth.

Nobles recruited private armies; law and order at times disintegrated, and the country was involved in a civil war during which some 100,000 were killed in battles across the country, including many noblemen. The powers of Parliament were diminished, and the way was opened for a return to a more despotic form of monarchy. None of the events in this dynastic struggle involved Shrewsbury Castle. Indeed it was falling into disrepair.

Richard, duke of York, as heir of the Mortimers (his father had married Anne Mortimer, the sister of the last childless Mortimer earl of March) was based in Ludlow in the 1450s, but it appears that he was eager to forge and maintain a relationship with the town of Shrewsbury. He visited in 1446, in 1450, and again in 1451, making gifts of venison, and feasting with the bailiffs and other worthies of the town. Although he himself never achieved the kingship he may have hoped for, two of his sons were crowned in turn.

Richard's son, Edward, earl of March, was living at the riverside House of the Dominican Friars – adjoining the old Watergate at the bottom of St Mary's Water Lane – when he received news of his father's and brother's deaths at Wakefield. He spent Christmas at Shrewsbury, but shortly afterwards is thought to have gone to Wigmore, Herefordshire, the heart of his power base, where he could readily form an army to confront a Lancastrian force advancing on him from Pembrokeshire. The resulting victory of Mortimers Cross and subsequent advance on London was to set him on the throne as Edward IV (1461-83).

Edward's second son, Richard, was born to his queen, Elizabeth (Woodville) at the Friary, which later excavations have shown to be an elegant and well-appointed set of buildings.

In 1471 Edward had set up a council to look after the affairs of his eldest son, the infant prince of Wales, and a few years later he gave it judicial powers. This was the beginning of the Council in the Marches into which were gradually subsumed the powers of the Marcher lords. Although the council originally had its headquarters in Ludlow, it was of great importance to Shrewsbury, especially in its later years.

When Edward IV died in 1483, his 12-year-old eldest son Edward, who had also spent some time at the Friary in 1480 but was then living in Ludlow Castle, was proclaimed king. As was customary, he was taken to the Tower of London to await his coronation, and as a concession, his younger brother Richard was allowed to go with him. However, there they suffered the unknown fate of the 'Princes in the Tower', as a result of which their uncle, the duke of Gloucester, claimed the throne as Richard III.

Shrewsbury was directly involved in national events when Richard's rights were challenged. Opponents sought to displace him with the rightful heir but, when it was realised that the 'Princes in the Tower' were no longer alive, Henry Tudor was the only surviving alternative, being the grandson of Henry V's widow, Katherine de Valois, who had remarried Owen Tudor. (Owen had been captured at the battle of Mortimers Cross and executed in Hereford.) Henry returned from exile in France, landing near Pembroke. He came straight on to Shrewsbury – where he found the gates shut and the portcullis down. His unusual entry into the town is one of its well-known stories, related in quaint detail in the contemporary chronicle known as the Taylor MS.

A statue, often believed to be of the duke of York, father of Edward IV and Richard III, was probably placed over the gateway to the town during the repairs to the old St George's Bridge in 1458. It was removed when the bridge was taken down in 1791 to a place on the old Market House. However, the statue is now generally believed to be of the Black Prince.

A painting by Alfred J. Hulme showing the entry of Henry Tudor into Shrewsbury. Thomas Mytton, Sheriff of Shropshire, had sworn, the previous evening, that Henry would only enter over his dead body. Thinking differently the next morning, this painting shows Mytton 'lying belly-up' allowing the future 'rightful king' to step over him, thereby allowing him to keep some faith with his oath, though probably not his dignity.

Master Mytton, the chief bailiff, had found himself in an embarrassing position because of previous events. Henry, duke of Buckingham, had been instrumental in putting Richard on the throne but, feeling aggrieved by lack of reward, he raised a revolt to depose him, and to place Henry Tudor, earl of Richmond on the throne. When the plot was discovered, Buckingham fled to his estates in Shropshire, where Thomas Mytton, then Sheriff of Shropshire, was involved in his capture and subsequent execution. Now, challenged to open the gate to 'his rightful king', the stout Master Mytton refused, swearing, 'only over my body will you enter'. By next morning, he had been persuaded by the townspeople to change his mind but, to save his oath, he duly lay down, belly upward, we are told, and Henry stepped over him on entering.

Henry lodged overnight in a house on Wyle Cop, now known as Henry Tudor House. Next day he marched out on his way to Bosworth Field, where Richard was killed and he was crowned on the battlefield. Henry Tudor, the last of the

Henry Tudor House on Wyle Cop would only have been completed two or three decades before Henry stayed in it and is one of the finest specimens of half-timbered buildings in the town. This illustration also shows one of the later water conduits being used.

Lancastrians, married Elizabeth of York (Edward IV's daughter), so uniting the two houses of York and Lancaster, and bringing the Wars of the Roses to an end.

This 4-light traceried oak window lit the principal room of the first-floor hall of Henry Tudor House. It is of a later date than the house and was discovered hidden under plaster (possibly to avoid payment of window tax in the 18th century) during alterations at the beginning of the 20th century.
(Stephen de Saulles)

The King's Head in Mardol, dating from the mid-15th century, lies close to the old Welsh Bridge crossing of the river where Henry Tudor entered the town. An example of the early timber-framed buildings that once filled the town, it is still a popular 'drinking house'.
(Stephen de Saulles)

6 THE TUDOR TOWN

'The towne of Shrobbeshyri standithe on a rokky hill of stone of a sadde [dull] redd earth, and Severne so girdethe in all the towne that savinge a little pece ... it were an isle.'

John Leland, visiting the town in 1539

Henry VII maintained the royal connections with the town. One of his first acts as king was to set up the Guild of St Winefride by royal licence, to offer daily prayers at her shrine for the king, the abbot and the guild. Although members had to recite the Pater Noster and Ave Maria in Latin, they were assured that prayers for their souls after death would be in English. The establishment of the guild was probably in recognition that the abbey had sheltered and supported him on his way to defeat Richard at Bosworth Field.

The king visited in 1488 with his queen and his eldest son, Prince Arthur, and kept the Feast of St George at St Chad's in 1490. When they came again in 1495, they lodged as Abbot Mynde's guests at the abbey, together with the royal court, including minstrels and actors. The royal party were lavishly entertained by the corporation, and Prince Arthur attended one of the Whitsuntide theatrical productions, to which the various craft fellowships contributed. These were held annually in the amphitheatre formed in the Quarry. (Later, Thomas Ashton, headmaster of Shrewsbury School, raised their profile and renown and was himself chief actor in the 1560s. Queen Elizabeth intended to attend on one occasion, but having reached Coventry, rumours of plague in the area meant she stayed away.)

The Abbots and the Abbey

Abbot Richard Lye, probably from a local family, was the youngest monk in the abbey when he was elected abbot in 1498. His main problem was the continuing dispute with the bailiffs over rights and privileges in Monks Foregate, which resulted in two hearings in the Star Chamber in 1504 and 1509. The first confirmed the abbot's rights over Monks Foregate, the second determined that Shrewsbury inhabitants could cross the Stone Bridge toll-free, but that their rights (as townspeople as opposed to abbot's subjects) extended only to the end of the bridge. Richard Lye's successes earned his epitaph: 'by his industry, great expenses and labours, he recovered those liberties of his

Abbey'. However, after his death, some personal transgressions came to light. He had been assisting various relatives with gifts of properties and life-long supplies of bread, ale and firewood, and even portions of tithe incomes. This was at a time when the abbey was becoming agriculturally less self-sufficient, causing expenditure on provisioning to rise to £250 in 1509. The abbey was buying, instead of selling, in Shrewsbury market, and its assets were being depleted.

The following abbacy, that of Abbot Richard Baker (also known as Richard Marshall), suffered from problems created in the previous one. Official visitations between 1518 and 1525 reported that the infirmary and dormitory buildings were in disrepair, that there were unauthorised property dealings, that proper accounts were not being kept, and that the monks were running up debts with local tradesmen. While Abbot Richard Lye had perhaps been too young to understand economic realities, Abbot Richard Baker was perhaps too old to be able to deal with them. He resigned, with a £10 pension from the king, in 1528.

The next abbot, Abbot Thomas Boteler (or Butler), was sub-prior during his predecessor's abbacy. From the records it appears that, far from helping Abbot Baker to deal with the abbey's problems, Boteler was probably adding to them. The bishop of Lichfield found that he was stealing glass from other buildings to use in his private chamber, and demolishing some of the minor buildings and selling off the tiles and timber.

As the later royal church inventory figures for income (£572) and outgoings (£98) showed, it was poor financial management rather than actual poverty that was causing many of the problems. Meanwhile, the choir roof leaked, no monks were being sent to university, regular masses were being neglected, and Boteler failed to attend Parliament, a right that had been granted to Shrewsbury abbots since the 13th century.

The Dissolution

In connection with the Council in the Marches, Prince Arthur, with his wife Katherine of Aragon, had taken up residence at Ludlow Castle, where he was taken ill and died. To avoid losing her dowry, the king betrothed the widow Katherine to his younger son, then still a boy of 11. When Henry VII died in 1509, this son succeeded, as Henry VIII, and was duly married to Katherine. Later he 'developed scruples' about marrying his brother's widow. When the pope refused to sanction a divorce, the course of events began which came to be known as the Reformation. It had personal implications for Henry, freeing him to marry Anne Boleyn, and created fundamental political, economic, social and religious consequences for the country as a whole. Freed of control from Rome, Henry initiated the Dissolution of the Monasteries.

It was an astonishing turn of events. In 1521, Henry VIII was declared 'Defender of the Faith' by the pope, yet the pope's authority had been formally abolished by 1536. The resultant changes must have been bewildering to a community accustomed to the all-embracing religious traditions of the time. Priests were suddenly allowed to marry; chantry chapels were abolished; clergy were instructed to teach in English, and the recent invention of printing made it possible to distribute copies of Coverdale's Bible to

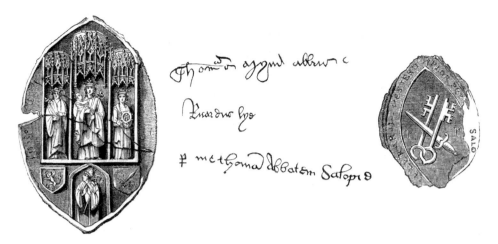

In 1539, when the dissolution of the abbey was imminent, Abbot Boteler and the townspeople petitioned that the buildings should be retained for entertaining royalty and for a free school. Here is his signature, with those of Thomas Mynde (abbot 1460-98) and Richard Lye (abbot 1498-1512), with Mynde's seal and that of the cellarer.

every church. It was the first Bible to be printed in England, and was based on Luther's German and Tyndale's translation of the New Testament, as Coverdale knew no Greek or Latin. From 1548, services had to be conducted in English, and the first English Prayer Book was available in 1549. As well as helping fund his new navy, Henry VIII intended to establish cathedrals with financial gains made from the Dissolution, including making Shrewsbury a diocese with the abbey to be the cathedral. In the event, six new dioceses were established, including Chester and Gloucester, and Shrewsbury had to wait till 1851, when it became the centre of a (Roman Catholic) diocese.

Abbot Thomas Boteler had not attended Parliament when Henry VIII's divorce from Katherine of Aragon was being moved – heralding the break from the Catholic church. Nor was he present in 1536 when the Act was passed for dissolving abbeys and taking their lands and wealth for the crown. However, in 1540, he was the abbot who, with his 17 monks, was summoned to the chapter house to surrender Shrewsbury Abbey to the king's commissioners. After the Dissolution, the burgesses allowed the nave, that is, the part of the abbey church that had also served as the parish church for the surrounding community, to be left standing to continue in use as the parish church, now properly known as the Church of the parish of Holy Cross. The choir, transepts, high altar and lady chapel were all demolished.

Property that had belonged to the monasteries was now sold for the benefit of the royal coffers. In Shrewsbury, the shrine of St Winefride was destroyed, and the associated guild disbanded, (it was re-established in 1987), while the colleges of St Mary's and St Chad's, together with the friaries, were also dissolved. The king's commissioners had reported on each establishment, but whatever the lax situation elsewhere, Richard Devereux could find little to criticise in Shrewsbury's friaries. The Black (Dominican)

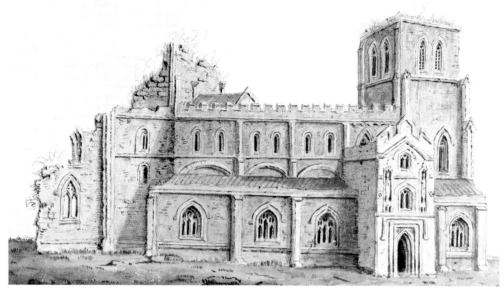

A copy of a drawing made by Sir W. Dugdale showing the nave as it was at the Dissolution together with fragments of the great middle tower and north transept. (SA 6001-198-411)

friars by the Watergate, had always, it seemed, 'maintained themselves in good repute'. In his letter to Thomas Cromwell, he mentioned various other houses that he had 'taken into the kyngs handds', but says of 'Schrewysbery', 'I could fynde no gret cause in them to cause them to gyve up'. He added that the Austin friars' house was 'In ruyne' and that the Grey friars 'wer glade to gyve up all In to the kyngs handds' but were of 'lytyll valur'. The abbot's house was handed over in 1540 and quickly sold into private hands, despite

An engraving by J.C. Buckler (1822) of the remains of the abbey after the Dissolution, showing the silhouette of the town beyond the river. In 1542 the town received a new charter from Henry VIII granting 'all the liberties, franchises and privileges' previously enjoyed by the abbot 'for the intimate affection which his majesty states himself to bear towards the town of Salop.'

the bailiffs' plea that it should be retained for entertaining royalty and other important visitors to the town, the castle being in a fairly ruined state by that time. Leland, writing a few years earlier, was more interested in the bridges over the Severn than the abbey, which he must have passed and simply noted: 'There is a Stone Bridge of 3 Arches over Mele [River Meole] as I entred into Shrosbery hard by the Abbey, and hard beneath the Bridge is the Confluence of Mele and Severne.'

The burgesses soon felt one practical loss, in the education of their sons by the abbey's monks which would have probably included religious instruction, Latin, mathematics and geography. Although Shrewsbury had not been included on the commissioners' list of proposed new schools, the bailiffs pleaded its cause.

The Aftermath and Education

Most medieval schools were attached to monasteries, collegiate churches or cathedrals. The schoolmaster who taught Ordericus Vitalis before he went away to university is known to have been Sigiward, the schoolmaster of the abbey. Henry III had even appointed one Roger de Abbedesle to be 'Rector of the Schools of Salop'. In Shrewsbury, schools seem to have been under the jurisdiction of the local authority from an early date. In 1448 the bailiffs had dismissed a Thomas Fillilode from 'any longer teaching boys or keeping a school within the town'. It is also known that in 1492 the Drapers maintained a school kept by Sir John Pleyley.

The remains of the group of 16th-century buildings belonging to the Franciscan (or Grey) Friars in the group of stone cottages near the present Greyfriars' footbridge. The ruins may have been part of the refectory and must have been almost new at the time of the Dissolution. (Shropshire Archives)

For a while the merchants in the town had been seeking to replace and even improve upon the existing practical training in accounting, literacy, modern languages and other basic education for their sons, so as to enable them to take part in the administration of their sometimes international businesses. With the loss of schooling due to the king's Dissolution of the abbey and the friaries, petitions were now presented to the Lord Chancellor and king for the founding of a grammar school. These petitions were on behalf of not only the bailiffs and burgesses of Shrewsbury, but also the inhabitants of all the surrounding country. It was suggested that the revenues of the lately dissolved colleges of St Mary and St Chad would be available. Henry VIII had died in 1547, but on 10 February 1552, Edward VI granted the necessary charter for the foundation of a school in Shrewsbury, to be called the 'Free Grammar School of King Edward VI' – 'free' in the sense of being free of ecclesiastical control. It was to become Shrewsbury School.

Grammar schools taught the grammar of language, and were based on a strictly classical education. They concentrated on Greek and Latin literature, poetry and the discipline of composing verse. Classical languages were held to be the necessary gateway to learning of all kinds, a feeling retained into the 18th century. Knowledge of Greek and Latin was essential for access to the law, the Church, medicine, science and the learned world in general. Those who wanted to pursue a trade entered into an apprenticeship.

The first school list of the new free grammar school included a high proportion of the sons of gentry. It consisted of 266 boys of whom half were 'oppidans', or town boys, and half were 'aliens', some from as far afield as Buckingham. The proportion of local boys increased in the mid 1600s. Thomas Auden, rural dean in the early 1900s, writes: 'For the first ten years the school had but a troubled existence, owing to various causes, but in 1561 Thomas Ashton was appointed Headmaster.' It was he who laid the real foundations of the school. A Fellow of Trinity College, Cambridge, he was probably introduced to the school by Sir Andrew Corbet. It is thought he had been tutor to Sir Andrew's two sons, and returned to the family as tutor when he retired.

Thomas Ashton's policies were advanced for his time. Unusually, sport was encouraged, in the form of archery, running and 'leaping'. The school's fencing facilities were also used by the town's apprentices. Although 'Maths' was not part of the initial curriculum, there must have been some interest in the subject, and at least one Elizabethan master, because the school produced two mathematicians in the Jacobean period. By 1570 there were 663 names entered, of which only 106 were from the town. By 1586, it was claimed to be the largest grammar school in England, with over 350 scholars. Between 1571 and 1583 around 10% of the school's pupils went on to university.

In short, the school proved to be highly successful, and pupils in the 1560s and 1570s included many names that became well known. Philip Sidney and Fulke Greville were two of its earliest pupils. Sir Henry Sidney was president of the Council in the Marches for 26 years. While based at Ludlow, he made many visits to Shrewsbury with his court, staying at the Council House, where his son was then at school. When he was there for the St George's Day celebrations in 1581, Thomas Ashton's boys honoured him with speeches and other entertainments, including a riverside send-off in Latin verse.

His son, Philip, proceeded to Christ Church, Oxford, and later earned a reputation as poet, scholar, and soldier and, as Sir Philip Sidney, one of the most admired of Queen Elizabeth's courtiers. He was regarded by many as the perfect example of the Renaissance gentleman. With his uncle, the earl of Leicester, Sir Philip took part in a military expedition to the Low Countries, and was fatally wounded in the relief of Zutphen. According to his biographer, Sir Fulke Greville, the wounded Sidney gave his own water bottle to a dying foot soldier, saying, 'Thy necessity is greater than mine'. He was greatly mourned by many writers of the day. His own remarkable works were published mostly after his death. Greville had his own distinguished political career, and was Secretary for Wales for several years.

Other pupils from that period included Lord Brooke, Chancellor of the Exchequer; Randolph Crew, Speaker of the House of Commons and Chief Justice of the King's Bench; Andrew Downes, a Greek scholar who worked on the Authorised Version of the Bible; Rowland Heylyn, puritan, alderman and Sheriff of London; and William Leighton, a poet and composer. Later names include Arthur Hopton, a mathematical prodigy whose astronomical tables were calculated on Shrewsbury's latitude; and Thomas Tomkys,

The meeting room (built in the early 1500s) of the Council in the Marches created by Edward IV, and presided over between 1560 and 1586 by Sir Henry Sidney. The president had his official residence at Ludlow Castle, but he and his court paid frequent visits to Shrewsbury. After the dissolution of the council, the Council House fell into disrepair but was later repaired and concerted into three houses (in Council House Court, off Castle Street). (Shropshire Archives)

playwright son of the public preacher John Tomkys. (More recent well-known 'alumni' have included Lord Heseltine, cabinet minister in Margaret Thatcher's government; Nick Owen, journalist, TV presenter and newsreader; Michael Palin, comedian, actor, TV presenter, travel writer and presenter; John Peel, disc jockey and radio presenter; 'Willie' Rushton, comedian, satirist, actor and author; and Sir John Stuttard, a Lord Mayor of London.)

The school's regional status and importance is also shown by the names of external donors to the school library, which itself became remarkable. Donors included university fellows, London merchants, and stationers with Shropshire connections, including (distantly) Edward Blount, friend of the playwright Christopher Marlowe.

Literacy in the town as a whole, however, was still low. In 1560 virtually all drapers, mercers and tanners were able to read and sign bonds, as opposed to about half of the shearmen, corvisors and weavers. Subsequent changes did show some improvement in the literacy in the farming hinterland and commercial classes, with those only being able to 'put their mark' standing at 27% by 1589, reducing to 13% by 1609, and down to 9% by 1709.

Book ownership was largely confined to merchants, professional men and better-off tradesmen. It is recorded that, in 1585, the stock of the Shrewsbury bookseller, Roger Ward, included over 500 items. It contained not only the classical and grammar school texts, but also books of poetry, music, medicine and devotional manuals. Shrewsbury School, meanwhile, was stocking its own library even before the founding of the Bodleian Library in Oxford.

Religious Changes

When Henry VIII died in 1547, he was succeeded by his son Edward VI, then a boy of nine. Those who managed affairs on his behalf permitted extremes that Henry VIII never intended. Churches were stripped of images, pictures, furnishings and even some stained glass. Decorative and valuable church plate that had been donated over the previous centuries was destroyed or confiscated, ostensibly on religious grounds, but in fact as a way of raising revenue. This was followed by a strong Roman Catholic reaction under Queen Mary which saw the symbolic re-erection of altars and rood screen at St Mary's, and the return to Latin masses and other customs. This was followed, in 1559, by a return to Protestantism when Mary's sister, Elizabeth I, became queen. The rood and altars were again removed, and ties with the pope and Rome were finally cut.

Through all these changes, Shrewsbury escaped the excesses of religious persecution which took place elsewhere. Only a few books and pictures were burned in the Square, and then only to comply with orders from outside the county. It appears that generally the same clergy held their positions under all the changing religious regimes. The laity came to dominate the church, which had become impoverished academically as well as financially. However, this situation changed with the improvements in education during Elizabeth's reign. In the meantime, extreme Protestants were not content with the Reformation changes, and puritan clergy drew large congregations and began to have considerable influence. By the 1580s, they were removing the crosses from outside

St Mary's and St Julian's, some of the stained glass windows, and also the stone altar from St Mary's – which they claimed had been 'used for idolatry'. The way was being paved for the various non-conforming religious sects which were to break away from the established church in the next century.

Commercial Changes

Although the wool trade was still dominating the commercial scene and export, the workshop trades based on leather, involving its preparation, processing and products, continued to provide for local demand. Hides would have been brought in from Wales for processing in Frankwell and at other sites. The noxious tanneries – they used oak bark and urine – on that side of the town were sited near the water, as was the Dominican friars' riverside tannery, which provoked objections from the abbey's monks on the river's east side. Prepared leather from the continent would also have been an important import, passing through Bristol and then brought up the river. Cordovian leather from Spain was the origin of the word Corvisor for the shoemakers in the town, Corvisors Row on the west side of Pride Hill being where they had their workshops.

Leather goods were in constant demand, not only for weather-proof and hard-wearing footwear and clothing, but also items such as saddlery and harness. The leather working would have become more skilled as the public's taste became more sophisticated, for example in accessories such as fashionable footwear and fine gloves.

But the principal commercial activity was the wool trade and the associated manufacture of cloth, and this was the basis of Shrewsbury's great prosperity in the latter half of the 16th century. The wool trade was prospering across England, with products from Yorkshire and the Cotswolds being shipped out through London; but the situation in Wales was different. Welsh sheep-farming, and its associated cloth industry, were not based on nucleated villages, whilst the grass and climate produced wool of limited quality, which did not make it worth merchants' while to journey to Wales to buy from the isolated farmsteads or hamlets. The Welsh needed a local centre, and Shrewsbury was ideally placed to fill this need. By the mid 1580s the town was the centre of a prosperous business.

'Welsh cloths' were so named from the origin of the wool, with many being made in Shrewsbury. Other cloths were brought into Shrewsbury, where they were washed and dried, stretched on tenter frames. The nap was fluffed up by scuffing with, preferably, teasel heads held in a frame at the end of a hand-held staff; wire carding-brushes tended to damage the cloth. The cloth was finished by the Shrewsbury Shearmen, who were employed by, and therefore depended on, the Drapers, the wholesalers in cloth. Normal practice was then to send the finished cloth to London wholesalers who shipped it abroad.

Although the Shrewsbury Drapers, with their charter of 1462, were a fairly late trade guild compared with other trades, they rose by luck, wealth and cunning, and came to dominate the other guilds concerned with wool processing. Inevitably they also began to hold positions of influence and power in the town itself. During the 16th century there was some rivalry over the trade with Oswestry and Chester, but gradually Shrewsbury gained monopoly of the wool staple.

After the Reformation the religious obligations of the guild were swept away, and by the Chantry Act of 1547 chantries were confiscated. The Shearmen and Mercers lost theirs – but not the Drapers, and the suspicion of bribery and 'oversight' by Draper-member officials in the town is inevitable.

George Leigh was one of the leading Drapers in the town in the mid 1500s, and his career is bound up with the fortunes of the Drapers Guild. In 1551, he was known as a 'Merchant of the Staple' when sworn in as a burgess. Two years later he was sworn in as a member of the Drapers Guild, and in the same year he was elected as a Member of Parliament. In 1555, he became a councilman, between 1564 and 1565 he served as bailiff, in 1565 he was an alderman, the same year that he negotiated a contract with a Llanymynech farmer and employed agents to travel around farms looking for supplies. In 1566 he may have played a part in the passing of an Act giving the Shrewsbury Drapers Guild a monopoly of the Welsh cloth trade. A fine was to be charged for every transgression, and the goods confiscated. One of the mercers, a Mr Ireland, was also behind the Act, and unsurprisingly, the following year Ireland and three of his brothers were all admitted to the Drapers Guild. In 1564, 1568 and 1574 he again served as bailiff, and over his lifetime he was elected one of the town's two MPs on a further five occasions.

In 1576, the present Drapers Hall was built on the site of their existing hall, overlooking St Mary's church, an extension being added just four years later. Although stone was now being used for public buildings, the Drapers chose timber for their hall, which provided the opportunity for elaborate carving and other embellishment to display their wealth. Pitchford Hall near Shrewsbury, completed c.1560, (said by Nikolaus Pevsner to be 'the most splendid black and white building in Shropshire'), was built by rich draper Adam Otley, and his master carpenter Adam Sandford. Sandford's son worked on the new Drapers Hall, so Pitchford could have been influential in their choice of material and the family of craftsmen. The new two-storey Guildhall included a meeting hall on the ground

The Drapers Hall was the headquarters of the powerful Shrewsbury Guild of Drapers. The building was started in 1576 and an extension constructed in 1580. The Drapers chose to build in timber, rather than in brick as was becoming fashionable, to allow for the carving and decorative detail appropriate to their importance. (Stephen de Saulles)

On the left is the rear of Weale's House, the front of which was rebuilt by William Jones, alderman and draper, father or uncle of Thomas Jones. The house has since been demolished. Thomas Jones (*c*.1568-1642), pictured on the right, was also a Shrewsbury draper and was made their master several times, becoming known as 'The Rich Jones'. He was sheriff of Shropshire in 1625 and served as bailiff six times. After Shrewsbury obtained the right to elect its own mayor, (in place of the two bailiffs), he was made Shrewsbury's first mayor in 1638. He built the timber-framed 'Jones's Mansion', now part of the Prince Rupert Hotel.
(SA 6001-200-414 & SHYMS FA-1999-09, courtesy of Shropshire Museums)

floor, with a raised dais at the street end. The 'great chamber', above, is open to the roof, with its decorated roof truss and prominent gable. (The ground floor still contains the original furniture and is now used as a restaurant.) The long dais table was known as a 'withdrawing table', because its leaves could be pulled out to extend its length to 17ft (over 5m). The kitchen and buttery were at the rear. The three-storey extension included a new entrance on the ground floor, and chambers on the upper floors.

In 1582, despite the Drapers' unpopularity for having cornered the market, the townspeople joined them to defeat an attempt by Chester to divert trade there. Although the guilds still engaged in charitable work, the religious aspects had given way to commercial principles and aspirations. From their headquarters the Drapers were able to dominate the town, their prominent members also founding a number of families that had influence within the county over succeeding generations. William Jones, David LLoyd, Robert Ireland, Richard Owen, and William Rowley are names which are still familiar, commemorated in the timber-framed buildings they built in the town.

Building Work

For around three centuries up until 1500, the design of domestic buildings had been simple and undecorated, and after about 1500, for nearly three-quarters of a century, there was very little new building. There were three plague epidemics between 1500 and 1550 and the town was in a generally poor state, not helped by a reduction in the wool trade. The latter was partly caused by a commercial challenge from Oswestry, to which town many farmers in Wales were now sending their wool, and due to a general disruption and subsequent changes to the pattern of trade caused by the Wars of the Roses.

Many of the 14th- and 15th-century open-hall structures in the town have been lost, either by later redevelopment of their sites or by concealment, by later conversion. Floors and ceilings had been installed to provide more rooms, and sometimes partitions to form more accommodation. Later brick chimneys had been inserted in many, although the scorched, smoke-stained timbers, the result of fires on open hearths, can still be seen in many attics. A typical example of such sub-division was revealed when the civic society discovered, in the 1960s, that completely hidden inside the group of tiny old tenements they were saving from demolition in St Alkmund's Square, was an original 13th-/14th-century timber-framed hall structure. It can now be seen, converted to present-day use, as one of the earliest examples in the town.

With the advent of the Tudors, things began to change. Henry VII (1485-1509) had succeeded in uniting the country by bringing together the warring factions of York and Lancaster in marriage. His son, Henry VIII (1509-1547), apart from instigating the Reformation and encouraging the culture of the Renaissance, set about reorganising the country's affairs. In 1522, Cardinal Wolsey was ordered to draw up an inventory of all men aged between 16 and 60. Distinguishing between those 'able' and 'unable', together with listing details of their property, armour and arms, Henry's emphasis was on building up his military potential. The survey also revealed the impoverished state of the country. In Shrewsbury it noted that the wool trade, previously so prosperous, had collapsed; that buildings were falling into disrepair; that the abbey roof was leaking. It was even reported that water was pouring into the choir, and that townhouse chimneys had toppled into the streets.

As a result, an Act of Parliament was passed in 1535 with the aim of revitalising the main towns, including Shrewsbury 'which was in great ruine and decay', and forcing the owners of buildings to repair their properties, on pain of confiscation. Either this dire threat, or other factors, brought about recovery. Between about 1570 and 1600, the Drapers, for example, their fortunes reviving, began a new burst of construction, at the same time adopting a more sophisticated style of timber-framed building.

By this latter part of the 16th century, living standards had risen, and there was a greater emphasis on rooms having a specific function and on personal privacy. The 'main hall' element was reserved more for the owner's use, as for example in the Old Cross Keys in the High Street, or for meetings and ceremonies where the building was used by an organisation, as in the case of guild halls. It was often placed on the first floor, allowing for retail or business uses at ground level. Feature windows in the halls would overlook the street.

The hallmarks of the Shrewsbury carpenters included close and broad vertical timber studs; cross-rails including the quatrefoil motif set in a circle with sunken spandrils within a square; curved S-shaped braces; twisted cable or 'barley sugar' upright pilaster shafts having simple bases and intermediate collar-moulding, terminating with carved heads; also dropped moulded sills; and all crowned by dominant gables enriched by carved vine-leaves and fruit on the barge-boards and tie-beams, and herringbone framing within the gable. Sometimes it included star forms in the upper panels. Door and window heads to all openings, passages and fireplaces show the flat Tudor arch, and bricks were introduced to form chimneys. Typically, the chimneys were set diagonally, with elaborate cornice cappings. This was the high period of timber prefabrication, for the main frames were constructed off site, given the coded carpenter's marks we still see, taken apart, and reassembled on site, matching the coded marks.

Although much of the work of the 'School of Shrewsbury carpenters' largely carried out between 1570 and 1600 has been destroyed, a few examples remain, giving character and quality to the street scene. The prototype seems to have been Pitchford Hall, a building that is generally acknowledged as 'the most splendid piece of black and white timber-frame building in Shropshire', about 6 miles from Shrewsbury. Pitchford was the work of Shrewsbury carpenter, John Sandford, in 1549. Three of his sons

The stone-built Shearmen's Hall in Milk Street, with its Early English lancet windows, appears to date back to the 14th century, although nothing of the original frontage now remains. After Elizabethan times it was converted to a theatre, and has been put to various commercial uses since then. The Shearmen's apprentices used to erect a maypole 'decked with garlands gay' on their feast day until 1588 when Puritans made objection to the revelry. In 1591 some young men defied the bailiff's order and were put in prison, but were later released and the dancing permitted – provided it was done 'soberly and in good order'. In Elizabeth's reign, 600 Shearmen were occupied, under the Drapers, in dressing or raising the wool on one side of a coarse kind of cloth called Welsh webs. The cloth went chiefly to America to clothe negro slaves and to Flanders, where it was worn by the peasants. (Shropshire Archives)

followed him into the trade and they and other carpenters continued his style and details. Below are details of some of the most famous examples of their work in Shrewsbury.

LLoyd's Mansion (demolished)

This mansion stood in the Square, at the corner with old Kiln Lane, now Princess Street. Bearing the date 1570 and initials D.LL, (for David LLoyd) this was the earliest example of the Shrewsbury School of carpentry in the town, and one of their finest. It bore their hallmarks in the short curved braces, cable mouldings and the sunken quatrefoils let into horizontal rails.

David LLoyd was a member of the Drapers and was bailiff in 1575, 1586 and 1594. The Mansion was demolished to make way for the enlargement and rebuilding of the (1785) Shirehall in the 1830s.

Old Cross Keys, now a coffee shop, 15 & 16 High Street, on the corner with Grope Lane

This residence, built in 1575, had a hall on the first floor, with an oriel window at the raised dais end overlooking the street. The building extends for a considerable length up Grope Lane, and would have had a shop and kitchen on the ground floor. It has internal 16th-century panelling and staircase. There is a projecting cupboard on the first floor which was supported by a porch on the ground floor before a shop window was inserted in about 1900. The porch formed the original entrance, but the present one is near the corner of High

An array of carved timberwork on LLoyd's Mansion, demolished to make way for the Shirehall extension in 1905. (SA PH-S-13-S-33-26-2)

The Old Cross Keys, 16 High Street, shows the same quatrefoil and cable motifs and also the star pattern of adjacent Owen's Mansion. The building extends up Grope Lane where examples of the carpenters' marks, by which these pre-fabricated buildings were put together on site, can be seen. (Stephen de Saulles)

Street with Grope Lane. The High Street front shows the star pattern for the first time in Shrewsbury. Some years ago it was an inn, hence its name.

Plough Vaults, *Nos.5 & 5A in The Square*
This was originally a pair of two-storey houses, known as The Shields, and built in 1570. One of them was occupied by Richard Powell, a mercer, in 1573. A third storey was added in a sympathetic idiom in 1880-90. It included three oriel windows, each one including moulded wood transoms and mullions, and supported on corbel brackets. The gables were given the traditional enriched bargeboards.and steeply pitched roofs of the late 16th century. The building was restored in the 19th century with alterations to the ground floor.

String of Horses, *New Street, Frankwell (moved to Avoncroft Museum of Buildings)*
This L-shaped building was built in 1576 as a private house by the Frankwell constable, John Worral, a prosperous leather worker. It had long frontages on to Frankwell and also to New Street, and an unusual feature of a large arch rising the full height of two storeys, allowing a cart or coach and horses to pass through to the rear. The property was later recorded as an inn in 1786.

The old 'String of Horses' was 'one of the most notable of Shrewsbury's diminishing store of 16th century timber frame houses' wrote L.C. Lloyd in the *Inns of Shrewsbury*.
It was demolished and 'put into store', to make way for the Frankwell roundabout.
A complex old structure, (original timber-frame on the upper floors, later cast-iron columns, steel beams, and old brickwork on the ground floor), was re-erected and provided with modern amenities as the reception building at the Avoncroft Museum of Buildings at Bromsgrove in 1972. (Shropshire Archives)

When demolished in the 1960s to make way for a roundabout, it was found that the partition walls retained the original wattle and daub, and that the clay was mixed with flax-stalks instead of the more usual straw.

The structure was eventually rescued by local architects and the Avoncroft Museum of Buildings at Bromsgrove. The timbers were taken out of store, adapted, and re-erected to become their main entrance and café building in 1972.

Ireland's Mansion, *High Street*

Robert Ireland was a draper, and served as bailiff in 1556. His house, built in 1580, has a most complex and rich façade with varied components. Ireland occupied the two centre bays, using the more prestigious close vertical studding on his own part and open studding on the rest of the building. He built a tenement block at each end for revenue, and perhaps additional presence. It had four projecting bays, with four oriel windows shaped as semi-octagonal bows in the side bays. The projecting bays are surmounted by handsome dormers in the top storey. Braces were generally straight, and there was enrichment only in the carved bargeboards. On the ground floor there are two original four-centred moulded timber archways with enriched heads. (A third one has

A postcard of *c.*1900 shows Ireland's Mansion. The building is attributed to Robert Ireland, bailiff in 1566 and 1579, described as a stout protestant, helper of the poor, a good housekeeper and one that 'kept good countenance in the town'.
The building in Pride Hill, facing, was replaced by Lloyd's Bank. (Courtesy of Rob Oakley)

disappeared, and the upper windows are not original, probably dating from about 1700.) An interesting and unsolved Shrewsbury mystery is the considerable space which has been found to exist between the ceiling of the second storey and the floor of the third storey.

Perche's Mansion, *Castle Street*

John Perche was bailiff in 1579, 1588, 1598 and 1602. His house, built in 1581, seems to have occupied originally two sides of a courtyard. The frontage to Windsor Place is about 85 feet (26m) long. (The initials I.P. are carved on a tie-beam of a partly hidden small gable in the courtyard along with the date 1581.) It is three storeys in height and was completely covered with plaster above the brick ground floor. The roof has a steep pitch with four small dormers. There is an overhang throughout at second-floor level, with brackets at each side of four windows. The windows on the ground floor in Windsor Place are old sliding sashes, and on the two upper floors, old double-hung sashes.

Several rooms are panelled with oak, and two have very fine old plastered ceilings with geometrical mouldings, within which are various devices: among them may be distinguished lions rampant, roses, doves, and groups of three pea-pods; each design on a separate raised oblong label. Alterations include a Georgian staircase.

The 85ft (c.26m) long curved frontage of the surviving part of Perche's Mansion to Windsor Place, off Castle Street, originally occupying two sides of a courtyard. John Perche was bailiff of Shrewsbury in 1579, '88, '98 and 1602. In 1676 a 94-year-old Sir Timothy Turneur, an eminent lawyer, King's Sergeant and Recorder of Shrewsbury lived in what was then known as the Old Raven. Later stucco added to the upper floors has been removed to reveal the timber frame, leaving the 'keying' scars in the timbers.
(Stephen de Saulles)

The façade featured in the film of *A Christmas Carol*, starring George C. Scott as Scrooge, made in Shrewsbury in the 1980s.

Owen's Mansion, *22-25 High Street*

Described as an Elizabethan town house at its best, it was built in two stages, the earlier dated 1592 (Nos. 23-25 High Street), the second dated 1598 (No. 22 High Street). The first storey has straight timbers like Ireland's Mansion, but otherwise is different in several ways. There are no bow windows, but each storey overhangs the one below. It has applied cable mouldings at the corners, and baluster-shaped studs appear for the first time. The main horizontal beams have the faces carved with sunken quatrefoils, whilst the gables have elaborately carved bargeboards, brackets and finials, the latter recently renewed. The tie-beams are also carved. The entire surface of the upper storey is divided into square panels, each sub-divided by cross bracings forming a star-like pattern.

Rowley's House, *Barker Street*

A large three-storey building with gable dormers was revealed, 'terribly dilapidated' and propped up with brickwork, when an area of wretched housing was cleared for improvements in the 1930s. It had been built by businessman William Rowley when he

Rowley's House, seen behind Rowley's Mansion, was the earliest brick house in Shrewsbury, built in 1618 by William Rowley, a newcomer to the town, elected a burgess in 1594. Wool merchant and brewer, he was one of the enlarged group of aldermen created under the charter of 1638. The mansion, presently part of the museum, exhibits the Jacobean characteristics of stone dressings and windows, small bricks and, originally, elaborate chimney stacks, regrettably not yet properly reinstated.

came to Shrewsbury in 1590, being admitted as a burgess in 1594. (The family also built the adjoining brick residence in 1618.) Stairs had been removed, and empty windows covered with corrugated iron. It was well restored under the direction of Arthur Ward, architect and civil engineer to the borough, and became the town's museum, but during part of the 1980s it was closed whilst awaiting work to upgrade its fire escape provision. Two local architects saved the building again, devising a less intrusive staircase than that originally proposed. More recently, public opinion has prevented its sale by the local authority to developers, but the building's future is still uncertain.

Merivale House, *Abbey Foregate (demolished)*
This L-shaped two-storey house built in 1601 presented an imposing gable end, with the typical diagonal infill timbers, facing the road. The staircase was a fine example with spiral balustrade, which, if contemporaneous, was probably the earliest of its type in Shrewsbury. There were two hiding places inside the property, one of them leading beneath the roof to a back staircase with an exit behind the house. The house was demolished by the local authority in the 1970s to clear the ground for a play area for the Wakeman School, with the assurance that it would be stored and re-erected on another site. It was later reported as 'lost'.

Castle Gates House
This is a large Elizabethan timber-frame and plaster town house built *c.*1620. It was originally built on Dogpole by Sir Francis Newport, who later offered King Charles support in exchange for a reward – which is how he gained his title of earl of Bradford. The house has two storeys plus an attic, and has a moulded timber doorcase with a four-centred arch with spandrils decorated with carved foliage. Three projecting moulded timber transomed and mullioned bay windows were inserted when the house was restored by Lord Barnard in 1912. The earl of Bradford used it to house his mistress, and he left it to her in his will, together with other Shropshire property.

This timber frame house was dismantled and re-erected as 'Castle Gates House' when the earl of Bradford built his new brick house in Dogpole in 1696. (Stephen de Saulles)

The Tudor Town Layout

The layout of the Elizabethan town at this time, illustrated in Burghley's map, shows how it can be said that Shrewsbury has one of the best conserved medieval town plans in the country. It plainly shows the two main bridge approaches, the surrounding river, and the entry to the loop through the narrow neck of land, guarded by the castle, where railway lines now cut across. It includes the main cross-town route, from south to north, Wyle Cop to Mardol, between the bridges, and clearly shows the original small joggle as it is crossed by the main spine route from east to west. (That main spine route now carries seven or eight different names as it passes, from the Castle Foregate entrance to the town, through to the river apex, down Victoria Avenue in the Quarry.) The link between the 'eastern arm' and the 'southern arm' in front of St Mary's church to Mardol Head is still the same.

Only minor additions have been made to the road network. Part of the town wall circuit is now built upon, but a remarkable area of the Elizabethan open land shown alongside the river is still retained as parkland, called the Quarry. The original small quarry seems to be indicated on the map. Even St Mary's Water Lane, the route flanked by stone walls that led down to the river from one of the city gates still exists, and with its lower gateway, still preserved. Two of the friaries, shown destroyed by Elizabeth's father, Henry VIII, have gone, but their names have been preserved in later building work. Fragments of the original stonework can be seen incorporated in nearby walls.

The castle had been described as a ruin in 1514, but a lease of the castle was granted to Richard Onslow, Speaker of the House of Commons from 1565 to 1596. He may have introduced the windows to the top storey, and perhaps also the richly carved roof beams in the main hall. But precisely who built the top floor and when is unclear. When the lease expired, Queen Elizabeth granted its

The gatehouse to the Council House built in 1620 by Sir William Owen of Condover after acquiring the property. It guarded the entrance to the Council House when the King or Council in the Marches was in residence, and acted as a prison. The whole building shows the amusing combination of the new continental Renaissance motifs with the existing Elizabethan traditions, typical of the Jacobean period. It is full of interesting detail: round-headed blind arches, baluster studs, ornate carving on corner posts and carved devices such as griffins and mermaids. (Stephen de Saulles)

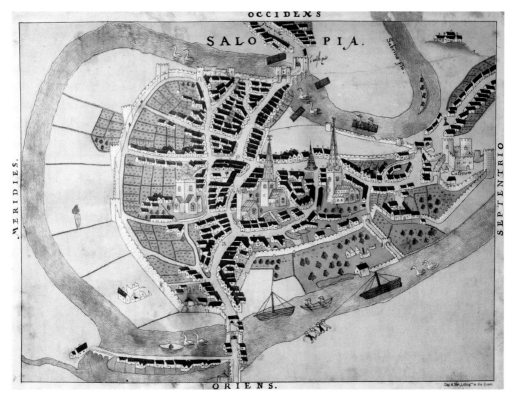

The Burghley map, so-called as it was found in Lord Burghley's private collection, was drawn in pictorial style between 1560 and 1580 and shows many features of the town in Queen Elizabeth's reign, including the use of the river. It is thought that it was specially prepared for her before her proposed visit. (Shropshire Archives)

ownership to the bailiffs and burgesses of Shrewsbury – perhaps for it to be used as council offices – and it is possible that the construction of the top floor and its roof was not yet complete. One theory suggests that the windows and roof were built after Onslow's time, because Burghley's pictorial map, supposed to be of 1575, shows the castle as roofless. But, as it also shows the entrance in the wrong place, the map may not have been very accurately drawn.

River Navigation
By Tudor times the town was beginning to be dependent on the river, which was used to bring in supplies of fuel, first peat and timber, and later coal. In the late 1500s there was a fuel shortage, and faggots for the communal baking ovens were brought downstream, but in general records of the river trade for this period are scarce. Naturally, the damming and obstructing of the river for fisheries and mills was a nuisance to traders. As early as 1425 a commission was appointed to see that dams did not obstruct the river traffic. There were spasmodic attempts to clear gravel from the shallows, and in 1575 the Commissioners for the Severn made various orders for removing obstructions, and some

obligations were put on fish weir owners to maintain gutters along which barges could pass. Fish weirs, built of timber and wickerwork, had been constructed across the river at shallow positions from very early times to trap fish in nets fixed across the funnel-shaped gateways. One is shown on Burghley's map, and another was downstream where Holywell Island still exists. Henry Pidgeon said of the river that it had 'long been celebrated for the excellency of its fish – salmon, pike, grayling, trout, perch, and many others but sport spoiled by poaching with illegal nets'.

The River Severn was remarkable for being navigable for all its 160 miles down to Gloucester and the Severn Estuary, without hindrance of locks. Vessels went downstream with the current, sailing where possible, but sail alone could not provide enough power coming upstream. In any event, barges had to lower their masts to pass under the various bridges. Thus men were used to haul the barges upstream, working in teams of six or eight, scrambling over rocks and through mud, without any harness, as was provided later for the horses which replaced them. Sheep and game from riverside meadows and woods were evidently a regular part of their diet, and they used their ingenuity to extract portions of cider, wines and spirits from amongst their cargoes. There were often alterations to weight tickets and frequent complaints concerning the loss of consignments.

These 'bow-haulers' are shown on Burghley's map, also the way in which rafts were used to float timber downstream when the river was high to Shrewsbury, their 'terminus'. These rafts frequently caused damage to bridges, and were dangerous in time of flood. Floods, of course, delayed journeys, as did low water in summer, sometimes halting traffic for weeks at a time. During such times of idleness, bow-haulers were constant, if not good, customers at the local taverns.

Judging the conditions and timing were all important to successful business. For example, fish from the January Fair at Bristol, had to get to the upper reaches, travelling at night when necessary, before the river fell, otherwise Lent would be over and the market for fish would be lost. But transport by road was more expensive.

Living Conditions in Elizabethan Shrewsbury
There were similarities between the end of the Elizabethan period and our own recent rising standards of living and prices. It was a period of inflation, of fuel crisis and technical innovation. By the middle of the 16th century, supplies of timber had dwindled. Harmer Moss peat was brought in for bakers' ovens and, by the 1570s, rewards were being offered to encourage prospecting for opencast coal to be found in the region, whilst the town authorities instructed traders to ensure that they retained a reserve stock of coal.

Outbreaks of 'aigue', and what was referred to as the 'sweating sickness', which may have been a form of influenza, brought renewed fears of plague, and caused the first developments in public health since the departure of the Romans. Besides a system of quarantine for merchants returning from London, it was decreed that swine and dogs were to be confined, and some streets were to be swept clear of food waste and offal twice a week. Another innovation was the introduction of piped fresh drinking water in the 1550s – a generation before most other towns. This came from wells sunk at Crowmeole, beyond Kingsland. The water was brought under the river to the centre of the town through elm wood pipes, later replaced by ones of lead. By 1574 there were five public draw-off points to supplement the town wells and river water, which had inevitably been suffering for some time from pollution caused by overcrowding. Many wells were also near to sources of pollution such as drains and cemeteries.

Health was also improved by the steps taken by the bailiffs to compensate for the series of bad harvests at the end of the century, which caused fluctuating prices and famines. Action had to be taken in order to prevent both rioting and speculation in grain and the magistrates were sent round local farms, instructing the farmers to bring a certain quantity into market each week in order to limit their hoarding of grain while waiting for the price to rise. In the latter 1590s such measures were insufficient, and the authorities had to arrange for imports of grain from the Baltic countries. It was shipped up the Severn and sold at subsidized prices.

There was also a gradual increase in knowledge as to the cause of some cases of 'mental illness'. For example, it was understood that rye, often then used to make bread, when damp developed a mould that contained ergot which if eaten would cause poisoning that could result in hallucinations and attendant irrational behaviour, convulsions, and even death.

Besides dealing with these problems, the bailiffs' accounts give details of various forms of entertainment enjoyed at the time. Dancing bears and minstrels were popular; and there were wrestling matches and cockfighting bouts attended by noblemen and gentlemen as well as everyone else. Various visiting noblemen's minstrels and players gave public performances. Tightrope walking in the Square is also mentioned, and there are various stories relating to the mysterious 16th-century phantom 'Bank's Horse' and its alleged supernatural powers.

In September 1591, a Master Banks, a Staffordshire gentleman, brought a white horse to Shrewsbury which he said would perform 'wonderful and strange things', including telling, by use of his foot, how many coins were in a man's pocket. Gathering a crowd to witness such acts, he said to the horse: 'Sir, there be bailiffs in this town; the one of them bid me welcome unto the town, and used me in a friendly manner, I would have thee go to him and give him thanks for me.' The horse duly sought out the right bailiff and bowed to him, also 'makinge curchey [curtsy] to hym with hys fote in suche maner as he coulid'. (Owen and Blakeway wonder whether it was stories about Bank's horse which Shakespeare drew upon in Act 1, Scene 2 of *Love's Labour Lost*: 'How easy it is to put years to the word three, and study three years in two words, the dancing horse will tell you.')

The new Market House
In 1595, the poor weather and a series of disastrous harvests prompted the bailiffs to commission Walter Hancock to build a new Market House, or Hall, where corn could be stored and sold under cover. The upper floor was to be used for the weekly wool sales. The structure now stands as a perfect lesson in good building. Although its purpose was strictly functional and it was built in record time, it is still one of the town's architectural gems, four hundred years later. It was built in good materials, to an excellent design for

The Square and old Market Hall at night. (Stephen de Saulles)

its original purpose; and sufficient funds were allocated to allow for quality of detail, and to provide a good investment. It also included innovative design features, such as the unusually large windows to allow good lighting for the inspection of cloth quality. During restoration work in 2000, it was discovered how Walter Hancock had solved the problem of building on soft ground. 'The Square' was created as a new market place in 1221, when the King's Market by St Alkmund's church got too congested, by draining the old marvellously named 'Gumblestolemore', or ducking-stool mere. When building the new Shirehall, alongside, in 1783, workmen had dug down 19ft (6m) trying, without success, to find solid ground. Haycock's foundations, laid on timber beams soon failed, and cracks were appearing everywhere. In constructing a replacement building in 1832, Smirke went down a further 10ft (3m) before reaching the firm base he sought for laying a very deep 3m solid concrete raft. He did not know of Hancock's earlier, simpler methods. It was found that Hancock's foundations of 1596 had not been taken down to solid ground but, more cleverly, had been laid with only a shallow cut, but by spreading the load over a 7ft width his structure suffered little or no settlement in four centuries. One wonders if Hancock in 1596 was instinctively aware of the information that the later exploratory deep borehole revealed in 2000.

This building and the later Shrewsbury School's building (the present library) at Castle Gates, show the influences of the Renaissance that originated two centuries before in Italy. These ideas were slowly reaching Shrewsbury, and merging with the local Elizabethan style of building – creating another phase in the development of the town.

7 STUART SHREWSBURY

'And that the said town may shine and be encreased, as well in honour and dignity as in privileges and authority, and that the wicked beholding the ensign of justice may be witholden from the lust of sinning, the King grants that the mayor, aldermen, and burgesses may have a sword bearer, who shall from time to time be attendant upon the mayor, and shall carry and bear before him one sheathed sword ordained and adorned as it shall please the mayor for the time being, in all places where maces have in times past being accustomably borne before the bailiffs, (so as the said sword shall not be borne erect in any church or chapel consecrated to the honour and worship of God). Three serjeants at mace to bear maces of silver gilt, engraved and adorned with our arms.'

One of the privileges granted to the town by King Charles I
in the charter of 1638

The Tudor period, for which Shrewsbury is renowned through its buildings, ended when James VI of Scotland succeeded Elizabeth I as James I of England in 1603. A new phase of history, under the Stuarts, began. The neglected castle was still in existence, but its walls and defences were no longer required. The scattered ruins of religious buildings constructed and valued during the previous 500 years had meanwhile come to be regarded as only useful quarries for dressed stone and other building materials incorporated into buildings elsewhere in town.

The Renaissance reaches Shrewsbury

The first hint of the Renaissance design idiom had shown itself, at the end of the Elizabethan period, in the design of the stone-built Market House in the Square. But for domestic purposes, timber frame continued as the traditional building system for another 30 years. However, in the short Jacobean period, there is a characteristically quaint combination of medieval and classical detailing and decorative motifs. The gatehouse to the Council House is an excellent example. It was erected in 1620 to provide an imposing new entrance because it was being used increasingly by the Council in the Marches as its headquarters. Arthur Ward described this property, built in 1620, 'as one of the architectural gems of the town ... its timbers are richly decorated with grotesque designs; two gables soar above the eaves and, being placed close to each other, give to the whole the semblance of an elegant three-storeyed house'. Among the carved devices adorning it are griffins, mermaids and grotesque figures; the inner gable features the usual vine. The panels are divided into geometric patterns. One of the finials included a device of a key, symbolic of the fact that part of the building was used as a prison for criminals sentenced by the council. It was built by Sir William Owen of Condover for times when visitors to the Council House (including Charles I in 1642) had to be closely guarded, and all strangers entering the town examined.

Shortly after the date of Speed's map, 1610, there was a change of direction in the visual appearance of the town. It is one that is now accepted as part of the town's tradition, and yet then was an entirely new departure. In 1590 William Rowley had come to Shrewsbury and started business as a draper, dealing in Welsh cloth, and also as

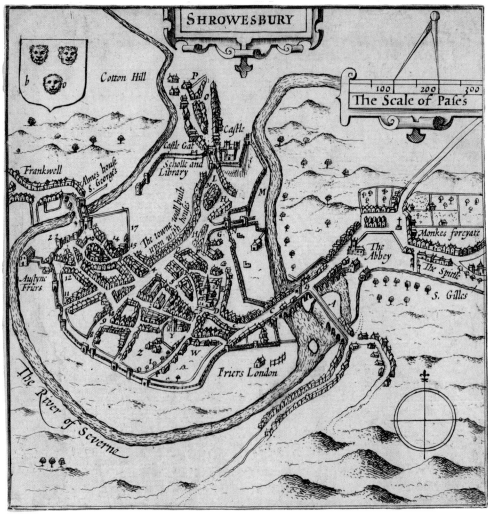

John Speed is one of the best known English cartographers, creating maps of many English counties and county towns. Here, in 1610 he used a pictorial style 'bird's eye view'. Foreshortening, and a smaller scale, allowed inclusion of suburbs for the first time. He named main streets – but filled blank space with decorative 'hills'. (SA 24330–PR-1-546)

a brewer and maltster, constructing the timber-framed building still known as Rowley's House. Yet he, or his son Roger, just a few years later in 1618, built a further house, Rowley's Mansion, reflecting the arrival of Renaissance style.

Brick construction was late coming to the borderlands. Brick-making was a long outdoor process and the six to eight weeks of firing and drying needed settled conditions in the brickfields. Brick had been used before, but only in small quantities for flues and ornamental chimneys. Mr Rowley's mansion used the small bricks of the period, (thicker would have distorted in the firing methods of the time), with stone dressings, and transomed and mullioned windows. Originally it had a parapet, but this was removed when it became dangerous early in the 19th century. Although there were functional, and decorative, projecting stone string courses to throw the water off the wall faces, the whole mass introduced a different form of design, and colour, into the town. There was a certain mistrust of brick as a structural material in those days, as can be seen by the insertion of timber whenever strong structural support was needed, and the use of stone quoins to hold the corners together, as they thought.

In the 1620s, the Grammar School embarked on an ambitious rebuilding project, in order to provide further accommodation as pupil numbers grew. The original timber

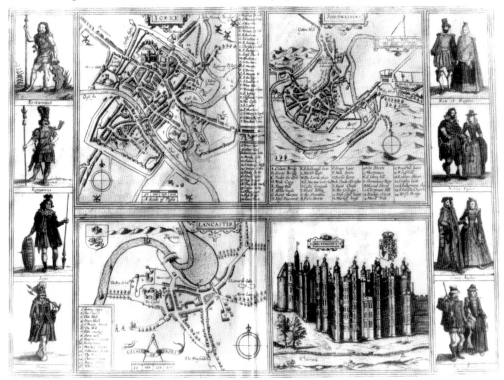

Map of Shrewsbury by Braun & Hogenberg published in 1617 showing the town, based on Speed's map of 1611, compared with York, Lancaster and Richmond. Pictorial in style, it includes the suburbs (by shortening Abbey Foregate), names streets and features and also shows that houses had been built up on the town walls in the half-century since Burghley's map. John Speed's patron was Sir Fulke Greville. (Shrewsbury Civic Society)

Shrewsbury's Royal Free Grammar School, founded by Edward VI in 1552, was first housed in timber-framed buildings. The stone chapel and library block was completed in 1612. In 1630 the main new school house block was finished. The restrained stone façades are decorated with unusual carved string courses and the delightful crested parapet is similar to Walter Hancock's old Market House, but he had died in 1599. It is possible that this was the work of his son. (Shropshire Archives)

classroom was demolished and in its place an imposing three-storey stone block was constructed, completed in 1630, thereby providing higher standards of accommodation, comparable with the Oxford and Cambridge colleges of the time. Again, there are Renaissance elements, and the mixture of classical and gothic detailing characteristic of the English interpretation of the continental Renaissance of some 200 years earlier. The whole group of buildings exhibits a pleasing dignity, achieved by combining a subtle balance of ornament and three-dimensional detailing, with a restrained and ordered surface treatment. The front of the new extension was in local ashlar, with emphasis on the main entrance archway and a decorative crested parapet similar to that installed on the Market House by Walter Hancock 35 years earlier. Walter Hancock had died in 1599, but it is thought that the school building could have been the work of his son, who evidently carried on the craft. Fluted Corinthian columns on decorated pedestals flank the elliptical entrance arch. The decorated string course breaks forward over each, to provide bases for the two carved figures which give such character to the frontage – one a scholar and the other a graduate, each in the costume of the time. Shared between them is a quotation from 5th-century BC Isocrates, '*Philomathes* [if thou art a lover of learning] *Polymathes* [thou wilt become very learned]'. The story is told that the bailiffs then in office in the town had expected their own initials to be inscribed over the entrance. However, John Meighen, the headmaster at the time, was not on good terms with them, and relegated their initials to 'a small building devoted to more ignoble uses which stood near at hand' – which has long since been demolished. Now, Isocrates's message is 'read', even if not fully understood, by many hundreds every week.

Originally, the new block housed the principal schoolroom, known as Top Schools. Many years later it held the town's Natural History Museum's collection of stuffed animals in glass showcases, and later still it was occupied by the local studies library. The chapel, forming the northern wing, was consecrated in 1617. Prayers were read twice a day on schooldays. Above the chapel was the library, which contained a collection of printed books and manuscripts, now held by Shrewsbury School in their present Kingsland

The two stone figures at the main entrance to the old Grammar School (now the library) represent a scholar and a graduate dressed in the costume of the day. The quotation is from Isocrates: '*Philomathes*' and '*Polymathes*' – 'Those who love learning – become very learned'.
(Stephen de Saulles)

Top Schools, the senior form room at the top of the schoolhouse block, as it appeared c.1880, and probably in the 17th century. (Shropshire Archives)

premises. The whole building complex included the early 16th-century timber-framed Rigg's Hall at the rear.

In the early 1600s the school's, and therefore the town's, connection with London had become important. Communication was through men such as Shrewsbury bookseller Roger Ward, who was important in the London printing trade, and Richard Meighen (son of the headmaster of the school), who was admitted to the London Stationer's Company in 1614. London news and ballads and reports came hot to Shrewsbury through their press contacts. By the 1630s men from Shropshire living in London were holding an annual dinner, a precedent for the Shropshire Society formed in the capital in 1899 (and still active).

Timber-frame building was not abandoned altogether but, apart from Porch House (1628), in Swan Hill, the last of the larger timber-framed houses, there was very little new domestic building at this time. Rather, it was a period of alterations and additions, and of inserting intermediate floors in existing hall-type buildings. This explains why the considerable increase in population is not reflected in the amount of extra development shown on John Speed's map of 1610. It does, however, show that houses had been built upon the old town walls, on the precipitous side of Pride Hill, then called High Pavement.

River Trade

The early 16th century had seen the beginnings of the river trade, but it became more organised in the 17th. Mardol Quay would have been one of the busiest of the river communities, with crowded inns, storehouses, chandlers, lodgings, and other amenities typical of a port – which Shrewsbury used to be, trading, through Bristol, with the continent. A quayside appears here in the Borough rental of 1610, and would then have consisted of wooden jetties probably constructed by a Mr Roland Jenks in 1607. He built Frankwell Quay the following year, and paid for the work by collecting tolls for goods landed. 1605 is the first year that a vessel is registered in British port books as having begun its journey in Shrewsbury.

Before the increase in activity created by the new quayside, the Frankwell community was made up of a variety of trades and crafts. Elsewhere there were clusters of particular occupations: there were more tanners and leather workers in Coleham, and brickfield workers and labourers in the Castle Foregate area, whereas Mardol's curved burgage plots show that as many properties as possible had direct access to the riverside. Some of Mardol's residents would have been involved in fishing, and others with the river trade, benefiting from direct access to the town centre. The fortunes of Frankwell, a planted town, and outside the loop, were initially more mixed. Tolls had to be lowered to encourage the use of its quay as opposed to that at Mardol. Later, however, Frankwell quay benefited from the establishment of malting and brewing activities nearby, as well as newer and larger storage provision not available on the crowded Mardol side. The Frankwell community gradually included river workers as quayside use developed.

Barge owners were important people in those days and were addressed by the title 'Owner', as we use the title 'Doctor' now. In the 1630s there were seven barge owners in Shrewsbury, and the number rose to ten some time later.

Traffic coming downstream from above Shrewsbury included the timber floats which remained familiar until the end of the 18th century, from which time barges were used instead. Goods also included lead and lead ore from Pool Quay and Llandrinio, slate for roofing, and bark harvested in mid-Wales for use in tanning, as well as wool, butter and cheese, and pickled oysters from Milford Haven which must have taken a rather circuitous route to reach Shrewsbury. In the 1830s and probably earlier, Grinshall stone was brought by road to Shrewsbury, where it was loaded on to barges. Coming upstream were goods mainly for domestic use. Coal was being imported from the early 17th century. Sometimes it came from Ironbridge, with quantities being transported by road to Chester. Other goods included iron and common groceries, drink, soap and snuff. Building materials such as lime and brick tiles came from Ironbridge and Stourport.

Commercial Centre and Social Change

Shrewsbury was, at this time of its life, one of the larger towns in the country. It had gained importance in connection with the Council in the Marches, which met here after 1571. This, together with the quarter sessions, began to make the town a political, as well as a commercial, centre. It was not only the collecting centre for Welsh goods, handling their transfer to Bristol and overseas, but also the distribution centre for luxury goods brought up river. There was an increasing trade with London, and suburbs were developing.

The early 17th century was a time of fundamental social change. The gentry were entering various forms of commerce, while wealthy drapers were founding new land-owning families. Meanwhile, in the 1630s the country as a whole was experiencing a constitutional crisis. Charles I succeeded his father in 1625 and now decided to rule without Parliament. He was already unpopular for supporting Spain and the Catholics, and when he required a contribution to the army, there was a reluctance to comply. Shrewsbury resisted the king's commands to send troops to fight in Scotland, making the excuse that they had no money. It was probably more a matter of lack of interest in military affairs. Tellingly, by this time the town was no longer guarded by gates, and citizens were permitted to take down sections of the walls, gaining access to useful grazing and market gardening land beyond – although this was soon to change.

In 1638 a new charter was offered to, some say forced on, the town, requiring the surrender of the previous one. The cost payable to the king for the privilege was thought to be excessive, and Archbishop Laud had inserted clauses that increased the power of the Church and reduced that of the local authority. It is said that the attractive part was the added privilege to the town of a mayor in place of the two bailiffs – and the entitlement to have a ceremonial sword of state. William Rowley was one of the first of the new aldermen to be appointed, which indicates the level of influence he had gained.

8   The Civil War and Commonwealth

'The king declared ware at Nottingham and when his Majesty arrived at Derby he heard from the loyalists of Shrewsbury, that the town was at his disposal. Therefore, because of its strong and pleasant situation, and by reason of its neighbourhood to North Wales, and the use of the river Severn, he determined to repair thither.'

From a report by Edward Hyde, Chancellor of the Exchequer and Privy Councillor, later Lord Clarendon, chief minister of Charles II

The differences between king and Parliament increased, and armed conflict became inevitable. Apart from the constant fears of Catholic riots, there were many elements that contributed to the strife, social and religious as much as political. Many people found it difficult to decide which side to support. Very few felt personal enmity towards the king; they only sided against him when he acted unconstitutionally. Of the twelve Shropshire Members of Parliament, eight fought for the king, and four sided with Parliament. But the main strength of the king's support came from the country squires supported by the peasantry, while that of Parliament came from the middle classes, on whom Puritanism had taken its firmest hold. The country as a whole was roughly divided geographically in its allegiance: the east supported Parliament while the west was broadly Royalist. Wales was almost solidly for the king and therefore a useful source of recruits. Within this broad overview, Shropshire was divided. The landowners tended to support the king, while the merchants, concerned about loss of trade with the continent, tended to support Parliament. In the town of Shrewsbury, there were also both elements.

As rumours ebbed and flowed, the first precautions against attack – from either side – had been commenced during 1641. The gates were reinforced; breaches made in the walls were blocked up again, and the walls repaired in places, which probably included the castle. A night watch was instituted, and firearms purchased. Significantly, the Watergate was to be chained, locked and guarded.

The royal standard was set up at Nottingham in August 1642. Shrewsbury had agreed the terms of the charter of 1638 so when Civil War broke out, the king calculated on the town taking his side. Also, it seems that Richard Newport of High Ercall, the richest of the local landowners, had written to the king, offering him a large sum of money (but indicating that a title would be acceptable in return), and promising Charles support. The king evidently accepted the offers, and his terms, and before he left Nottingham

The council chamber in the Council House, furnished for the period when the Council
in the Marches was meeting in Shrewsbury, and when the king visited during the Civil War.
(Shropshire Archives)

he directed a troop of footsoldiers to Shrewsbury, 'where I doubt not you will be well received', and he himself followed. He arrived in mid-September, some say to cheering, at the head of an army of some 6-8,000 men.

Charles took up residence, not in the castle, but at the Council House nearby. This property was already well-appointed and comfortable, used as it was by the Council in the Marches. The king's courtiers were provided with accommodation by the masters of the school opposite, and various leading citizens. During their three week stay, Charles appointed the vicar of the abbey as his chaplain, visited Chester, and also addressed a general muster of troops at the Gaye Meadow. (This was land across the river, opposite St Mary's Water Lane, once part of the abbot's garden and orchard. Later still it was a site for carnivals and circuses; and for some recent decades Shrewsbury Football Club's ground, now moved to the outskirts.) Addressing the townspeople, the king expressed his satisfaction in coming to such a loyal part of his country, and announced that he had sent for a mint, and a printing press. He told them that he was having all his own silver plate melted down for coinage to pay his troops, and appealed to them to do the same. On the Sunday before he left, he took an oath on the sacrament in St Mary's church, in which he promised to defend and maintain the true Protestant Religion, as established by Queen Elizabeth and James I, and the privileges and freedom of Parliament.

The silver that formed the materials for the Shrewsbury coinage was partly from the private plate belonging to the king, partly from the collections of the Oxford and

The bedchamber in the Council House, with its heavily decorated Jacobean interior decoration and furnishings, used by presidents of the Council in the Marches, King Charles during the Civil War and King James II in 1687. (Shropshire Archives)

Cambridge colleges (brought via Worcester and the first skirmish of the Civil War at Powick Bridge), and partly from the gentry of Shropshire and the plate from Shrewsbury School. Many also presented Charles with considerable sums of money and, among other contributions, was a loan from the school's chest of £600 – which the king acknowledged in a letter addressed to his 'trusty and well-beloved' Richard Gibbon, late mayor of the town, and Thomas Chaloner, schoolmaster of the Grammar School. He promised that he would cause the same to be repaid whenever they should demand it, but he never did.

The town itself, where there were many among the elite who sympathised with Parliament, was less generous in the matter of financial support. It became necessary to adopt free quartering for the troops, under which householders had to house and feed soldiers allocated to them in exchange for a ticket that would supposedly be redeemed for cash at a later date, but rarely was. This was a constant cause of resentment and hardship during the course of the war.

When the king left on 12 October, the whole army moved on to Bridgnorth and Wolverhampton. After the first major engagement at Edgehill, he had intended advancing towards London, but was checked at Turnham Green. He retreated to Oxford, which he then made his headquarters. The mint was brought from Aberystwyth and duly set up in Shrewsbury, where it worked for several months before following the king to Oxford.

Two of the king's most enthusiastic supporters in Shropshire were Richard Newport and Sir Francis Ottley of Pitchford. The latter was appointed governor of Shrewsbury.

When the king departed Shrewsbury in October 1642 he left Francis Ottley of Pitchford in charge of the town. Here he is with his wife, Lucy, and children Richard and Mary.
(Stephen de Saulles, courtesy of Shropshire Museums)

Ottley insisted on a strong protestation of loyalty from the town's chief inhabitants, in which they declared that, 'without any mental reservation, they detested and abhorred the notorious rebellion which went under the name of the Parliamentary army, and would, with their whole force and means, withstand it'. Backed by his military authority, he was able to silence those sympathetic to the other side. Ottley had evidently promised the king to set up a musket manufactory in the town, but this was never done.

The local militia was untrained, and lacking in enthusiasm. Training sessions were more an excuse for social gatherings, being described as 'more like country fairs'. The militia, or trained bands, included peace-time farmers; they were willing to be members when there was no fighting, but when the actual fighting started, they would absent themselves, hiring others to take their place – which was not very satisfactory from a military viewpoint. Not only that, but the garrison in Shrewsbury had only two professionals amongst its eight officers. Accordingly, the king appointed Lord Capel as commander-in-chief of his troops in Shropshire and the neighbouring counties, with responsibility to organise affairs effectively.

Lord Capel ordered houses outside the castle walls on the north side to be demolished so the river as a moat could be used around the castle bailey with a clear field of fire. A drawbridge was built across the moat at the castle gate, and Lord Capel caused the castle to be repaired and strengthened, making it once again suitable for military use. The main hall was divided in two by a substantial partition, which still exists at its eastern entrance. A stone postern gate structure with a room above was built, also a wall from the original motte, where Laura's Tower now stands, to the east tower of the castle.

He also had a deep trench dug from the present Smithfield Road up to the castle bailey, so creating a moat flooded by the river, and complete with drawbridge. The main gate was provided with new iron-studded double doors, and musketry embrasures and slits were inserted in the adjoining walls. He ordered additional work to the town walls, closing the gaps which had been made in them over the years to gain access to the lands beyond. A new section of wall was built from Castle Foregate to Mardol Quay along the riverside, known as the Roushill Wall. A strong fort was also created at the top of Frankwell, of which no trace remains.

Shrewsbury was thus strongly held for the king. The town was important strategically for several reasons. It was a central assembly point for troops raised from the north, the south-west and Wales. There was a magazine (ammunition store), which made it a desirable place to capture. It housed the garrison that protected essential iron manufactories of shot and cannon at Leighton and Coalbrookdale, and, in this connection, it was on lines of communication with Oxford and York. Shrewsbury was also important for supporting Chester, which was under almost continual siege. Moreover, it was a political centre, and considered to be a place of refuge in case of a Catholic uprising. Finally, in case of emergency, Shrewsbury was well placed on a possible escape route to Wales and Ireland, or down river to Bristol, and the Continent.

Prince Rupert by Anthonis van Dyck.
Rupert, the king's nephew, was based in
Shrewsbury at the beginning of 1644

Early on in the struggles, Parliamentary forces took Whitchurch and so acquired a large store of arms and ammunition, as well as a sum of £2,000 which had been held there for paying Capel's soldiers. Capel took Oswestry as a counter-stroke, where he established another strong garrison. Parliament decided that Wem would be a good base from which to harass Shrewsbury, and for their communications with the forces besieging Chester. Wem duly became their headquarters, under the command of Colonel Mytton. In order to guard against surprise attacks on Shrewsbury from Wem, Sir Francis Ottley placed garrisons in Moreton Corbet Castle, and in the moated manor house of Albright Hussey, just north of the town.

Towards the end of 1643, Capel suffered a serious reverse when he failed to capture Wem, suffering heavy casualties and losing many of his best officers. Back in Shrewsbury, his troops faced a riot in which several townspeople were killed. Capel was replaced by Lord Byron for a while, and then in January 1644, by Prince Rupert, the king's nephew. Rupert seems to have been dissatisfied with Ottley's preparations in the town, for he wrote to Ottley ordering him to mobilise the gentry and townspeople to get certain work done at the castle, including the partitioning off of spaces and rooms for receiving and storing ammunition and equipment. Rupert himself took up his quarters in the house of Jones the Lawyer opposite St Mary's church, now part of the well-known Prince Rupert Hotel. The prince gave fresh impetus

In January 1644 Prince Rupert, together with his brother Prince Maurice, took up quarters in the house of Master Jones the lawyer, the mansion now incorporated in the Shrewsbury hotel named after him. (Stephen de Saulles)

to the royal cause, deciding to replace the system of free quartering with a land tax on everyone to pay for the troops' board and lodging – although accepting cheese or grain in lieu. However, the soldiers' pay was much in arrears, and the men were discontented. At the same time, both gentry and townspeople were almost at the end of their resources, and were unable or unwilling to pay much more, and against this background Prince Rupert now gave orders that a levy should be made, sufficient to provide one month's pay to each soldier in lieu of arrears. This proved impossible to raise and the soldiers resorted to helping themselves to what they considered their entitlement, causing further resentment in the town and countryside. In addition, Rupert's horses were ruining the pasture-lands outside the walls.

Early in 1644 year Rupert opted to replace Ottley with Sir Fulke Hunckes, an officer who had served in Ireland, but he soon proved to be widely unpopular with the townspeople, and in August had in turn been replaced by Sir Michael Erneley. Erneley was soon reporting to Rupert: 'The edge of the gentry is much blunted, the county's loyalty is strangely abated; they begin to warp to the enemy's party.' Elsewhere in Shropshire, risings of clubmen were happening, as people tried to protect their possessions from plundering by soldiers of either side.

By the end of 1644, matters in the town were approaching a crisis. Many of those who had been among the king's warmest supporters grew lukewarm under the financial and other strains, which included the necessity to increase 'the watch' (the night guards) and constantly repair the walls. Meanwhile, neither Prince Rupert, nor his brother Maurice, who came to support him, was able to make any progress against the Parliamentary forces.

Early in 1645, the governor weakened the garrison by sending a detachment for the relief of Chester, and was himself ill in bed, unable to maintain his normal vigilance. This state of affairs was allegedly communicated to the Parliamentary garrison at Wem from an unexpected source, a hitherto staunch and ostentatious Royalist, Sir William Owen, the owner of the property called Council Gates, which had been important for guarding the king when he came to Shrewsbury. Owen was even captured by the Parliamentarians, and subsequently fined, but with mysterious leniency. It later emerged that he had been passing information on Royalist plans to Wem for two years, and even offering them the use of his property in Condover as a garrison. On receipt of the latest information, plans to take Shrewsbury were immediately put in hand.

Under cover of darkness, on the night of 21-22 February, a mounted force of around a thousand men reached Castle Foregate at about 4 o'clock in the morning. Here they divided. The main body advanced to the north gate, to await admission. A small party led by Lieutenant Benbow (a native of the town), made their way to the left, towards the river below the castle, scaled the wall using the light ladders they had brought with them. They then made their way over to the north gate, to let down the drawbridge and allow the cavalry into the town. Colonel Reinking, 'with the main body of 350 foot, ... filed along the narrow footpath by the river ... and reached the bottom of Water Lane. This bold step led them to a spot ... commanded by two forts. ... No military commander ... would have led his men [into] such a situation, had he not been assured of finding [both] gates in [the] lane left open for his admission. This was the case, ... and up this lane, Reinking entered the town, ... indebted to treachery for his success.'

By midday, the castle had surrendered, on condition that the English present should be allowed to march out to Ludlow unmolested. Of the 50 Irish Royalist troops left, 13 were chosen by lot and hanged the same day without a trial; Irish soldiers were widely, but wrongly, believed to have carried out barbarous acts on Protestants in Ireland. The fort at Frankwell, called Cadogan, held out a while longer, but once they heard the castle had surrendered, they followed suit. Apart from the death of the Irish soldiers, casualties were light. The Parliamentarians lost two men, the Royalists six, including a captain. But crucially, the Royalists lost 14 pieces of ordnance, several barrels of gunpowder, several hundred stands of arms and a store of munitions that belonged to Prince Maurice.

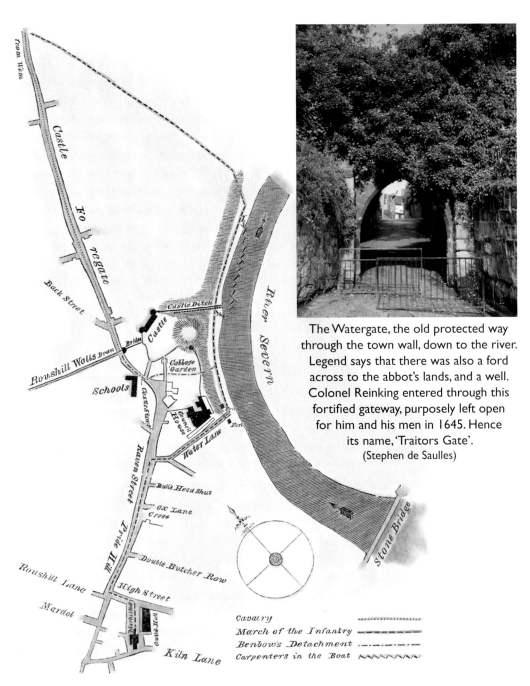

The Watergate, the old protected way through the town wall, down to the river. Legend says that there was also a ford across to the abbot's lands, and a well. Colonel Reinking entered through this fortified gateway, purposely left open for him and his men in 1645. Hence its name, 'Traitors Gate'.
(Stephen de Saulles)

Cavalry
March of the Infantry
Benbow's Detachment
Carpenters in the Boat

A diagrammatic map showing the method of attack on Shrewsbury by the Parliamentary forces on 21-22 March 1645, led by Lieut-Colonel William Reinking supported by Colonel Thomas Mytton. The 13th-century Watergate had been reinforced by a blockhouse on each side. However, Reinking, with the main body of the infantry, gained entry through the Watergate and proceeded up the hill to St Mary's Gate, joining the cavalry who had been let in over the drawbridge, and made their way to the Square where they overcame the guard.

As the fortified town had been generally regarded as a safe place, the gentry from around had fled to Shrewsbury for refuge from the insecurity of their country seats. Parliament-supporting townsmen knew where to find them, and the prisoners taken as the day wore on included eight knights and baronets, 40 colonels, majors and captains, and 200 private soldiers. Governor Michael Erneley, already ill, died a few days after being taken prisoner.

Parliamentary Rule

In London, Colonel Mytton was formally thanked in the House of Commons for his victory and a day of thanksgiving was ordered for the fall of this, 'one of the King's principal strongholds'. Indeed, the fall of Shrewsbury began a collapse of Royalist strongholds in the county. The castles at Caus, Stokesay and Shrawardine fell in July, followed by Lilleshall Abbey and Dawley in August, and Moreton Corbet in September. Bridgnorth was captured in March of the following year. Ludlow was the last to fall, in May of 1646.

Changes were now made in the government of the town, and it seems that they were almost all welcomed. Several suspended aldermen were able to return to office, while a number of prominent Royalist families, including the town clerk, were obliged to leave. But the Drapers' trade with London had been ruined, and also that with Bristol, because of blockades at Bridgnorth, Bewdley and Bristol. The town was de-garrisoned, but Parliamentary orders in 1647 meant that a garrison of 100 foot soldiers was to be maintained in the castle, as there was widespread fear and rumour of Royalist uprisings. Indeed, when the future Charles II led a largely Scottish army into England in 1651, he sent an envoy to demand, in vain, the surrender of Shrewsbury. Soon afterwards, Cromwell won a decisive battle at Worcester, and Charles escaped to France. Though times were more peaceful, many problems remained. Outbreaks of plague which struck the town in 1650-51 caused high mortality, probably on account of the years of malnutrition. Then, in 1654 and 1659, there were unsuccessful attempts to retake the castle for the exiled king.

The capable and much respected Humphrey Mackworth had been appointed governor shortly after the town was taken; his lieutenant at the castle, a recently promoted Captain Hill, was less respected. In fact he was evidently much hated by the garrison soldiers and in the town – and considered 'a prodigall drunken fellow who before the warrs was a pitiful barber in this towne'. A story is related 'which illustrates the social condition of Shrewsbury at the time', that he was lured to a drink with a townsman at the Loggerheads. While he was away, the soldiers locked the castle gate, and cast Hill's boots and clothing over the wall. In fear for his life, Hill fled the town that night, never to be heard of again. Governor Mackworth, a member of Cromwell's Privy Council, died in 1654 and, in contrast, was given 'a stately funeral in Westminster Abbey'.

Sometime between 1649 and 1652, the north wall of the abbey suffered considerable damage from cannon fire believed to have been directed at the building as a warning not to make use of it for military purposes. The abbey was used, however, to house Scots taken prisoner at the battle of Worcester, as records remain of the cleaning costs after they left.

One of the prisoners taken at Worcester was Lieutenant, then Captain John Benbow. It is said that, like many others, he had been appalled to find himself associated with the execution of the king, and had therefore changed allegiance. So, as 'a traitor to their cause', he was one of three marked men brought to trial at Chester. Cromwell had issued an instruction to the Court Martial, which included his previous commander Colonel, now Major General Mytton on the panel, that they were to be made an example. John Benbow, still only 28, was sentenced to face a firing squad on the castle green – where he had led his assault-party six years before. He was buried by the footpath across the churchyard of old St Chad's church, which was then still standing. Given Cromwell's personal interest in his execution, and the example to be made of him, it is surprising that such a burial was permitted. Benbow obviously had friends then – and for many years after. When I first came to Shrewsbury, and lived in Belmont, there was still an elderly inhabitant who used to put out breadcrumbs for the birds on his tombstone every day, in memory of him, though on the basis of which allegiance I cannot now remember. Perhaps it was out of respect for the courage that Benbow had shown in his very change of allegiance.

Under the Protectorate, Cromwell raised a new and standing militia, levied a decimation tax (tax of one tenth), and imposed restriction on travel without a permit from the local (military) magistrate. He also banned bear-baiting, cockfighting and 'other dissolute assemblies', set men made wartime captives 'free upon security', and appointed Colonel James Berry as Major General for Shropshire, Hereford and Worcester. Saints were abolished, and the town's churches lost the St in their titles and became simply Chadd's, Marye's, Alkmund's and Julyan's for a while.

In King Charles I's time Presbyterianism was predominant, but it was replaced by Independency during Cromwell's rule. Both groups wished to suppress episcopacy, as represented in the Church of England. In 1644 it was made a crime to use the Prayer Book, which was replaced by a new Directory of Public Worship. The first Quakers and Baptists appeared in Shrewsbury in the 1650s in place of the uneasy coalition between 'high' and 'low' church.

Cromwell died in 1658. The mayor and aldermen happily accepted his son, Richard, as Lord Protector of this Commonwealth, but Richard, unable to bring together the different parties in Parliament and the army, resigned in May 1659. Matters continued in a confused way until General Monk, in 1660, declared for the king. Richard Ottley, son of the former governor (who had died in 1649), went to Dover to meet and congratulate his new sovereign when he arrived from France. Afterwards, he wrote a letter to his mother, to be delivered to the King's Head in Shrewsbury, apparently having brought the king with his two brothers, the dukes of York and Gloucester, to Whitehall: 'My most deare and ever honoured Mother: I met them at Calais, and had the happiness to be the lifeguard since Friday last; wherein my content over ballanced the paynes I underwent.'

9 RESTORATION SHREWSBURY

'It was my good fortune to be ordered some time ago into the place which is made the scene of this comedy. I was a perfect stranger to everything in Salop but its character of loyalty, the number of its inhabitants, the alacrity of the gentlemen in recruiting the army, with their generous and hospitable reception of strangers ... The Kingdom cannot show better bodies of men, better inclinations for the service, more generosity, more good understanding, nor more politeness than is to be found at the foot of the Wrekin.'

George Farquhar 1705, in his dedication to *The Recruiting Officer*

With the restoration of the monarchy, political fortunes in Shrewsbury were again reversed. Royalists were able to return to positions they had been forced to relinquish, and Parliamentarians were obliged to sue for pardon. Charles II bestowed the castle on Sir Francis Newport (later earl of Bradford) as a reward for supporting his father's cause, and the castle was to remain in private ownership until 1924. Although it remained fortified until 1686, the arms and ammunition were taken away in due course, and the outer bailey defences were demolished.

The charter which James II granted in place of that granted by Charles I gave the king new powers to remove any officials or elected councillors of which he disapproved. This caused ill feeling, but in spite of this the king was received, with all due ceremony, when he came to Shrewsbury on a royal progress, arriving from Ludlow in August 1687. It had been some few years since a royal visit, and the corporation sent to Gloucester and Worcester to seek their advice on appropriate preparations. This included the suggestion that every householder gravelled the street in front of his property just before the king's arrival, and this was duly done.

James was given a loyal address and a purse of one hundred guineas. He in turn, when attending divine service at St Mary's the following day, performed the royal duty expected of him, in touching people to cure them of the 'king's evil', or scrofula. It seems that a Friday meal of fish was prepared for the king, mayor and corporation, but that James left in haste by a back stair, without dining, in order to reach Whitchurch that night. The town was thus not able to present its prepared list of grievances. However, the old charter was restored a few months later, when James was trying to garner support shortly before William of Orange's landing on the south coast. After this

The High Street from Pride Hill drawn in 1821, but showing the timber-framed buildings, and probably the activities, much as they would have appeared at the time of the Restoration. The etching shows the emphasis on first-floor accommodation, with shops below and sleeping rooms above. Ireland's Mansion is along the view on the right. (SA 079 6001-200-376)

visit, the Council House fell into disrepair, for with the Dissolution of the Council in the Marches in 1689, it had no further purpose.

Despite religious toleration, there remained tensions between Puritans and Anglicans. The Church of England was no longer the only church, and even within it, high and low church preferences were emerging. The first Presbyterian congregation in Shrewsbury had been formed during the Commonwealth years, and in 1691 they built a meeting house in the High Street. Out of this grew Unitarian and Congregational groups. In 1692 a Quaker meeting house was established, although meetings of Friends had been held since the 1650s. There was a Roman Catholic chapel and, from the end of the century, a Baptist group. The Declaration of Indulgence in 1672 permitted dissenting places of worship, and seven were registered in Shrewsbury.

Although the town's border and military importance had now passed, Shrewsbury had become a principal provincial city. It was already the social centre for the county, and had gradually become so for much of central Wales. Wealthy families in the surrounding countryside had houses in the town, and it was their presence which helped the town to recover from the disruption to commerce caused by the Civil War, as various trades, crafts and professions were necessary to meet their requirements.

Even so, between 1650 and 1695 there was a marked decline in the leather and textile industries, hitherto so important to the town; also of rural occupations, as Shrewsbury dwellers became more urbanised. No longer did troupes of hardy mountain ponies laden with bales of cloth pour into the Market Square every Thursday morning. Set against these declines were sharp increases in the clothing, food and drink trades. Also on the increase were the building trades, and there was a doubling in service industries, luxury trades and the professions as a whole. River trade thrived and by the 1680s the names can be traced of 11 trowmen, four watermen, two hauliers and a shipwright. These would have generated demand for chandlers and other services. In 1650 there were eight tailors, 14 glovers and 18 shoemakers, and by 1695 these numbers had increased to 52, 46 and 80 respectively.

New trades in 1695 included a furrier, a perfumer, a vintner, a bookbinder, a stationer, a drawing-master, a painter of portrait miniatures and a gunsmith; two each of distillers, booksellers, needle-makers, milliners, dancing-masters and comb-makers; three goldsmiths and no less than six watchmakers and nine tobacconists. Thomas Holland, a sword cutler, was making utilitarian items such as scissors and shoemakers' knives for other craftsmen, and also silver-hilted swords and decorative boxes ornamented with fish-skin for sale as luxury items. Household goods changed as standards of comfort and elegance increased. Apart from many additional items of furniture, bed-linen became the norm, and a well stocked linen chest, with 'three changes', became part of a well-to-do family's assets as recorded in their wills.

Records and Tax

An interesting and unusual set of records exists in Shrewsbury. Other towns sent their taxation returns off to London (where they were destroyed a long time ago), but for some reason Shrewsbury failed to comply with regulations, and so has an almost unique set of records on the town and its inhabitants from two periods in the 17th century. Some of them still await full examination and interpretation.

Under Charles II, a new tax was introduced: the Hearth Tax of 1672, based on the number of chimneys on each property. Like the window tax which replaced it, it was easy to administer, and eliminated any concealment of wealth, as windows and chimneys could be counted from outside a house. It appears that the population at the time was around 5,000, comprising about 1,000 households, with about 150 on poor relief. By the end of the century, the population had increased to about 6,000, some 5,000 of whom lived in the quarter square mile, within the river loop. Pastures encircled the town, which was still confined inside the walls, apart from the suburbs of Abbey Foregate, Coleham and Frankwell.

Amenities and Services

The town was becoming congested, but there were at least two urban amenities. The pleasant formal gardens were remarked on by visitors, and Shrewsbury enjoyed piped

A painting of the formal gardens behind properties adjoining the 'Old House' in Dogpole. It illustrates the arrival of the Renaissance in Shrewsbury. Ficino of Florence wrote in 1492 of his optimism, standing on the verge of a better future replacing the 'dark and dreadful times' of the Middle Ages. Gardens became works of art, not merely used for productive purposes, but laid out in axial, geometric designs to be viewed from windows, or strolling and conversing without being overheard. (Shrewsbury Civic Society)

Anthony Rocke's family's 'Old House' on Dogpole when Henry VIII's daughter, Princess Mary Tudor, later Queen Mary (1553-58) spent 18 months here as a child of ten in 1525. Rocke was a servant of Katherine of Aragon. Altered in periods since, but retaining its great chimney stacks, it has revealed hidden paintings incorporating Katherine's pomegranate symbol, behind a hinged carved Jacobean overmantle. (Stephen de Saulles)

water before most other towns. Pure spring water had been piped into the town from the wells beyond Kingsland since the middle of the 16th century, but most water for general domestic purposes had always been obtained from the Severn. Until the mid-17th century, the inhabitants, as in most other towns, had to find their own supply by sinking wells or carrying it from the river. By then, it seems that there was a reservoir for Severn water 'situate upon the Town wall, near Mr More's garden on Clarimond Hill [Claremont Hill]'. It was filled by a wheel, worked by horses, at the riverside. When the lease expired in 1705, another was granted by the corporation to Robert Aldersley of London. This entitled him to erect new works under the Stone (English) Bridge at a rent of five shillings a year – and he was allowed to keep the profit.

The water was raised by an undershot waterwheel activated by the flow of the river, and piped to a lead cistern installed over the arches of the then Market Cross, on the High Pavement, on the site of the later Post Office building. A 'useful market place' was to be formed underneath. The necessary pumps were housed in a wooden building on the largest bylet on the town side of the bridge. ('Bylet' is a local dialect word for the mid-stream islands in the river.) In 1669, a stone conduit was built in the Green Market, (the Square), and another two in Wyle Cop and Mardol. (They were both taken down again in 1703 because they obstructed the roadways.)

One of Shrewsbury's visitors in 1698 was Celia Fiennes, accompanied by two servants. She was undertaking what she called her 'Great Journey' from London to Carlisle, and so into Scotland, then down to Land's End, and back to London. She passed through Shrewsbury on her way south, approaching from Whitchurch. She writes of the distant view of the church spires and the castle with its walls, battlements and towers; and she admired the fine River Severn, 'which encompasses the greatest part of the town, and twines and twists itself about'. She refers to three bridges, one of which had houses built upon it, to the Council House and other buildings, to walks beside the river, to three free

Newport House in Dogpole was the town house of Lord Newport, newly created earl of Bradford. He had been rewarded by the king for his services to the Royalist cause, with a title and the castle, no longer required for military purposes. He moved his timber-framed house to the castle forecourt, it is said for his mistress, and built his new house on the site, based on London styles, and set a new fashion in the town. It was in fashionable brick, with sash windows, deep overhanging, decorated eaves, and the new idea of symmetry. (The portico was added in the 19th century.) Later it served as the borough's 'guildhall' when, as well as offices, it included the mayor's parlour, an appropriate setting for receiving official visitors to Shrewsbury. It has recently been recently sold off by the then council into private ownership.
(Stephen de Saulles)

schools and also to the finely-carved stone market cross. She also noted 'a good schoole for young gentlewomen for learning work and behaviour and musick'. This was one of the most celebrated educational establishments in the town, the Chambre-Saxfield Academy for gentlewomen, run jointly by a widow named Esther Chambre and her assistant Barbara Saxfield. It was situated near to St Mary's church in the 1690s, and took both boarders and day pupils, who were carefully groomed in 'behaviour and musick' as well as in 'learning work'. They were taught sketching, deportment, and how to step into and out of a carriage – a most important skill considering the latest fashion, which included hooped skirts several feet in diameter and whalebone bodices. The school seems to have won an enviable reputation among the county set. Celia Fiennes also admired the gardens of the abbey, which were laid out with gravel walks and fine grass areas, and the greenery with its lemon and orange trees, also firs, myrtles and holly, and a 'greenhouse full of all sorts of Curiosityes of flowers and greens'. She related how, every Wednesday, most of the ladies and gentlemen of the town 'walk there as in St James's Park'. She pronounced Shrewsbury 'a pleasant town to live in, and great plenty which makes it cheap living'. She finally noted that 'there are abundance of people of quality in Shrewsbury, more than in any town except Nottingham'.

The Recruiting Officer was written by Lieut George Farquhar in 1705 while he was himself fulfilling that duty and staying at the Raven Hotel. The hotel was demolished in the 1960s to make way for a national chain store. (Shropshire Archives)

Personalities

No doubt many of Celia Fiennes' 'people of quality' would have been tutored in deportment, manners and dancing by Shrewsbury-born John Weaver, sometimes called 'the Father of English Pantomime', and the son of a dancing master of some repute. His original interest was in ballet, or what he called 'scenic dancing'. He wrote books on the art of dancing and the scientific principles of teaching it, and developed a system of notation for memorising dance steps. John Weaver's first pantomime, *The Tavern Bilkers*, was produced at Drury Lane, establishing a new tradition, and some of his compositions were performed at Queen Anne's court.

The well-known Restoration comedy, *The Recruiting Officer*, was written by Lieutenant George Farquhar while staying at the Raven recruiting for the army, then engaged under Marlborough in fighting the French. The story is set in Shrewsbury, and Farquhar included many allusions to local features and personalities. Most were complimentary and he evidently enjoyed his stay. It seems he based his principal male character, Captain Plume, on himself. His Sergeant Kite remains unidentified, but one of the justices he introduces is said to be John Hill, a relative of Roger Rowley (of Rowley's House), a mayor in 1689, after whom Hill's Lane is named. The play opens in the Market Square, and another scene is set alongside the river. Although still some 15 years before the avenues of trees were planted, a character is able to exclaim, 'A fine river, this same Severn!' Sergeant Kite bids his latest recruits to meet him at the sign of the Raven, and refers to the potency of the hostelry's 'March beer'. Later he prevents a drunken pair from returning home: 'Nay then, I command you to stay. I place you both sentinels in this place, for two hours to watch the motion of St Mary's clock, you; and you the motion of St Chad's; and he that dares stir from his post till he be relieved shall have my sword in his guts the next minute.' This 'watching' could not be done today, as old St Chad's collapsed in 1788, but when the play was written in 1706 it would have been possible to see both clocks from the spot where the fictional sentinels were described as standing.

Another personality of the time was Shrewsbury-born naval hero Admiral John Benbow, believed to be a nephew of Captain John Benbow of Civil War fame. Originally a waterman on the Severn, he joined the navy in 1678 fighting pirates in the Mediterranean. With an irascible temper, he was soon court martialled for insulting a fellow officer, but returned to sea at the command of his own merchantman, during which time, after fighting off a pirate attack, he took 13 of their heads, preserved in salt, as evidence. At Cadiz, the customs authority insisted on inspecting what he referred to as 'salt provisions for his own use', and he rolled out the heads, offering them as gifts. In consequence, Benbow received an introduction to the king of Spain, who wrote to King James, commending him. He was soon in a position of command in the Royal Navy, protecting English merchantmen in the Channel against the French. After various other duties, he commanded the fleet in the West Indies as vice-admiral. In 1702, he was in action off Cape Santa Marta in South America, and was left unsupported by the other ships when pursuing the French. He died of wounds, and was buried in Jamaica. A public house in the town centre, first listed in the 1800s, is

Admiral John Benbow (born c.1653), described as 'of great temperance and great courage', lived at Coton Hill until he ran away to sea. (Courtesy of Shropshire Museums SHYMS FA-1991-112)

named after him. There used to be another interesting memento of him. He was born in about 1653, in a house on Coton Hill overlooking the river, and when this was demolished, the trunk of a poplar tree at the front was retained. On this trunk there hung a key to the house, said to have been placed there by Benbow himself when, as a lad, he ran away to go to sea. Sadly tree trunk, old signboard and key have all been lost in redevelopment for modern flats.

Shrewsbury Show

During the Civil War, the annual Shrewsbury Show was suspended, and probably almost forgotten. With the Restoration, and the change of mood which followed years of Puritan restraint, the show was revived, and reached its heyday over the succeeding decades. The religious significance had disappeared, and concentration was now on the identity of the individual guilds involved. The companies assembled to the accompaniment of their own show tune – the Butchers to the 'Roast beef of old England' – at the castle. Then, with exuberant noise and colour, they would process through the main streets of the town, each led by a 'king' and other figureheads, with boldly decorated banners, and flags decked

In 1591 'the trades began to go to Kingsland', the start of what was to become the Shrewsbury Show. The ceremonies lapsed with the rise of Puritanism and then the Civil War, but with the Restoration of the Stuarts and a resurgence of delight in entertainment, the Shrewsbury Show was likewise restored, reaching its hey-day in the 1680s-90s.
A long poem of 1770 includes the lines:
To Kingsland Arbours once a year they go,
In ordered elegance serene and slow; ....
And balls and banquets crown the genial night.
(Shropshire Archives)

with tassels and streamers, cheered and followed by the townspeople, all dressed up for the holiday, till everyone reached the unenclosed common land of Kingsland. There, each company had its arbour, enclosing its own meeting place, built of timber, brick or stone and furnished with tables and benches ready for feasting and entertainments. The mayor and corporation would assemble on horseback at the Guildhall, and follow to Kingsland, 'making a courtesy call' at each arbour, to share the banquet at each stop'. They all returned to town much later.

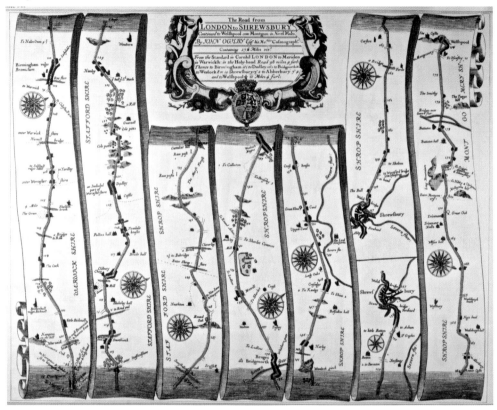

John Ogilby's strip road map of the route between London and Shrewsbury published in his *Britannia* atlas of 1675. (SA CM/2/34)

10   GEORGIAN SHREWSBURY

'Shrewsbury is one of the most interesting spots that man ever beheld ... It is curiously enclosed by the river Severn, which is here large and fine, and which, in the form of a horseshoe, completely surrounds it ... The environs of this town, especially on the Welsh side, are the most beautiful that can be conceived. The town lies in the midst of a fine agricultural country, of which it is the great and almost only mart. Hither come the farmers to sell their produce and hence they take in exchange their groceries, their clothing, and all the materials for their implements and the domestic conveniences. It was fair-day when I arrived at Shrewsbury ... I cannot quit Shrewsbury without expressing the great satisfaction that I derived from my visit to that place.'

William Cobbett, visiting the town in 1830

During the Georgian period, which lasted through the reigns of four Georges and William IV, Shrewsbury enjoyed its own company for a few years, happily relieved of involvement in many of the political, constitutional and overseas matters which were occupying attention at the capital. Although referred to as a 'garden city' at the beginning of this period, it was still only in the early stages of adapting from its status as a medieval border town to the market town and commercial centre of the early and middle parts of the 18th century – and, with the rise of the English gentry, on to being the fashionable leisure town of the later 18th century, when it could be said 'to go to Shrewsbury was to go to town'. John Tarbuck (a local Pepys), wrote about 'Shrewsbury as a Business Centre' in 1787: 'Shrewsbury having been the established road to Ireland, from London, Bath and Bristol causes much business to be done here, and is the means of an influx of money, as most of the travellers make a point to stop here to view the beauties of this delightfully situated town.'

Though itself now more on the sidelines of national events, the town not only supported reforms in the conduct of Parliamentary elections, but produced national leaders, industrial innovators, designer craftsmen and architects of national repute. New professions emerged such as surgeons from apothecaries, architects from builders, engineers from ironmasters and solicitors from lawyers.

Roads were poorly maintained and travel on them was slow. Cart-like vehicles carried goods, travelling in caravan trains, probably for mutual assistance and protection from

Abbey House, facing towards the west end of the abbey in Abbey Foregate, is a fine Queen Anne house with characteristic stone quoins and parapet roofline. Standing behind 'handsome wrought iron gates', it was built by Thomas Jenkins, sheriff in 1729, and remained in the family until 1861. Internally, the very large landing at the top of the staircase 'of noble proportions', was said to be designed for sedan chairs, used by ladies of the time, to be turned around with ease. (Stephen de Saulles)

robbers. The system of Turnpike Trusts started in 1662. Trusts were established by Acts of Parliament which gave them authority to collect tolls, using the money to organise and make the necessary repairs and improvements, including purchasing necessary land. The cost of maintaining roads was thus transferred from the owners of adjoining properties to those who used them. The first local routes, in the 1750s, were from Shrewsbury to Wrexham, and to Shifnal via Crackley Bank – as a first stage towards London.

The town pioneered coach travel, and the A5 route to Holyhead and Ireland, engineered by Shrewsbury-sponsored Thomas Telford, was described as 'the finest road in Europe'.

The town's involvement in military affairs reduced to strengthening the town's gates at the time of the '15 and '45 Jacobite Rebellions, and on one subsequent occasion. Otherwise, the town was only concerned in raising volunteers and the assembly of militia, although Shrewsbury has retained strong associations with the army ever since. (The Shropshire Regiment was founded in 1755.)

Swan Hill Court, built in 1762 for the Marquis of Bath, presents an imposing Georgian façade and beautiful walled garden to the Town Walls side. It is a fine example of the work of Thomas Farnolls Pritchard, originally a joiner. The interior was carefully restored after the war, but has since been spoiled. (SA Neg B4818)

Shrewsbury's long association with the county's military history and ceremonial is epitomised in the presentation of colours to the Volunteers in 1804. (Shropshire Archives)

An Administrative Centre and Town of Leisure

The Assizes and Quarter Sessions, held again in Shrewsbury from 1730, tended to be dominated by Tory squires, while the Lieutenancy was generally held by Whig gentry. As Parliamentary government strengthened, Shrewsbury was one of the most hotly contested boroughs in the county.

Shrewsbury had elected two Members ever since that privilege had been conferred on a few towns by King Edward I in 1283. The franchise was for many years restricted to those who had been admitted burgesses of the town, who, in 1774, numbered around 800 out of a population of some 9-10,000. Even then there were disputes as to whether burgesses retained their right to vote when they were not living within the required parish boundaries.

The election of 1774, so well lampooned by Hogarth and also by a local artist in an old engraving, illustrated the common happenings of the time. Only the very rich landed gentry could compete, for votes were bought and bludgeon men (thugs) were hired to intimidate the electorate and go to any lengths to secure the interests of the candidate who had employed them. Before other means of promotion or identification, 'colours' were an important feature of elections. On this occasion the three candidates were Charlton Leighton (later Sir Charlton Leighton of Loton), a Tory, who adopted

The old County Gaol, (in front of the present library), was built in 1705, replacing the prison cells in towers on the bridges. It was used until 1782 when John Howard's report on prison conditions caused the magistrates to put in hand the present building, started in 1793.
The scene shows a prisoner standing locked to a post, with a loaf stolen from a fellow prisoner; in the foreground provisions are being sold, and a woman cries her vegetables; a highwayman slips a letter to his wife into a woman's pocket; and a pick-pocket is at work.
The gaol keeper was largely paid, or bribed, by the inmates. (Shropshire Archives)

The Square from the Market House during the contested election of 1774.
The Booth Hall (which served the purpose of a modern guildhall), where a later statue of one of the candidates, Lord Clive, now stands was erected in 1547, enlarged and glazed in 1578 and graced with a clock including phases of the moon. The building on the left was later made part of the Plough Inn. (SA PH-S-13-5-28-1-1 b)

Robert Clive by Nathaniel Dance-Holland. Clive, born near Market Drayton, gained fame for his victory in India at Plassey, made a fortune and acquired Walcot Hall near Craven Arms.

blue and yellow; William Pulteney (later Sir William Pulteney), a Whig who lived in the castle, adopted light blue as his colour; and Robert, Lord Clive, a Tory whose seat was near Market Drayton, took purple and red. The polls were open for four days, with the candidates paying to transport their supporters from outlying areas to the town so that they could cast their votes. It was declared that Clive and Leighton had been elected, but Pulteney, who had many non-resident burgesses' votes, took the matter to trial in the Court of King's Bench, and the verdict confirmed the right of burgesses to vote irrespective of residence, a decision that saw Leighton unseated and Pulteney elected, resulting in much celebration in the town. (Pulteney remained MP for Shrewsbury until his death in 1805. Robert Clive died in 1775 and Sir Charlton Leighton was eventually elected in 1780.)

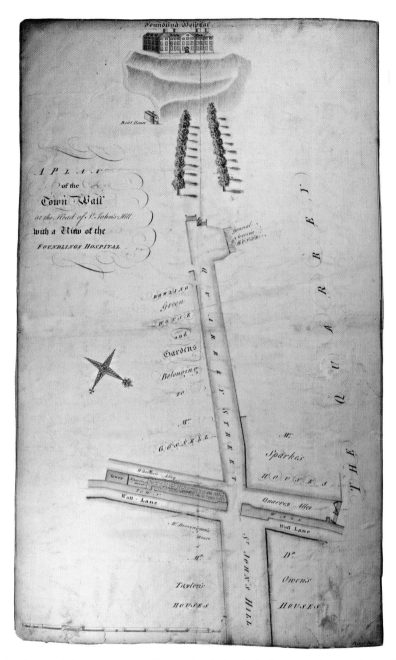

A sketch of part of the old town wall, including Wheeler's Tower and part of the Quarry, indicating some new tree planting on the avenue from St John's Hill and Quarry Place, and focusing on a view across the river (not shown) to the Foundling Hospital, dating it to between 1746 and 1794 when it was disused. Planting round the river walk had taken place in 1719. Legend has it that it was done by plantsman Thomas Wright's magic 'overnight', defying the corporation's wishes – but that they liked it afterwards.
(SA 6001-200-90)

Meanwhile, those elected appear to have spent most of their time squabbling with each other, certainly once the issue became which county family would be represented in Parliament at the expense of which other county families. The person who appears to have achieved most for Shrewsbury in Parliament in this period was a man who was never an MP. John Ashby, attorney, town clerk and three times deputy sheriff, and also a supporter of Robert Clive, was adept at coordinating Parliamentary lobbying in Shrewsbury's favour. By building the Lion Hotel, and adding the Adam-style Assembly Room in 1777 'to promote the general good of this town and county', he provided the town with a splendid social focus. Charles Dickens, Thomas de Quincy (author of *Confessions of an English Opium Eater*) and Prince William, later William IV, all stayed there, and it was the venue for an exhibition by Madame Tussaud.

Later MPs included Sir Rowland Hill, who was elected as MP in 1812, but he could not serve the constituency in Parliament owing to his military engagements abroad; he was the duke of Wellington's right-hand man at the battle of Waterloo in 1815. In 1819 John Mytton was elected. The author of his own 'Mad Jack' tales set in Shropshire – for example, of surprising his dinner guests by riding a pet bear, or some say horse, through his dining room, and of setting his nightshirt on fire as a cure for hiccups – served just one year. He is said to have attended Parliament only once, and then only for half an hour.

The social activity in the town generated by the Assizes and Quarter Sessions reinforced the changes already taking place. As the textile trade declined, so the leisure sector increased. When the wool trade finished in the 1790s, the administrative, financial and professional expertise for which the town is still renowned had become established.

The tree-lined walks, in 'one of the most celebrated promenades in the kingdom, called the 'Quarry'' were laid out as early as 1719. The Quarry was named after the dingle from which the town's first dull red building stone was quarried. *The Gentleman's*

The view c.1816 from the House of Industry or workhouse at Kingsland, now enjoyed by Shrewsbury School, across the river to the town centre. (Shropshire Archives)

Magazine thought the public walks, parks and gardens to be the finest in the kingdom, and many visitors, including Dr Johnson and Celia Fiennes, remarked upon the beautiful river walks. In 1722, another visitor wrote, less kindly, that in Shrewsbury there were 'the most coffee-houses ... that ever I saw in any town; but when you came to them, they are but ale-houses – only they think the name of coffee-house gives a better air'.

At the beginning of the 18th century, cockfighting was still patronised by gentry. A hunt, followed by dancing in the evening, was mentioned in Farquhar's play written in 1706 and by mid-century the tradition of the annual 'Hunt Ball for the Ladies' was established. It soon became linked with fund-raising for the Infirmary. On the morning of the hunt, a church service was held at St Chad's, followed by a champagne lunch, and it is said that the corks were sometimes heard before the blessing. It was the custom for a charity collection to be taken at the door by two young ladies clad, despite the winter season, in their evening ball dresses. One would be the latest bride in the county, for which honour there was some competition and manoeuvring; the other was a débutante. There were evidently other customs which furthered one of the underlying purposes of these social events: the married ladies wore pale blue, or some say red, trimmed with white, while for the unmarried, the rule was white, trimmed with the colour selected for their mothers' own dresses. The gentlemen were obliged to prove their eligibility as marriageable bachelors by the colour of their jackets. (How determined, or chosen, is now forgotten.) It was noted by one contemporary writer with satisfaction, or was it chagrin, that 'the officers of the army have pretty good success'.

The Shrewsbury 'Season' was firmly established by the 1770s, when those concerned with the legal sessions assembled with their families and enjoyed the sophistication of town life. Ladies travelled in sedan chairs, and socialising became a full-time occupation, as London ways spread to the provinces. By 1800, most county families maintained a town house for 'the season'. This was a period of improving standards of personal comfort, and the introduction of luxuries as well as fashions to be noticed and followed.

In 1780 the castle had become the private residence of Sir William Pulteney MP, allegedly the richest commoner in England. He befriended his fellow Scot Thomas Telford, then a promising young architect and engineer, when he first came to Shrewsbury, giving him an opportunity to establish his professional life when he commissioned 'young Thomas' to

Laura's Tower at Shrewsbury Castle, designed by Thomas Telford for use as a summer house. (Stephen de Saulles)

Thomas Telford, architect, engineer, 'Colossus of Roads' and remarkable administrator who made an unique contribution to Shropshire's history, and our country's roads and bridges as well as our canals. (SA PR-2-621)

make various improvements to his residence. Telford divided the interior into a number of rooms and installed a new main staircase. He also remodelled the windows, widening the previously very narrow slits to give more light, so giving the appearance seen today. In addition he moved the entrance from its position in the east tower to the centre of the ground floor (i.e. to present basement level), the position it had originally occupied in Edward I's castle. He also designed and supervised the octagonal stone tower on the site of the original motte, for use as a summer house for his client's daughter Laura – hence the present name of Laura's Tower (built *c*.1790).

An account of Miss Pulteney's coming-of-age celebrations reflects the time. Flags flew from the castle, by that time their private home. The castle and Raven Hotel, in Castle Street, were illuminated by flares set outside and candelabra inside. An ox was roasted in a nearby meadow; sheep were roasted in the streets; there was free drink, and a ball and supper, at the Lion. A boy from Shrewsbury School, writing home, described the scene as Miss Pulteney arrived by coach, and included the comments, 'she was dressed in a kind of chocolate coloured sattin, trimmed with ermine, she seemed to me to have no hoop [supporting the very wide skirts, perhaps going out of fashion then]. They say she is to have £16,000 a year in her own possession now that she is of age. Last week was the Hunt Week, too, when there were free dinners at the Lion every day, a concert on Tuesday, and a ball on Thursday'.

The major inns were advertising assembly rooms, and some public buildings were adapted to hold audiences for music and readings. There was card playing, many dinners and much socialising, especially amongst the ladies. The new coffee houses abounded, perhaps now no longer providing a front for ale-houses.

Shrewsbury had been a horse racing centre for centuries. From medieval times it had taken place on common land on Kingsland, otherwise used for grazing and recreation. By 1729 the racecourse was too small for the crowds attending and a new course was laid out on Bicton Heath to the west of the town centre, where it continued in use for over a century, leaving a legacy in the road name Racecourse Lane. It was not until the late 1830s that a larger course was laid out closer to the town on part of the earl of Tankerville's 56-acre estate in Monkmoor, on the east side of the town.

The Theatre Royal, Shoplatch, was erected in 1834 on the site of the ruins of Charlton Hall, previously used for stage events. The interior was richly fitted and decorated, as befitted the 'Season' in a fashionable town.

There were bowling greens in the Quarry and in Castle Foregate, whilst the tennis court near the Gullet Inn was one of the earliest outside London.

A guide to Shrewsbury was first published in 1784 for the benefit of visitors and shortly after the turn of the century, a later edition showed that the town enjoyed an elegant new theatre which replaced an earlier one. However, this soon appears to have become 'ruinous' and was purchased by its manager, Mr Bennett, in 1833. The following year he demolished it and built a new Theatre Royal on the same site but on a more lavish scale.

New Royal Baths were announced as commodious, and large enough for them to be used to learn the gentle art of swimming. The teenage Princess Victoria was brought to give royal approval to the imposing new library and improvements at the Boys' Grammar School, then under the headmastership of the much respected Dr Butler.

For the daughters of gentlemen, pages of the *Shrewsbury Chronicle* carried advertisements in 1773 for Mrs Gwynn's 'Boarding School for young ladies' and another establishment run by Mrs Jaquet in St Mary's Place where 'Young Ladies are instructed in every useful and genteel part of education'. French was taught 'grammatically' and 'proper masters' were provided 'for dancing, music, writing, drawing, etc.' Additional dancing lessons and French tuition could be had at Mr Gardiner's lodgings in Castle Street, while in Shoplatch 'near the Play House' Mr Rocke, formerly 'First Violin to the Court of Hanover', taught the violin, oboe, German flute, bassoon, guitar and harpsichord as well as 'vocal music'.

The Philanthropic Movement (and Public Buildings)

Contrasting with the gracious living and social round, but arising from it, was a new awareness of social problems and, fortunately, the resources to tackle some of them. As Thomas Auden wrote in 1905, 'The [18th] century was marked in Shrewsbury by two movements of philanthropy deserving of the highest praise. One was the foundation of what were known as 'Charity Schools' for the education of the poorer classes ... The other ... was the foundation in 1747 of the Salop Infirmary.' He goes on to state that 'this philanthropic movement, it will be observed, was essentially a town movement both in its origin and purpose'.

Some minor street improvements were made as the result of a few public-spirited gentlemen dedicating portions of their land to allow road widening. This was a significant contribution to movement in the town's busy streets before the days of planning legislation. Some were also subscribing money for more major works such as schools, bridges and hospitals. This was a time when the rich felt it right to use their wealth for the public good.

For example, a so called 'ragged school' (which referred to the children's clothing), supported by public subscription, had been established by John Pound for the benefit of poor children in Portsmouth in 1708. His lead was followed in Shrewsbury by two members of the Drapers Guild. John Pound aimed to take children off the streets and help to make them employable, putting emphasis on giving 'habits of order' and regular attendance. Besides reading, writing, arithmetic and bible stories, he included cooking, carpentry and shoe mending in his curriculum. Later, the concept was supported by Lord Salisbury, who formed the Ragged School Union in 1844. At the time, the existing 'Dame', and various denominational, schools were not catering for the poorest inner-city or town children.

Thomas Bowdler's or the 'Blue School' in Beeches Lane was founded in 1724, by the terms of his will, for the instruction, clothing and apprenticing of poor children in the parish of St Julian's, who were also to be taken to attend that church every Sunday. A decade later, in 1734, Shrewsbury Draper James Millington left money to found a school and almshouses in Frankwell. There, 20 boys and the same number of girls were educated, and given clothing twice a year. Apprenticeships were arranged when they reached the age of 14. Millington's Hospital, part designed by Edward Massey and the later central part by John Haycock, also provided two-room accommodation for 12 poor

Bowdler's School, established by Thomas Bowdler, alderman and draper, in 1724. This handsome, unspoilt building is on Town Walls. The new style of architectural symmetry is evident, while a doorway, with a segmental pediment and decorated window over, provides a strong central emphasis. The wide projecting eaves were later forbidden because of fire risk.
(Stephen de Saulles)

Millington's school and almshouses were built on the site of an old chapel that had become ruinous and was only used to house victims of plague. The central part with pediment and portico was that added by John Haycock in 1785.

men or women of the parish, each being given two gowns, three tons of coal and ten guineas yearly, and two loaves of bread each week.

The early Salop Infirmary, originally designed as a private house, was one of the first charity hospitals in the country. As Henry Pidgeon says, it 'had the distinguished honour of being the fifth in the kingdom to form the way in establishing a Provincial Asylum, on the basis of public benevolence'. It 'commenced its salutary operations' in 1747.

A new 'well-built structure', the Foundling Hospital designed by Thomas Farnolls Pritchard, (one of the first to describe himself as an architect), was erected on Kingsland,

The Foundling Hospital was built in 1760 for the reception of orphans from the Foundling Hospital in London. It was purchased in 1784 to serve as a House of Industry or Poor Law workhouse, and subsequently as a flannel mill. The building was later adapted and elaborated to form part of Shrewsbury School when it moved to Kingsland in 1882. (Shropshire Archives)

overlooking the town and river below, in 1760. It was to provide accommodation for orphans sent from the Foundling Hospital in London. The scheme was discontinued in 1774 when funds ran out. The redundant building was purchased in 1784, under an Act of Parliament, for use as a House of Industry (more commonly known as a workhouse) under the management of a board of directors. (In the next century it was adapted and enlarged, and became part of Shrewsbury School.)

Later examples of charitable institutions in this period of philanthropy were (John) 'Allatt's School', built under his will of 1799. Allatt had been treasurer to the corporation for nearly 40 years. Designed by John Hiram Haycock, on Murivance, the school provided education for 30 boys and 30 girls from 1805. This were followed by a Lancasterian School in 1812, located east of the Dana, where the construction of the railway later caused its demolition. The building of this school was inspired by a visit from Joseph Lancaster, a London-born educationalist who gave a lecture in Shrewsbury in 1811, his views attracting interest and, crucially, finance. His system of educating poor children used a minimum number of teachers, as it used the older children to teach the younger ones. The Lancasterian School, designed by Charles Bage, opened with 233 pupils. When demolition threatened, the school moved into the Union Wharf building until the completion, in 1851, of their new premises in Beacall's Lane. St Chad's Ladies' School for 154 girls was established in 1820, with the declared intention, typical of the time, of training them 'to do their duty, for conscience sake, in that state of life to which it shall please God to call them', in other words, to make them suitable for dairy or factory work, or domestic service – either in marriage or employment.

Allat's School on Town Walls was founded by John Allat, treasurer to the corporation. It was built in 1800 by John Hiram Haycock (1759-1830) and had separate classrooms for boys and girls. (Shropshire Archives)

The Drapers Almshouses built in 1825 to replace those built in the mid 1400s.
The 18 two-storey houses arranged around a courtyard were in turn replaced by new
almshouses built in Longden Coleham in 1964. (Note the water tower behind.)

Within the town, the old Drapers Almshouses in St Mary's churchyard had become 'wretched and filthy' and 'dangerously unwholesome', and were rebuilt in 1825 on the opposite side of the road, 'from a design by Mr J. Carline' in the then fashionable revivalist Tudor style, which was also adopted for the houses built for masters at Shrewsbury School in School Gardens. Although the earlier accommodation had become so dilapidated, the inmates had to be bribed with the payment of £2 to move. It appears that the initial offer of £1 was refused, which perhaps shows how much the earlier units had been appreciated.

The original Salop Infirmary was replaced by a new building in 1830. Designed by Edward Haycock, it was built on the site of the previous small infirmary erected in 1747. During its construction, patients were transferred temporarily to the House of Industry on Kingsland. The new four-storey infirmary was 170ft (c.52m) long and 80ft (c.24m) high. It provided for the latest standards of medical care and accommodation, and even included an early central heating system – described as a 'patent hot-water apparatus'. As described by Henry Pidgeon in 1837, it enjoyed a spacious terrace and balconies for the benefit of fresh air, 'from which a most expansive and interesting view presents itself'. The medical officers of the establishment 'gratuitously devote their time and apply their skill in promoting the benevolent design of the institution'. Pidgeon also noted that 'the mode devised for its [financial] support was very characteristic of the time'. Apart from subscriptions, and a church service with a special collection, there was an annual fox hunt one morning, followed by 'a Ball for the ladies' in the evening.

The Infirmary, 'liberally supported by subscriptions and benefactions', opened in 1745.
It was rebuilt in 1830, with an imposing Doric portico by Edward Haycock who, unlike his
father and grandfather, had had a formal architectural training.
He succeeded Thomas Telford as county surveyor. (Shropshire Archives)

Religion and Societies

Henry Pidgeon described the charity ethos of the time when he wrote: 'Several other charitable societies exist in the town, whose object is to afford gifts of money, clothing, medical assistance, and religious instruction, to the necessitous sick poor; as well as for the distribution of the scriptures and the public formularies of the established church, and for the propagation of Christianity both at home and abroad.'

There was a renewed interest in religion, and several national figures were active. Methodism was stimulated by frequent visits from John Wesley, who visited 18 times between 1761 and 1790, whilst Samuel Taylor Coleridge preached at the Unitarian Church in 1798. Coleridge spent some weeks in the town, during which time he may well have been working on his 'Rime of the Ancient Mariner'. There is a story that he read part of the poem at a supper party; allegedly this caused him so much excitement that he rushed out of the house at the end of the evening, leaving his hat behind, and was apprehended by a watchman who feared that a hatless, running figure was up to no good.

A number of societies and institutions were formed in the early 1800s. For example, there was a Prison Charity, established in about 1800, to help prisoners while in prison, and provide some practical assistance on their release. The Humane Society that had existed in 1786 was revived in 1824, the main purpose being to prevent the frequent fatal river accidents, which tended to result from swimming in the river during the bathing season, or skating unsafely in winter. The society aimed to provide a system of 'watch from the banks' and competent assistance in case of accident, whilst rewarding acts of bravery by members of the public.

A Mechanics Institute came into being in 1825, reflecting the new interest in science and engineering, and in contrast, both a Choral Society and the Horticultural Society were founded in 1834. A Natural History Society and Museum were established, followed by a subscription library in 1835.

Town Improvements

The population was increasing. This was partly due to a declining death rate in infancy and adolescence, and also to improvements in agricultural methods which resulted in better nutrition, especially for the poor. As the rich became more socially and politically conscious, they began to press for ways of dealing with the congestion and other problems caused by the increased use of the streets for open markets and the slaughtering of livestock. Although there had been a few building regulations designed to prevent the spread of fire, such as forbidding overhanging timber eaves and, after about 1730, requiring windows to be set behind the face of the brickwork, it was not until the 1754 Street Act that wider municipal improvements were first tackled. Under the Act, 'scavengers' were appointed to clean certain parts of the town twice a week, and the corporation instituted fines for throwing offal into the street.

The further Street Improvement Act of 1756 ordered the paving of some town streets, and appointed scavengers to clean them regularly. The constant traffic of horse-drawn coal carts, goods wagons and coaches, the activities of street trading and the cattle market, together with a lack of proper drainage, all created problems, and these, the narrow streets and the encroachments built onto the footpaths were constantly discussed.

In the background is the rebuilt St Alkmund's, designed and rebuilt by John Carline II, mason and sculptor and John Tilley, bricklayer, in 'modern Gothic' in 1795. In the foreground is St Julian's, designed and rebuilt by Thomas Farnolls Pritchard in 1749. (SA 6001-199-432)

Although there had been minor improvements to it over the years, the pitch of Wyle Cop was still very steep. In 1789 major works were carried out, and the top of the Cop was lowered by several feet. The alterations on the eastern side, though modified, are still visible, and form part of Shrewsbury's interesting present-day changes in level in the townscape. St Julian's church now stands high off the road, at the top of a long flight of steps, and 'retained' by a stretch of substantial stone walling. There is also a steep turn into Fish Street. The lower part of the Cop, nearest to the river and liable to flooding, was raised, and Coleham Head, which suffered the same problem on the other side of the river, was raised by 5ft, or about 1.5m.

132

Shrewsbury was the marketing centre for large areas of Shropshire and a deep hinterland into Wales, and Welsh produce was shipped on to London, Birmingham and other parts of the country. But the market lacked space, convenience and storage facilities, compared with other towns. Most display and sales took place on the open streets. The twice weekly market days, on Wednesdays and Saturdays, caused congestion and left clutter and mess afterwards. Monthly butter and cheese fairs, and the horse and wool fairs, caused even more. The upper well-lit floor of the Market House in the Square functioned well as a cloth market, but the arcaded ground floor space below was too dark for the proper inspection of grain samples, and was not completely sheltered from the rain. The open space between the Market House and the High Street was used for the 'Green' or 'Apple Market', sometimes called the 'pannier market', where farmers' wives brought their fruit and vegetables to sell. It was fully exposed to all weathers.

Country butchers clustered round the open sides of the Market House, wielding sharp knives and choppers. Horse dealers, although forbidden to do so, trotted their animals up and down alongside, to demonstrate their good points. Traders, buyers, children and no doubt hungry dogs would have added to the confusion. A farmer wrote to the *Salopian Journal*, complaining of the potential danger, a letter which probably typified a rising tide of complaint.

Powers had been obtained to construct a towpath along the Severn from Worcester to Ironbridge in 1772, although none was built until the 1790s, and it reached as far as Shrewsbury only by 1811. In 1784 there had been proposals for the construction of

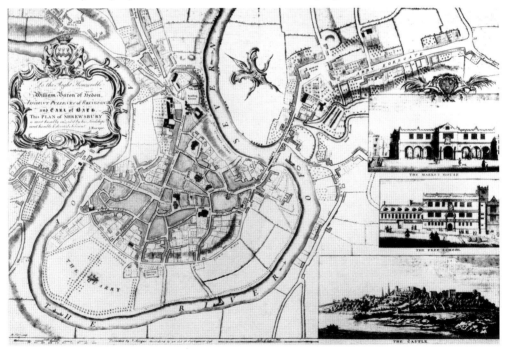

Map of Shrewsbury *c.*1746 by John Rocque in new blockplan style,
important buildings shaded dark, and with accompanying views.

locks and weirs which would have provided a good depth of water at all seasons, but there was so much opposition from the Shropshire barge owners that the scheme was abandoned. They also objected to the idea of paying tolls. (Locks were eventually built below Stourbridge after 1842.)

By the 1820s rates were being paid by property owners. In consequence, they were bringing various matters to the attention of Shrewsbury Corporation. For example, in the past an Act had required night soil to be emptied into the Severn, but in summer it piled up on the banks, and unsurprisingly raised complaints.

It was only under the second Street Improvement Act of 1821 that the corporation was empowered to lay down a number of local regulations concerning such matters as the watch, and also its first planning regulations, which covered paving, lighting and the cleansing of the town. Many of the rounded brick corners, to ease circulation by carriages, date from then. An Improvements Commission was appointed to implement the Act, and this spawned a number of sub-committees, each covering an activity that needed attention. The commission included a number of public-spirited people with time to offer, and was initially chaired by Rev John Brickdale Blakeway. From its deliberations came the first movement towards combatting dirt and disease, and the concept of 'public health'.

The Streets Committee of the Improvements Commission took action to change the street markets: horse trading was excluded from the Square, Welsh Bridge and Dogpole, and allowed in Frankwell and the Abbey and Castle Foregate areas, where there was sufficient space. The horse fairs were to rotate between the three sites. Sheep sales were to be permitted in special pens set up on market days in Castle Street. Pigs were to be kept to an area between Swine Market Hill (later St John's Hill) and Claremont Hill. Cattle sales were moved from Ox Lane (later renamed St Mary's Street) to Dogpole. Significantly, dung was to be collected by contractors and taken to yards from where it would be sold for the benefit of gardens and allotments, the contractors guaranteeing to have the streets cleaned for Sunday churchgoers. The slaughtering of livestock in Butcher Row was also to be stopped, as was the display of raw meat in the street.

Public notices were issued and handbills printed urging people not to throw rubbish into the streets. The town-crier proclaimed that washing should not be hung on the railings around the churches, or on fences. Notices were served on residents to sweep the footways in front of their properties three times a week – under threat of a fine.

There was an urgent need for somewhere for the sale of butter and cheese from the dairy farms of north Shropshire, and it was temporarily moved from the small shelter under the Butter Cross (the present High Cross) to the Butter and Poultry Market on Pride Hill, erected in 1819. (This was found to cause obstruction to the thoroughfare on market days, so was taken down in 1830 as being 'unsuitable and incommodious'.) By 1822 a butter and cheese warehouse had been built by Henry Newton, a brewer, at the Circus Yard near Welsh Bridge. This was well-placed alongside the river for produce to come by barge, and for carriers bringing goods across the bridge.

The Street Acts of 1821-25 imposed certain planning and building regulations for the benefit of safety and convenience. Bow windows were to be replaced with flat ones, and any structures projecting into the street, including steps, were to be set back behind the building line. Coal hole gratings were to be laid flat or vertical, the same rule applying to cellar windows and trap doors. There was a general prohibition on displaying goods or wares outside one's property. Handbills were published and distributed giving details of all the new regulations.

Shoplatch and Mardol were widened. The frontages of some properties on the High Street, Mardol and Pride Hill were compulsorily purchased to allow for widening where necessary. An elementary form of macadam was used for road surfacing for the first time, replacing the earlier mud or dust. Where new sections were required, graded layers of broken stone, each smaller than the one below, were compacted and laid to a camber, with a system of side drains, all based on Telford's method – which, as he probably knew, had been used by the Romans.

Several stretches of the road were lowered, to make travel easier for the horses, and safer in frosty weather. This was by as much as 10ft (3m) in the case of the Belmont/Belmont Bank junction around old St Chad's, and also St Julian's on the High Street frontage.

Mardol in 1820. The first three properties on the left, with another one set back, were destroyed for the building of the new General Market in 1868. The 'Dutch gable' on the right-hand Mardol Head corner survives, but apart from property boundaries little else remains of the frontages. The 6-floor timber structure on the left strikes one with wonder.
(SA 6001-200-394)

In 1823 a special meeting was held to decide whether to make alterations to Castle Gates. The route then went through the present School Gardens and it was agreed to create a new, lowered route through the school's land, largely paid for by subscriptions. But, as laymen, they did not realise they were weakening the foundations and removing part of the support of the school buildings. (This danger to the Library was only discovered, and narrowly averted, in the 1970s by the county architects department.)

A new Butter and Cheese Market, 'elegant and commodious', was designed by Fallows & Hart of Birmingham, and built in 1836 on a sloping Howard Street site in Castle Foregate at the terminus of the Shrewsbury Canal. The Wappenshall-Norbury Junction of the Birmingham & Liverpool Junction Canal (now the Shropshire Union) linked it with the national network, providing a waterway to London, Birmingham or Lancashire. Taking advantage of the slope and two internal floor levels, it provided a convenient transfer point for goods between the adjoining canal and road wagons. Apart from butter and cheese, it also handled other agricultural produce and merchandise.

Perhaps as an expression of the new sense of civic pride, many of the old street names were made to sound more genteel. Ox Lane, so named when cattle fairs were held there, became St Mary's Street; and Pig Hill, earlier Swine Market Hill, was renamed St John's Hill, in deference to the refinement of its householders.

Public Services

The Watch

One of the sub-committees established under the Improvements Commission was concerned with the watch. The earlier watch had included the duties of 'crying the hours', before all households had clocks and pocket- or wristwatches, and of checking that no candles or oil-lamps had been left unsnuffed. But the system, like the candles before them, had fallen into disuse, whilst the watchmen had fallen into bad habits of going off home early or sleeping on the job. In the meantime, burglary had probably become worthwhile. In the system established by the commission, a superintendent and 12 watchmen were employed with duties more akin to those of a police force, protecting property and keeping public order.

Lighting

By around 1726, a few oil-lamps had been set up in parts of the town centre, by 1739 they had been erected at each end of the Market House in the Square, and by 1744, the chief streets were lit in this way. By the end of the century, there were more than 200 lamps in the principal areas of the town. In 1820 a company was formed which raised sufficient capital, by issuing 800 shares at £10 each, to supply the town with gas, and gas lighting was introduced in 1821.

Water

In the early 1700s, the stone conduits in Wyle Cop, in Mardol and in the Square were found to be obstructing the increased traffic in the streets, and were replaced by smaller wooden ones. In 1705 piped water was pumped from the river by a horse-operated wheel to a reservoir attached to the town wall on Claremont Hill. But in 1736, the pillars supporting the reservoir in the new market collapsed due to the excessive weight of water, and it was replaced by a larger one capable of holding 600 barrels of water, and two or three elsewhere in the town. In 1768 new wells were developed in Broadwell, but the population was increasing and, by the end of the century, the amount of drinking water was proving inadequate. By 1790, the Claremont Hill reservoir had to be demolished to make way for the new St Chad's church, and a replacement was built opposite the Quarry-keeper's house.

In 1827, under an Act of Parliament, the Shrewsbury Waterworks Company was formed. This company purchased the existing equipment and erected new works at Coton Hill. Although the proprietors had undertaken to supply clean water to the town, it was so thick and muddy it was unsuitable for drinking. River water was therefore pumped up to a brick tower behind the old Post Office in St Mary's Street, but during the summer months, the water was only available for a few hours in the week and people had to rely on water from the old source at Broadwell. It was then decided that the state of that supply should be examined. Two 'officials' accompanied by William Eccleston, the plumber's foreman, 'walked the whole length of the pipe and found no wet or faulty place to indicate the imperfection of any part of the pipe', whilst 'the reservoir was at the Quarry full and overflowing with the most pellucid water and perfectly clean'. Their report did however note the need for fitting and protecting an air pipe and more stopcocks so that any future 'impediments' could be 'easily discovered for want of these' and, finally that 'there is a great quantity of water at the Conduit (Head) which runs from a spring ... down a ditch into the road to Radbrook House and the Hanwood Turnpike Gate'. It was therefore decided to bring this old source back into use.

Sewers & Drainage

One of the Improvement Commission's sub-committees was required to consider the subject of sewers and drainage, and after due consideration plans were made for sewers to be laid, also with drain connections to drain the cellars which had habitually been used to store each household's sewage. The costs quoted by Carline's proved to be too high for immediate universal implementation, so the work was carried out in stages. Property owners were obliged to pay for their own drain and connection to the sewer.

Fire Services

A fire service was formed following a damaging fire in Abbey Foregate in the 1770s. This fire broke out between 2 and 3pm on Good Friday, the first day of April 1774, and continued raging for five hours, destroying 47 houses, 16 barns, 15 stables, four shops and several stacks of hay, and damaging a further five houses, which were 'much injured'. The sum of £794 18s 9d was raised by subscription for the relief of the sufferers, towards which the Drapers contributed £50. It is recorded that, of this, £326 8s was paid out, and £426 7s 4d returned to the subscribers, the balance presumably being spent on administration.

Newspapers

Thomas Wood published his first tentative news sheets, entitled the *New Chronicle*, a liberal-leaning newspaper, in 1772, in small format, hoping to avoid the 'tax on knowledge' as the tax on newspapers introduced by Parliament in 1712 to curb seditious publications was generally called. Publishers found a variety of ways of either covering the extra cost, or getting round the rules by altering the frequency of publication or its size. When the tax office ruled against him, Wood increased the size and cost of the *Chronicle* to cover the tax, and it thrived. It carried columns of advertisements for the patent medicines of the time, and foreign news brought from London. One of the most dramatic local stories was the collapse of old St Chad's church at 4 o'clock one morning in 1788. It appeared under the restrained headline 'Shrewsbury, Friday, July 11th', and most of the 13 column inches devoted to it were taken up by a description of the church taken from Thomas Phillips' *History of Shrewsbury*, published in 1779 – and included the hint that a few copies were still available at 10s 6d each.

When Thomas Wood died in 1801, his wife continued in his place, probably the earliest woman newspaper proprietor anywhere. In 1790, the printers J. & W. Eddowes launched their own *Salopian Journal* but, as it was of conservative persuasion, the *Chronicle* was not affected and has continued to the present day, introducing several innovations on the way, not least in the post war period as will be described in chapter 16.

The Industrial Town

Boatbuilding

On the banks of a river rich in fish, coracle-making and boat-building must have been traditional activities in the town, but there is little mention or evidence of them. However, whether as an industry or a craft, boatyard activity took place downstream of Welsh Bridge on the town side in the 1730s.

Several generations of John Harwood's family were known as boatbuilders before, during and beyond the 1700s. John Harwood, a ship's carpenter, died in 1708, and an Edward Harwood, boatbuilder, voted in an election in 1806. They were probably engaged in producing craft for fishing and other local uses. An engraving in the 1730s, either by the artist John Bowen, or based on one by him, shows a view of a vessel under construction in an open area downstream of Welsh Bridge, but it suggests an area available for such use, rather than an established boatyard.

Forges, Foundries and Mills

Foremost among the seven Shropshire forges was the one listed in 1710 at the confluence of the Tern with the Severn in Atcham, an area that has been called 'A Forgotten Industrial Valley'. It included a mill for rolling brass plates and iron hoops, a slitting mill, a wire mill, and a steel furnace. By 1717 it was producing 300 tons of iron a year.

This was an early sign of coming changes. By the 1790s, Shrewsbury had lost its role as a finishing and commercial centre for the Welsh woollen trades, but the loss was being replaced by other activities. Shrewsbury had become a manufacturing town.

A combination of circumstances towards the turn of the 1700s brought together a formidable group of men of outstanding entrepreneurial skills and intellectual ability who contributed forcefully to the wealth and vigour of the town. Included amongst their number were Charles Bage, a surveyor, factory designer and wine merchant described by Telford as a 'treasure of talents and integrity'; Thomas and Benjamin Benyon, who had experience in flax spinning and cloth marketing; and William Hazledine, whose Shrewsbury foundry employed nearly 500 people at its height, and provided ironwork for many major engineering works, such as the Chirk and Pontcysyllte aqueducts, the Spey and Menai bridges, and the lock gates on the Caledonian Canal. (He also became one of Shrewsbury's more influential citizens, owning much property in the town by the time he died in 1840.) Then there was John Marshall of Leeds, son of a linen merchant, and himself a flaxmaster and inventive manufacturer; William Reynolds of Ketley, an ironmaster who had experimented with Telford on iron construction for the Longdon aqueduct on the Shrewsbury Canal; William Strutt, of Belper, a cottonmaster who had already pioneered the use of cruciform cast-iron columns in mills in Derbyshire; along with Thomas Telford.

In 1793, John Marshall had developed a method of spinning flax mechanically, to produce yarn and thread. He shared a factory in Leeds with Thomas and Benjamin Benyon, and they built a second factory there in 1795. Like other mills at the time, it was constructed with timber floors and beams and was therefore a high fire risk. Indeed, it was destroyed by fire within two years.

The Benyon Bage and Marshall Flax Spinning Mill, Ditherington, begun by Charles Bage in 1796. As the first iron-framed building in the world it is probably Shrewsbury's most important building, being the forerunner of the skyscrapers in America.
Bage was familiar with structural experiments being carried out by Telford and with the manufacturing methods of Hazledine and Abraham Darby III. (SA PC-S-12-F-1-1)

John Marshall with the Benyons, his main investors, and Charles Bage, therefore decided to build a new factory at Shrewsbury. This was a more attractive location, alongside the Shrewsbury Canal, giving access to the Coalbrookdale coalfield and Merseyside. Charles Bage, in consultation with William Reynolds, who was well versed in the design and strengths of cast-iron columns and beams, and with the help of Hazledine's new iron foundry would produce the innovative design for the new multi-storey and fireproof Ditherington flax mill. It was built in 1798, the first iron-framed multi-storey building in the world, and the forerunner of the world's skyscrapers, and is now one of the UK's most important historic buildings.

Through the use of cast-iron, the span could be increased beyond the previous limits of timber. The width was thus increased to 39ft 6in (12m), and it was 177ft 3in (54m) long. Instead of using timber, the floor was formed on shallow brick barrel vaulting, carried on iron beams supported on slender cruciform columns. The column heads were designed so that shafting to drive the machinery passed through them. The original doors and window frames were also of cast iron. (Many were filled in later when the building became a malting house as malting demands far less light.)

The first 20hp steam engine, supplied by Boulton & Watt, was installed in the bays at the south end of the building. A second engine, of 40hp, was set up at the north end in 1799. Then the original engine was replaced by one of 60hp in 1810, set up in a separate engine house close to the south end. At the same time, the building became one of the first to be lit by gas, nine years before the town itself.

In 1808 the Ditherington property was valued at £17,000 and by 1816 the figure had reached £90,000. Between 1811 and 1814 it briefly manufactured canvas and other fabrics and employed up to 48 weavers, but in the main it concentrated on producing flax thread, with a workforce that numbered over 500. By the 1830s, what had become Johnson Marshall & Son were so successful that they were replacing machinery. The mill was converted to a new process of wet spinning, and also made thread for the boot and clothing industries. Later, steam for the engines in the main building was supplied by boilers sited on the banks of the Shrewsbury Canal to which coal could be brought by barge. The mill remained part of the Marshall industrial empire – 'the largest firm of flax spinners in Europe' – until 1886, by which time the business had gone into decline under John Marshall's sons and grandsons, and production ended.

During the 30 years after 1790, the right bank of the river in the suburb of Coleham was the most industrialised part of Shrewsbury, as indicated by the Hitchcock map of 1832 (see p.160). In 1790, John Carline sold a site at the junction of Longden Coleham and Coleham Head to the firm of Powis & Hodges, who set up a woollen mill with two multi-storey buildings. Both measured about 33ft (12m) wide, while one was 93ft (34m) long, the other a bit less at 86ft (31m) long. A steam engine and waterwheel provided power for the carding engines, spinning jennies and fulling provision, but the enterprise was not successful. The buildings were left empty in 1799, and remained unused for a few years, advertised as 'new, with a steam engine'.

In 1803, John Carline showed the buildings to Charles Hulbert and his potential partners from Manchester, who were looking to lease premises for a cotton manufactory.

Hulbert's cotton works, set up in 1803. Part of Shrewsbury's Industrial Revolution, cotton weaving grew up in Longden Coleham linked with spinning in Llangollen. However the workers resisted the introduction of steam-driven looms, and so he turned to printing. Three large buildings were sited on Carline Fields, including one five storeys high and nearly 100ft (30m) long. (Shropshire Archives)

It is said that after entertaining them to a meal, John Carline, acting more commercially than professionally, tempted them by offering his architectural services at no fee! Thus, the buildings escaped demolition and the Carline family were able to lease the redundant buildings to Charles Hulbert for weaving cotton calicoes.

The mill opened with 97 workers and soon employed about 200, but Hulbert lacked sufficient resources to retain the workers, who would often leave to earn higher wages in Lancashire and Cheshire. When he attempted to introduce 30 steam looms in 1812, the workers resisted and threatened him with violence. As a result Hulbert found it more profitable to turn to retailing and in 1814 he moved into the town centre. He finally gave up the lease of the mill in 1825 and took up alternative occupations, as an auctioneer and writer of antiquarian books. The buildings reverted to the Carline family and were converted to workers' cottages.

Besides the cotton mill in Coleham, there were several smaller linen and flannel spinning mills elsewhere in the town. Another iron-framed flax spinning mill was set up by Benjamin Benyon and Charles Bage in 1804 in Castlefields. This measured 208ft by 35ft (63.4m by 10.7m), accommodated 39 hand looms and 24 power looms worked by a steam engine, and employed more than 500 people. Bage left the partnership in 1816, and the Benyon brothers died in 1833/4. By 1837, the mill had been sold and demolished.

Charles Bage had left to set up his own flax/linen weaving business in Kingsland, where he built a single storey building, 90ft (27.5m) long with a 30ft (9.1m) span brick vaulted roof. It housed 30 hand looms and another 24 looms powered by a steam engine, but the business was not a success. He died in 1822 and his wife closed the factory in 1826. Thomas Burr, a London plumber who had established himself in Beeches Lane in the town centre where he made lead pipes, purchased the redundant mill property in 1829 and set up a lead factory, which, when further developed by his two sons, proved a constant source of nuisance to the town.

Breweries

In the first half of the 19th century, a few large breweries provided employment, including the Salopian Brewery. This was large for its time and its products were loaded into barges on the river for transport elsewhere. Similarly, the Coleham Brewery, by the river upstream of English Bridge, shipped its beers from Union Wharf. Trouncer's Brewery, established in Coleham in 1807, became very successful through three generations of the family, and owned many public houses in the town. They too were able to use the river for delivering grain to the adjoining maltings and transporting their barrels of beer.

Brickmaking

During this period, most domestic buildings were built with local bricks made in small brickworks sited around the outer areas of the town. In 1821, the business of the brickmaker was said to be 'carried on in open fields and its mode of operation may be seen in the neighbourhood of most large towns', and locally made bricks created part of the character of the various suburbs. After 1797, the local kilns could be fired by coal brought in from Coalbrookdale by canal.

Fellmongering

Fells, or dressed skins, were brought into the town from rural Wales on the backs of pack animals. The skins were washed in the river and processed and prepared for sale in the fellmongers' building in Frankwell, which had been built in 1590, and was about 70 feet (21m) long. The building provided room both for dealing with the skins and for the storage of wool, as well as having shops on the ground floor and workshops on the first and second floors. The Civic Society restored and converted it to community use.

Glass-stainers

John Betton of Shrewsbury (1765-1849) started making stained-glass in 1806, and in 1815 he formed a partnership with David Evans and established a workshop in the old Gibbon's Mansion property at the bottom of Wyle Cop. H.E. Forrest wrote in 1972 that 'they were amongst the first to revive the art of staining glass in this country, and were most successful in copying the beautiful colours obtained by the medieval workers of the Flemish School'. They restored the Jesse window in St Mary's, and executed new windows in the abbey, in St Mary's and St Julian's churches in the town centre, and also in St George's in Frankwell and St Giles's in Wenlock Road. They also undertook commissions for Lichfield Cathedral, Winchester College Chapel and Lord Hill. Their work was usually of biblical scenes, in strong colours, and copied from paintings. John Betton retired in 1825, but David Evans continued to work, assisted by his sons, until his death in 1861.

Malting

Malting had been important to Shrewsbury for decades, if not centuries. A certain Mary Hampton, who died in 1626, had derived her income from a malthouse, while the Taylor family were maltsters over several generations. William Taylor was born in 1756, and the family tradition continued into the 1900s. Frankwell was particularly associated with malting, and in 1786 twelve malting businesses were listed in the area, some attached to the inns there. The malting complex known as The Glen was a range of three-storey buildings, constructed with typical low ceilings, and small barred window openings. They were able to process nearly 250 bushels (c.9000 litres) of barley every four days. Many inns, however, such as the Dun Cow in Abbey Foregate, made their own malt and brewed their own beer.

Ropemaking

There were three Rope Walks in Shrewsbury in the 1800s. The one in Castle Foregate, near the canal, was owned by Richard Lyster in 1812. The other two were further out of the town, one near Copthorne Road, and the other at Meole Brace. Rope had long been required in connection with the river trade, and was also used in mining, and to a more limited extent, in building and agricultural work.

Stonemasons

John Carline II (1761-1835) settled in Shrewsbury in 1780. With partners John Tilley and then Henry Linnel, he worked as an architect and stonemason from their yard by English Bridge. (His, father, John Carline I, had come to Shrewsbury in the late 1760s as foreman mason on Gwynn's English Bridge – see below – but he returned to Lincoln.) The business employed about 70 men, some working in the yard and others out on the various building sites. The business was carried on by John Carline III until c.1850, by which time it had produced a large proportion of the stonework in the town, including that for replacing the flood-damaged Coleham Bridge and building the new Welsh Bridge in 1795.

Small traders

Besides the larger or more formalised industries, there were many small traders and individuals providing a great variety of crafts and services to the town's wider community, often from their own premises. They illustrate the self-supporting aspect of the social structure of the town. They included candle-makers, cork cutters, pewter-makers, tinsmiths, soap-boilers, and probably several laundry women and sweeps, besides all those employed in stabling and services. Craftsmen included shoemakers, several nailers, cabinetmakers, upholsterers and tailors, some of whom worked from home for masters based in the town centre. One, James Phillips, was perhaps exceptional. He lived in New Street, had a shop in High Street, and employed 50 tailors. There were also glovemakers working from properties in both the lower Mardol area, and also the western end of Abbey Foregate, which gave them rear access to running river water. In Abbey Foregate, the old abbey fishponds had been adapted for use as a tannery dealing with calf and sheepskins. That area became a centre for the glovemakers, until that part of the old abbey site was taken for building houses in about 1730.

Professional services and the 'leisured classes'

There was also a growing number of professionals, chiefly lawyers, offering their services, many taking up residence in the Belmont and St John's Hill area of the town. Analysis of trade figures from 1747 show that, in the previous hundred years, the 'leisured classes' had increased from an eighth to a full sixth of the population, while the proportion engaged in the food and drinks trades had almost doubled.

New Buildings and Alterations

In the last few centuries many building façades have been modernised according to the fashion of the day. Timber frame has been faced with dignified brick, or plastered over and marked with 'courses' to give the appearance of even more costly stonework. In later years fashion reversed, and 'timber-framing' was painted over the previously fashionable brickwork. An example of this is in the approach to the Library, in terraces of houses in School Gardens related to the old Shrewsbury School. They were originally of Georgian design, built in brick. Their façades, dating from 1825-30, were rendered within a few years in an imitation 'Tudor' style.

Some major alterations were made to the abbey church, making it more suited to its use as a parish church. Between 1704 and 1706, the dilapidated heavy walls and parapets of the nave were demolished, and a new roof was constructed above the triforium gallery. A few years later, in 1729, the single pitch, lean-to aisle roofs were replaced on the north side with a specially designed multi-gabled roof, allowing the aisle windows to be enlarged to let in more light.

In the late 1700s, the abbey church became the repository for various monuments and furnishings from the collapsed old St Chad's and demolished St Alkmund's churches in the town centre. Nevertheless, by the end of the 1700s the abbey church was in a poor and neglected state, which probably lessened any reluctance to allow the destruction caused by taking Telford's 'new A5 road to Ireland' straight through the south transept, completely destroying the cloisters.

The 'extraordinary affair' of the collapse of old St Chad's church in 1788 had the unforeseen consequence of enhancing three reputations, those of the *Chronicle*

The Liberal Club building in Belmont shows clearly the addition of a Georgian brick façade to a timber-framed building.
(Stephen de Saulles)

Old engravings show St Alkmund's church to have been of great architectural interest. However, after the collapse of St Chad's in 1788, and despite a professional structural survey, parishioners resolved on demolition in 1794. It proved so substantial that gunpowder had to be used. The tower and tall spire were reprieved, but it was still rated later as 'an act of vandalism', although not the only one in Shrewsbury. (SA 6001-199-359)

(see p.138), Thomas Telford and George Steuart, the architect for the replacement church. The churchwardens had sent for Telford to report on their leaking roof. He inspected it and reported back to them that that was the least of their troubles. He had found that due to 'injudicious gravedigging' too close to the shallow medieval foundations, the

Old St Chad's church sketched in July 1762 showing its considerable size. By legend, it was built on the site of the 'habitation of the Cynddylan wrapped in flames' of the old Welsh sagas, also associated with a British prince and poet Llywarch Hen, from Cumberland, who 'sought refuge with Cynddylan'. After the collapse of 1788, only the Lady Chapel remains.
(SA 6001-199-110)

structure was subsiding, especially under the north-west pier supporting the great tower. Large cracks in the walls confirmed the gravity of the situation. At the parish vestry meeting held in the church, Telford told them it was pointless to think of repairing the roof until emergency measures were taken to secure the walls. The response was indignation and ridicule, and protestations that the cracks had existed since time immemorial. When people started making remarks about professional men having a tendency to create work for themselves, Telford lost patience and left the meeting, saying as he left that if they were going to continue their deliberations, they would be wise to adjourn to the churchyard before the church fell down on their heads.

Old St Chad's in 2012, with the tower of St Alkmund's to the left and St Mary's between them, across a shallow valley. (Stephen de Saulles)

Having dismissed Telford, they engaged a local stonemason to do some repair work. Three days later, in the early morning, the mason was in the porch waiting for the sexton to bring the key when the clock began to strike the hour. As L.T.C. Rolt wrote in his book on Thomas Telford, 'The effect of the Israelite trumpets upon the walls of Jericho was not more startling. At the very first stroke of the bell the entire tower collapsed with a tremendous roar and crashed through the roof of the nave, demolishing completely the whole of the northern arcade.'

Understandably, an architect other than Telford, George Steuart, (who had designed Attingham Park at Atcham in 1785), was engaged to design the new St Chad's on a new site, overlooking the Quarry. It was intended to build a 'Gothic edifice' on a conventional rectangular plan. However, an alternative circular design proceeded, owing to an error in the minuting of the responsible committee's decision. When the misunderstanding was discovered, Steuart was instructed to prepare working drawings for the rectangular scheme. When he requested a second set of fees for the new drawings, the committee, not wishing to meet the cost, reluctantly, but fortunately, decided to accept the consequence of their oversight. The resulting church, the new St Chad's, completed in 1794, has an approximately 100ft (30m) diameter circular nave, expressed externally by a dramatic dome topped by a large golden cross. Internally, it includes an unusual gallery supported on a double row of slender Ionic columns. Once the initial shock had passed, it was and continues to be generally admired as a great asset to the town: 'Its style is Classic, but its round design is almost unique.'

New St Chad's, built in 1788, is a remarkable church achieved in spite of a committee. Architect George Steuart prepared four designs: one rectangular and three circular. The committee chose the rectangular option but, through neglect in minuting, Steuart proceeded with working drawings for a circular church. When their mistake emerged, the committee baulked at further fees, so let the matter ride. (Stephen de Saulles)

Thomas Telford, meanwhile, was initiating excavations at *Viriconium*. His discoveries of Roman work were to bring about a stop to the random 'quarrying' of building stone from historical sites for local construction work. Telford obtained authorisation, and sponsorship, to undertake the excavation work 'in order that men of learning might satisfy their curiosity'. He made ground plans and drawings of the buildings he discovered and so became a pioneer in the new profession of archaeology.

In 1836, Telford was also engaged in national work. His design for the new high-speed coaching 'A5' road from London to Holyhead via the facilities in Shrewsbury cut through the remaining abbey cloisters in order to avoid the sharp turns in the existing route to the north of the abbey church. The work was done after his death, and political requirements took priority over amenity – or thoughts of 'conservation'. The

The abbey, showing how Telford's pioneering route to Holyhead destroyed the southern transept and cloisters. Stone toothing was left in the hope of rebuilding the transept.
(Stephen de Saulles)

scheme also destroyed the pleasant gardens which had been laid out on the south side of the church. The scars left by dismantling the transept can still be seen, for coursing stones for possible toothing-in a future replacement wing were left projecting, but funds have never been available to fulfill the hope. The temporary in-fill wall still presents its blank reproach to the passing traffic.

Towards the end of this period, and during Telford's lifetime, three major reconstruction projects were undertaken, including both bridges. Defensive narrow gateways and provisions were no longer necessary, and obstructions on the bridges were impeding the increasing flow of packhorses and cart traffic. The renewal of both bridges had become necessary.

The old East, or Stone Bridge (now the English Bridge), much repaired and greatly congested, was replaced by a new bridge in 1769. It was designed by John Gwynn, a Shrewsbury-born London architect, and a founder member of the Royal Academy. When he died in March 1786, the *Shrewsbury Chronicle* compared his talent to that of Christopher Wren and wondered what he might have achieved if he had received the same level of patronage. The bridge was described by Henry Pidgeon, a gentleman of culture and borough treasurer in the 1830s: 'Its elegance and beauty of architecture is probably surpassed by few bridges in the kingdom, and is in every respect an ornament to the town, and an equally noble monument of the public spirit and generosity of

The old medieval stone 'English' bridge had been designed for packhorses and was only 10ft (3m) wide. (It included a waterwheel to pump water up to the cistern at the High Cross. The wheel caused problems in times of flood, but was not finally removed until 1830.) In 1765 it was decided to rebuild the old bridge, an operation shown in progress here. The Meole Brook was diverted, and some low-lying land filled so that the new bridge only needed to be about a third the length of the old one (Shropshire Archives)

The new English Bridge was completed in 1769. The illustration shows the original water level it was designed for. (It was raised by 3ft 6ins, about a metre, in the 20th century.) The high centre arch, to allow freer flow for floodwater, caused road gradient problems in times of frost, and was eventually lowered. (Shropshire Archives)

the gentry of the county, who so laudably exerted themselves to further its erection.'
Now altered slightly, the original scheme included ways down to the river on each side,
where coaching horses could be washed. It needs to be borne in mind that the river was
normally 3.5ft (about 1m) lower than the present level, which has been raised by the
construction of the weir.

The keystone on the central arch on the north, facing upstream, bears the head of
Sabrina, goddess of the river; that on the downstream side bears the head of Neptune
watching the waters flow towards the sea. The river is said to be in flood when the level
reaches the mouths of the dolphins on the flanking piers of the central arch.

The Welsh Bridge, which had been for so long the approach for trains of Welsh ponies,
each laden with two huge bolts of cloth, bearing their loads to the market place every
Thursday, driven by 'stout Welshmen in their country coats of blue cloth and striped
linsey waistcoats' (linen warp and woollen weft), was replaced in 1796. The battlemented
form of the bridge tower on the far side of the bridge was highly ornamented as can be

In 1785 the new Shirehall, with its ordered façades and pedimented 'engaged' (attached)
Ionic portico, was one of the finest examples of neo-classic design by John Hiram Haycock,
with stonework by John Carline and plasterwork by Joseph Bromfield. An Act of Parliament
allowed the approaches to be improved. Accordingly High Street was widened, St Julian's cut
back and the top of the Cop lowered by a further 2-3ft (almost a metre). Built on a 'moss
pit' left by glaciation, the foundations sank, damaging the building beyond repair according
to Telford's survey, and it was replaced by the County Hall of 1837 by Sir Robert Smirke
(designer of the British Museum), built on a concrete raft foundation 10ft (3m) thick.
(SA PR4-11)

seen in Buck's engraving of 1732. Leland, who was Henry VIII's antiquary travelling in the 1530s, reporting to the king on what he saw, described the old bridge as 'the greatest, fairest and highest upon the stream'. No longer necessary for reasons of defence, and having become an obstruction to traffic, the main gate was taken down in 1773, and the one at the Mardol end about ten years later.

The new bridge was sited, against the professional advice of Thomas Telford, a short distance downstream of the old medieval structure, and obliquely to the flow of the river. It was designed by Carline and Tilley in the town but, as Telford predicted, it was subject to serious river scouring and soon required very expensive remedial work to strengthen, and then protect, the foundations which had been undermined. It was not the first time that Telford's professional advice had been ignored with negative consequences.

In the town centre, the Shirehall, designed by John Hiram Haycock in an Italianate style, was completed in 1785. Its siting, on the north side of the Square and facing the High Street, struck deep soft ground which involved creating 10ft (3m) deep foundations. Nevertheless, by 1832 cracks were appearing in the walls and Telford was engaged to investigate the causes. It was another expensive problem. He found that the timber piles had decayed, and it was decided that repairs would be more costly than complete rebuilding. The replacement building designed by Sir Robert Smirke was finished in 1837.

Personalities

Most fortunately for Shrewsbury, these physical changes were wrought during a period of awakening public taste and strong local architectural influence. The period of 'Shropshire enlightenment', as Barrie Trinder wrote in 1983, in his *History of Shropshire*, 'lasted only a few years into the 19th century, but its effects were far reaching'.

It was a remarkable period. Those particularly influencing Shrewsbury included a number of men of wide culture and expertise, many of whom used to meet at Longnor Hall, a few miles south of Shrewsbury, the home of Archdeacon Joseph Plymley. He wrote *A General View of the Agriculture of Shropshire* in 1802, was a trustee of the turnpike roads and became involved in the anti-slavery movement. Among other personalities were Archibald Alison, philosopher and author of *Essays on the Nature and Principles of Taste*; Dr Samuel Butler, bishop and headmaster of Shrewsbury School; John Carline II, architect; Robert Waring Darwin, physician, a leading members of the group, and father of Charles Darwin; Thomas Eyton and Rowland Hunt, promoters of canal building; Edward Massey, architect; the Rev. Hugh Owen, author of *Some Account of the Ancient and Present State of Shrewsbury*; John Tilley, architect; William Reynolds, ironmaster; and James Wyatt, architect. Others met before in this chapter included the lawyer John Ashby; Charles Bage, designer of the Ditherington and Castlefields flaxmills, and one of the founders of the Lancasterian School; William Hazledine, ironfounder; Charles Hulbert, writer and mill owner; John Gwynn RA, architect and a founder member of the Royal Academy; Thomas Farnolls Pritchard, architect; and Thomas Telford, later elected a Fellow of the Royal Society of London and the first President of the Institution of Civil Engineers.

A National Transport Centre

Transport improvements played a vital part in the development of the 18th-century town, and the foundations for the 19th century. The improvements in roads, the number converging on the town, increased river traffic, the extensive carrier network and the coming of the Shrewsbury Canal in 1790, made Shrewsbury into a nationally important transport centre, even before the advent of the railways. Wagons from London, Birmingham and Manchester used to arrive here, and goods were then sent on to all parts of the country.

In the 17th century the Severn was the second busiest river in Europe, but it was in the 18th century that it reached its peak volume of goods transported. Those shipped downstream from or through Shrewsbury were very important to the activity in Coalbrookdale and the Ironbridge Gorge, and included timber for pit props, oak and ash for rails and sleepers, wood for the Coalbrookdale pumping engine, hay and straw for the ironworks and charcoal for the forges. Similarly, raw materials were taken upstream to the isolated forges in the Welsh hills. Iron cooking pots, grates and china also went upstream destined for Welsh homes. In 1756 the normal freight charge for goods from Shrewsbury down to Bristol was 10 shillings (50p) a ton, and the return rate, upstream, half as much again at 15 shillings (75p). A 12% surcharge was made when the river was low. A downstream voyage to Gloucester was reckoned to take between 11 and 24 hours. (By 1850 it was said that one should allow a fortnight for a return trip to Bristol.)

A view downstream from below the Infirmary at the bottom of St Mary's Water Lane with its protecting stone walls and Watergate on the left, before the construction of the Union Wharf and associated buildings in 1823. In 1810 the ironmaster, William Hazledine invested £500 to extend the towpath from Coalbrookdale to Shrewsbury. (Shropshire Archives)

The pulley wheel on Welsh Bridge, built in 1796, is one of the few reminders left of the town's river-trading days, when this area of Shrewsbury was surrounded by quays, warehouses and all the trappings of a busy port, including minor boat-building and repair work. The wheel assisted in hauling the 'trows' upstream. (Stephen de Saulles)

At the end of the 18th century, timber and fuel, oak bark for tanning, lead, slates and limestone were going downstream. Shrewsbury was importing a wide variety of merchants' goods, including wine, brandy and tobacco, and tropical products such as cane sugar and foreign fruits. Barges were bringing coal from the Severn Gorge and raw materials for the iron industry. The vessels on this upper section of the Severn were comparatively small, up to about 30 tons. On the lower section, below Bewdley or Gloucester, where goods could be transferred, the larger trows were up to 80 tons.

But problems in using the river for transport were mounting. By 1717, the new mill at Atcham (see p.138) was producing 300 tons of iron a year, requiring more regular servicing by barge. In the early 1700s a large load of pig iron would have lasted a forge for a month or more, and a year's supply could be delivered in a short period of good water levels; but water flow in the river was becoming less predictable. Telford pointed out that due to the enclosure and drainage of water meadows in north Shropshire, they could no longer act as a sponge in times of heavy rainfall, allowing water to reach the river slowly. Instead, rain ran off quickly, causing floods and depriving the river of its natural supply in dry periods. By the 1790s, Black Country forges and foundries were developing a need for regular weekly deliveries, which could not be met. Production was being held up. In 1795 there was one of the greatest floods ever remembered and yet, in the following year, there were only eight weeks in which navigation was possible during the whole year. Again, in 1803, the water level was recorded as being 'lower than ever remembered by the oldest and most experienced waterman now living'. While fish weirs were in existence, boats were restricted to narrow passageways where the water tended to flow fast through the channels. Once they were decaying or gone, the waters slackened and silt could accumulate, eventually forming shallows that impeded navigation.

The first river passenger traffic recorded is the journey of a midshipman from Wales, travelling from Shrewsbury in a wherry, in 1750. A wherry was a large rowing boat, manned by two oarsmen, with a hooded shelter for the passenger. It is recorded that he left Shrewsbury in the early morning, breakfasted at Atcham, dined at Bridgnorth, drank tea at Bewdley and arrived at Worcester at 9 o'clock in the evening.

In 1823 the site of the old Dominican friary, next to the old 13th-century Watergate, was levelled for the erection of a house and warehouse, alongside a new wharf for the recently formed Union Wharf Company. They also created a new trackway (now called Back Lane) from the wharf up to Raven Street (now Castle Street). This was to avoid the old stone Watergate which was too narrow for carts. The longer, curved route also reduced the gradient for horses pulling goods up the steep slope to the town centre.

During the excavation for the new trackway, workmen found traces of the 'well-appointed' 13th-century Dominican friary building. This was the friary King Edward IV had chosen, in 1473, as a suitable residence for his queen, and birthplace for one of his sons. The finds included many fragments of stone mullions, of 'a very handsome late gothick', and many pieces of 'very small octagonal pillars of an elegant form'. Owen & Blakeway also recorded the discovery of a skeleton 7ft 2in (2.18m) tall, but they gave no further explanation as to who he might have been. (There were later finds in the 1975 conversion work, including skeletons of members of the nobility brought for burial from the battle of Shrewsbury, 1403.)

'Conveyance from Union Wharf', at the bottom of St Mary's Water Lane, 'to London, Birmingham, Worcester, Gloucester and Bristol, and all intermediate places, every Tuesday and Friday' was still being advertised in 1828, a year when the service was run by John Rees. Rees is also listed as a maltster in Coleham. Hitchcock's map of 1832 shows the new building and marks it 'Union Wharf' and the new Back Lane is shown. In an 1834 Directory, six Wharfingers & Owners are listed at Mardol and Frankwell and one, John Rees, at Union Wharf. It also lists him as a 'Porter Dealer (& cider) Union Wharf'.

Canals

The Ellesmere Canal Company, founded in 1793, had hoped to connect Shrewsbury with Chester, thus creating a major waterway linking the Severn, the Dee and the Mersey. It crossed the Dee and the Ceiriog by Telford's iron-trough aqueducts at Chirk and Pontcysyllte, but its planned link with the Severn was abandoned for commercial reasons in 1805 in favour of a junction with the older Chester Canal, to become the modern Llangollen Canal and Montgomery Canal. Meanwhile a number of small canals had been built in the area around what is now Telford between 1768 and 1791 to serve a number of coal mines and ironworks. In 1793 an Act of Parliament was obtained which authorised the creation of a canal to link the town of Shrewsbury with this canal network in eastern Shropshire. Josiah Clowes was appointed chief engineer, but died in 1795 and was succeeded by Thomas Telford.

Three main types of canal were developed in Britain in the second half of the 18th century. There were broad canals, with locks 14 feet (over 4m) wide, narrow canals, with locks 7 feet (a little over 2m) wide, and tub-boat canals. The eastern Shropshire canal network was the latter type, as they were designed to cope with steep gradients. Tub-boats were rectangular in plan, 19ft 9ins (c.6m) long, and 6ft 2ins (c.2m) wide, by 3ft (c.0.9m) deep, made of wrought iron plates rivetted together. They had a very shallow draught of only about 3ins (75mm) when empty, increasing by about 4ins (100mm) per ton, and could carry up to a maximum of about five tons. This allowed them to be raised and lowered along the canal by means of inclined planes rather than locks. (An inclined plane consisted of two sets of rails laid parallel to each other, on each pair of which ran a cradle, raised or lowered by a wire rope, and capable of carrying one tub-boat at a time. The descending cradle assisted in balancing the weight of the ascending one, and the extra power needed was supplied by a stationary winding engine.) Towpaths were provided, and the tub boats were hauled by horses in trains of up to 20 boats together. They were steered by a man walking along the towpath who kept the leading boat in the middle of the canal simply by pushing against it with a pole. The cost of operating tub-boats was low, for it was said that one horse and one steersman could manage a load of 120 tons (122 tonnes).

The Shrewsbury Canal was completed in 1797, but it and the short canals in eastern Shropshire remained isolated from the rest of the canal network. Then, in 1826, the Birmingham & Liverpool Junction Canal was authorised to link the West Midlands with Merseyside. A branch from Norbury, through Newport to Wappenshall, finally linked the Shrewsbury Canal to the national network in 1835. This enabled specially built narrow boats with beam width of 6ft 7ins (2m) to reach the town centre's Butter Market. The section from Wappenshall to Shrewsbury was subsequently widened, enabling the standard 7ft (2.1m) narrow boats to come right into Shrewsbury.

The existence of the Shrewsbury Canal was a primary reason for the siting of the Ditherington Flaxmill, for the canal was able to bring raw material and fuel to the mill, and ship products away for distribution. Indirectly, therefore, it provided employment, foodstuffs and prestige for the town. The canal was also used to transport farm produce from the rural farmlands to the north of Shrewsbury into the Butter Market terminus, the boats returning with products manufactured in the town for distribution in those areas.

Coaching Services

Roads had received little attention since the Romans left, and the Civil War had made them worse. In 1730, it took a party of ladies, gentlemen and servants 12 days to travel from Shrewsbury to London. Matters had improved by 1753, when the first regular weekly direct service from Shrewsbury to London was launched from the Red Lion (the forerunner of the Lion); before that, the service had involved making connections at Coventry and Oxford. Nevertheless, it took four days, cost 18 shillings, and was most uncomfortable, yet coach travel was regarded as being 'for the ladies'. The following year, Mr Fowler at The Raven was offering three and a half days at 21 shillings inside, and riding outside at 10s 6d. By the summer of 1764, the journey time was reduced to two and a half days, with only one over-night stop at Coventry, and therefore much more economical overall. In 1769 the *New Fly*, with steel springs, came into service and took, via an overnight stop in Birmingham, only 24 hours at 12 shillings. Four years later, in 1773, the service offered was via Oxford for the overnight stop, and took two days for a cost of 36 shillings.

In 1780 Robert Lawrence moved his coaching business from the Raven to the Lion Hotel in Wyle Cop and pioneered the through route from London to Dublin through

Shrewsbury. In 1782 the Lord Lieutenant of Ireland, Earl Temple, arrived at the Lion on a new coach and is reputed to have said that 'he was extremely glad the Shrewsbury road had been recommended to him, as he found it, not only considerably nearer, but the accommodations were in every respect perfectly to his satisfaction'. Lawrence had achieved the cooperation of landowners and noble householders to set up inns on a new route he devised – via Wrexham, Mold, St Asaph and Conway. The service from Shrewsbury to Holyhead started in 1779, ran three times a week, and cost two guineas (£2 2s). The journey time was one and a half days with a night stop at the Lion. Lawrence went on to improve the service by travelling via Oswestry, Corwen and Llanrwst.

Prior to 1800 the whole route from London to Holyhead was under the care of about 24 separate Turnpike Trusts. The farther from London, the less the traffic, and therefore the less revenue taken in tolls, and so less there was to be spent on road maintenance. In 1800 the Act of Union between the Parliaments of England and Ireland increased traffic between the two capitals and so the revenue to be gained. Taking up the opportunity, Lawrence devised an even more direct route, over Capel Curig in the Welsh mountains. It took two years to engineer, but the service opened in 1804, two years before he died.

The coaching industry created by Lawrence was of great economic benefit to the town, providing fresh sources of income to many innkeepers, shopkeepers, caterers, farriers and drivers directly, as well as many others indirectly. A coach from the Lion was the first to cover 100 miles in a day. Teams of horses were employed, changing every seven or eight miles, done in less than a minute, and using about 150 horses for each journey. Lawrence had even organised a landlords' association by which he kept the whole route cleared of snow in the winter, each landlord clearing his stretch of road. His coaches had the reputation not only for service, but also for reliability and punctuality.

Meanwhile, in 1784, John Palmer, a Bath theatre proprietor, conceived the idea of sending mail by coach, rather than by post boys as was then the usual way. William Pitt, the Prime Minister, allowed him to carry out trial runs at his own expense; they worked well. The following year Robert Lawrence succeeded in establishing a similar service in coaches running between Shrewsbury and London. In 1786, Prime Minister Pitt appointed John Palmer as Surveyor and Controller General of the Post Office. Under the Royal Mail system he devised, coach drivers worked for contractors, but the guards were employed by the Royal Mail. By the late 1700s, 80 mail coaches, each drawn by four horses, left London every evening, each with four to six passengers whose fares

The Talbot Hotel, on the corner of Market Street and Swan Hill, designed by Samuel Scoltock and built in 1775, became one of Shrewsbury's leading coaching inns. Its main business was probably in the privately chartered 'post' coaches with up to 12, each with four horses, leaving the hotel each day. (In 1855 it was used to house the first School of Design.) (Shropshire Archives)

covered the cost of carrying the mail. Each coach had a guard armed with a blunderbuss. Because mails travelled free of turnpike tolls, (while expecting special service, such as having the gate ready open at the sound of the approaching post-horn), the Post Master General's requests for road improvements were not received very sympathetically.

In 1808 the Royal Mail tried to extend the mail coach service west of Shrewsbury to Holyhead and thence Dublin, but poor roads caused problems. In 1809 there were six major breakdowns of coaches and three post horses fell and broke a leg. In 1810 a Parliamentary committee was appointed to enquire into the state of the road and Thomas Telford was instructed to prepare a report. This he did the following year, but no action was taken. By 1815 the mail coaches were still taking 41 hours to travel the 276 miles from London to Holyhead through Oxford, Birmingham and Shrewsbury, and so the Holyhead Road Commission was constituted, empowered to spend money on improving the route, and determined that it should pass through Shrewsbury, Llangollen and Snowdonia. The Commission instructed Telford to survey the route; he completed this in 1817, and this time the necessary work was put in hand. Telford commenced by working on some of the most dangerous stretches of road in Snowdonia. Over the course of the next few years several Acts of Parliament were passed authorising the construction of the Menai Suspension bridge, a new road across Anglesey, combining the Turnpike Trusts west of Shrewsbury into a single body directly responsible to Parliament. By 1837 the journey time from London to Holyhead had been cut to 28 hours – with resulting economic benefits to Shrewsbury. An ironic consequence of the construction of the whole route, referred to as 'the finest road in Europe', was that it made possible, and indeed hastened, the development of the new railway network which made it redundant, at least for some decades.

Lord Hill's Column was funded by public subscription in 1815 to commemorate the military services of Lord Hill, a Shropshire general who had fought with Wellington in the Peninsular War and then at Waterloo. He was also, briefly, MP for Shrewsbury. A landmark for miles around, its 172 steps lead to a panoramic view. (Shropshire Archives)

After 1837 further cuts to travelling time were made possible by the railways, which gradually led to a decline in traffic on the road.

From 1816, coaches arriving from London would have passed Lord Hill's Column at the entrance to the town. This was erected to commemorate Lieutenant General Rowland Lord Hill, who served under Wellington in the Peninsular War and at Waterloo. To every coach it marked a point of 'arrival' or 'departure'. It is the largest Doric column in the world, standing 133.5ft (51m) high overall, and was designed by Edward Haycock. The colossal statue of Hill, modelled by Joseph Panzetta, is made from the mysterious 'coade stone' allegedly invented by Mrs Coade to an original secret recipe that died with her, and formed by Messrs Coade and Sealy, of London. The column and plinth are of the local Grinshill stone.

As well as the Lion and the Raven, the other chief coaching inns were the Britannia, rebuilt in 1820 with stabling for 150 horses, and the Talbot. At the peak of the coaching days of the 1830s, the great feat of Sam Hayward, who drove the London coach for about 16 years, was to bring the coach at full speed up Wyle Cop (then much steeper) past the entrance to the Lion yard, circling sharply and taking it through the narrow archway at the same high speed with, it is said, 'never a mishap', and 'never as much as ten minutes late'. No other coachman ever attempted it.

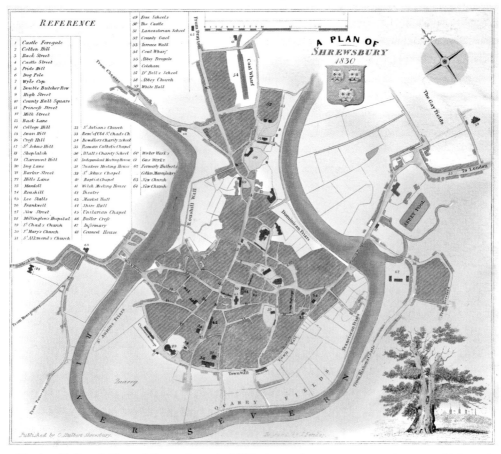

Charles Hulbert's Plan of Shrewsbury in 1836 shows the town centre changes which took place during the Georgian period since Rocque's map of 1746 (see p.133). (SA PR-2-419)

11   VICTORIAN TIMES

> 'We have the strangest little rooms, the ceilings of which I can touch with my hand. The windows bulge out over the street as if they were little storm windows in a ship, and a door opens out of the sitting room on to a little open gallery with plants in it, where one leans over a queer old rail.'
>
> Charles Dickens in 1838, writing to his elder daughter, while staying at the Lion Hotel with his illustrator, 'Phiz' (Hablot K. Browne)

A strong sense of patriotism developed during the new queen's reign, perhaps in reaction to the recent Prince Regent's reputation. One of Queen Victoria's first acts on behalf of Shrewsbury, within a month of her 1837 accession, was to create John Bickerton Williams, the mayor of Shrewsbury, a knight. Evidently Williams had been promised a knighthood by William IV in recognition of his book *The Memoirs of the Life, Character and Writings of Sir Matthew Hale*, but the king had died before carrying it out. (Hale was an influential English barrister, judge and jurist who served both Cromwell and Charles II. He did not confine himself to law, but also studied mathematics, physics, chemistry, anatomy and architecture.)

National celebrations were made the excuse for local holidays. The queen's coronation was celebrated in 1838, and her wedding to Prince Albert two years later. The marriage of the Princess Royal, which took place in 1858, was celebrated officially by the corporation with a dinner, served at 5pm in the Guildhall, terminated by a long list of formal loyal toasts. In the mayor's words, they were 'those which were invariably proposed when English gentlemen met together, proving thereby that the routine of their lives was one of loyalty and patriotism'. His sentiments were greeted, as would have been expected, by cries of 'Hear! Hear!' In those days, gentlemen were very verbose on formal occasions, and the length of their speeches would have reflected their feelings of self-importance. The dinner was also remarkable for the fact that it was the celebration of a lady by an all-male gathering. It was the subject of adverse comment, and a poem, in the *Echo*, which also celebrated the event, but less formally and with the inclusion of the ladies, at 'a ball' at the Shrewsbury and Hereford Railway sheds. Hearing that the corporation was proposing nothing further, the Nonconformist churches arranged a gathering of 1,500 children who, wearing white rosettes, paraded through the town, accompanied by brass bands, prayers and banners.

The Municipal Corporations Act of 1835 had abolished the regulatory powers of the Drapers, but although they lost both power and influence, they retained ownership of their Hall, and the records and furniture it contained. Although it had become an anachronism, it retained its original form, with master, wardens and freemen – who, as charitable trustees, administered their almshouses. Under the same Act, Shrewsbury became a municipal borough and was enlarged to include adjoining built-up areas. The area was divided into five wards, each of which was to elect six councillors. In turn the councillors would elect ten alderman to make up the municipal body, who then elected the mayor.

Although still a town of great vitality, Shrewsbury was not one of the Victorian boom towns. In the first half of the 19th century, the population of England and Wales increased by over 150%, while that of Shrewsbury rose by less than 60%. In the middle of the 17th century, it had ranked as the 13th town in England, but by the middle of the 19th century, it was not amongst the first 40. By the end of the century, the population had reached about 28,000, and had spread out into the suburbs of Castlefields around the railway, Copthorne around the new barracks, Cherry Orchard around the old Whitehall, and arcadian Kingsland after the construction of the bridge in 1882.

Hitchcock's map of 1832, with accurate block plans and boundaries, showing early stages of modern cartography. It shows the canal town before Telford's road or railways came, but industrial buildings in Castlefields and the suburbs of Ditherington and Coleham.
(SA 3073-1)

Social Change

At the beginning of Queen Victoria's reign, social structures and convention were rigid. Society was divided between those who received and those who gave service, and everyone 'knew their place'. There was a degree of paternalism in the attitude of the first, and a simplicity of expectation in the other, which only changed as working-class horizons widened. By the middle of the century, there was a segregation of the classes in the town which had not existed before; until then, rich and poor had lived cheek by jowl. The change was brought about by rebuilding work in Swan Hill and St John's Hill, and the creation of other areas of genteel housing such as Belmont. Until the mid 1860s, ladies made use of sedan chairs for their social journeys around the town. As the centre of the town became less agreeable, those who could afford to do so moved out into the nearby suburbs, which were then still within walking distance.

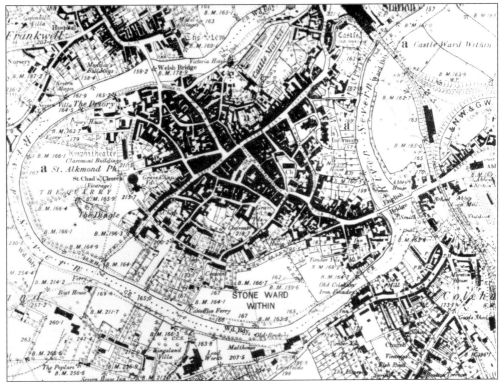

An extract from the 1884 6-inch to 1 mile Ordnance Survey map showing more accurate detail, including development along the main streets and on the old town walls, plot boundaries, and 'bench marks', related to a Datum, then in feet, at the Liverpool Victoria dock level. It shows major changes: the new railway, cutting through right by the castle, giving a 'town-centre station', a viaduct, signal box and routes of the different companies. New are the General Market, a Cattle Market, or 'Smithfield', and new riverside Smithfield Road. The larger scale allowed greater use of symbols and typographical styles, conveying a wealth of information still found useful.
(Shropshire Archives)

Belmont was the fashionable new street in the early 18th century. Left, a terrace of
two- and three-storey Georgian houses. No.6 is a handsome Queen Anne house, with
stone quoins and bands, built in 1701, used after 1821 as the 'Judge's Lodgings', with
Belmont House, of simpler style, set back behind original gate piers.
(Stephen de Saulles)

Coaching and Posting

Coaching and posting were both important features of the county town at the beginning
of the Victorian period. 'Posting', or the hire of coaches, employed many more people
and horses than the regular coaching services. But the new mainline railways, resulting
from the railway mania of the 1840s, almost ended the prosperity of coaching. By 1840,
there was a rail route from the capital to Ireland taken through Chester, so that the
demand for Telford's new A5 route was lessened. Nevertheless, it continued to provide an
excellent route between Shrewsbury and London. Where Lawrence had been the pioneer
in the 18th century, Isaac Taylor took his place in the 19th. He saw opportunities in the
challenge of the railways to Shrewsbury's trade and status, and ensured that the services
from the Lion integrated with the new rail routes and times, exploiting, for example, the
possibilities in providing feeder services to Birmingham.

   As part of their promotion, coaches were named after current events, for example,
the *Pickwick* in 1837 when the *Pickwick Papers* were being published; the *Prince Albert*
in the year of the queen's wedding; the *Nimrod*, the nom-de-plume of a popular racing
author of the time; the *Exhibition* in 1851, to draw attention to the Great Exhibition in
London, and even the *Nugget*, which ran from Shrewsbury to Wales during the Welsh
gold rush in the 1850s.

Isaac Taylor's enterprise was acknowledged in 1843 with a gift, when the following tribute was paid: 'The spirit with which Mr Taylor had carried on the coaching previous to the giant competition of steam was well known to everyone. All persons remember the first coach in England – the *Wonder*, with its six horses, the rapid *Stag*, and the swift *L'Hirondelle*, coaches that had been conducted in a style seldom equalled, and certainly never excelled. We need scarcely refer to the stimulus given to the trade of the town at that time, through the exertions of Mr Taylor, who was never beaten, until steam rose up in array against him.' Another leading personality in coaching was the Hon Thomas Kenyon of Pradoe of the Lion office, described as 'the most deservedly popular man in the County of Shropshire'. He once drove the *Wonder* himself to London, and Isaac Taylor described him as 'one of the kindest patrons, and one of the warmest supporters'.

The Lion led the field, with around 16 departures daily. The first two stops on the way to Birmingham, at Wellington and Shifnal, were at inns kept by two of Taylor's brothers. In 1878, there is a graphic account of a typical 5am departure of the *Wonder* from the Lion: 'Before the hour all passengers were required to be in their places, all luggage had to be safely packed and as the chime of the first of the four quarters rung out from St Julian's church tower Richard Ash, the guard, clambered to his place; behind, the coachman took his place in the box, and with the first strike of the hour, the four well groomed steeds dashed forward under the archway of the inn yard, the horse cloths were removed with a flourish, the skid [wheel brake] was put on as the corner was turned, and sharply went the heavy vehicle down the Wyle Cop.'

Although Shrewsbury's experience in providing especially good facilities for its visitors enabled the coaching industry to withstand competition from the railways for about 20 years, its end was inevitable. Ultimately the coaches could not compete with the creeping tendrils of the railway network, its speed and low fares. The era of the stagecoach finally came to an end in the 1860s. The Talbot, which had been one of the leading coaching inns, became a police station in 1854, with the Inland Revenue occupying the first floor and the building also providing accommodation for the new Shrewsbury School of Design.

River and Canal Use

Proposals for providing locks on the River Severn were firmly opposed by boat owners, who objected to the idea of paying tolls or having the navigation obstructed. By 1840, when Telford's attempts to provide for year round navigation had been frustrated by opposition, it was common for craft to remain aground at Ironbridge during dry periods. As the river rose, they went on to Gloucester in fleets of 20 or 30, hurriedly unloading and returning upstream quickly before the level fell again, travelling by night if necessary. With these unreliable conditions, it was only the cheapness of transport by water compared with road haulage that enabled the river trade to survive so long.

For a while during Victorian times the busy commercial use of the river continued, with boatbuilding and related activities continuing round the quays. Yet the Montgomery Canal had begun to whittle traffic away from the upper Severn from the 1790s, largely by diverting it to Liverpool, whilst the linking of the Shrewsbury Canal with the national canal network in 1835 diverted other trade away from the river. The 1837 *History of Shrewsbury* by Thomas Phillips and Charles Hulbert lists six boat owners with 20 vessels. One of the owners was John Rees at Union Wharf, downstream of English Bridge, who had three barges – *The Success* (40 tons), *The Betsy* (40) and *The Prudence* (35) – plus two unnamed boats of 10 and 8 tons. In 1841 there were 17 watermen, but in 1851 there were only two. One of them was still John Rees, a maltster who shipped porter and cider; his trade remained good and the wharfage buildings, store and bargees' tavern were enlarged in 1856.

But navigation on the upper Severn ceased around 1850 and gradually the wharves fell into disuse, and the last barge was seen in 1895. The Howard Street Butter Market warehouse remained well placed to enable goods to be despatched, now by rail instead of narrow boat, and the London and North Western Railway took over the market in 1857.

Ferries

In the 18th and 19th centuries, ferries linked the surrounding suburbs to the town centre. From 1809, when bow-haulers were replaced by horses to haul the barges upstream, new horse ferries were needed where the towpath switched from one bank to the other. The horse ferry downstream of the Underdale Island between Castlefields and Underdale operated from 1809, and was later replaced by one further upstream connecting from Bradford Street in 1882. This ferry also profited from carrying passengers to the racecourse, including those attending the Royal Show in 1884, and various other events held there. In 1897 an extra halfpenny was charged for ferrying a bicycle.

There was a ferry linking Longden Coleham to Greyfriars until 1880, when it was replaced by a 'footbridge' to take the increasing number of cyclists endangering the pedestrians on English Bridge at 'rush hours'.

A ferry also operated between the Quarry and the Kingsland Coffee House. In 1872 the Kingsland Bridge Company was formed, but the Act of Parliament permitting a bridge was not obtained until 1880. Designed by Henry Robertson,

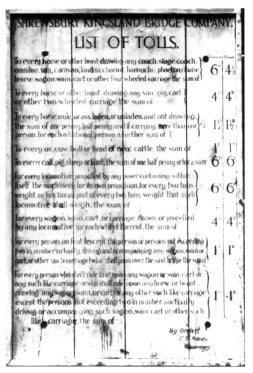

The Kingsland Bridge, built in 1882, has always been privately owned and operated as a toll bridge. The old tariff board indicated the range of traffic it was designed to carry. The bridge enabled the suburb of Kingsland to be developed with private houses, many of them originally for masters at the school. (Shropshire Archives)

engineer and the borough's MP, the single arch with suspended carriageway spans 212ft (64.6m) across the river and riverside walk on the town side. It opened as a toll bridge in 1882, coinciding with Shrewsbury School's move from its original town centre site to the healthier heights of Kingsland, overlooking the horseshoe town layout, across the river. The ferry remained in use by the boys to reach their boathouse from the Quarry.

When there were only two bridges into the town there were several passenger ferry crossing points, some of them still in use up to the last war. This one was used primarily by boys from Shrewsbury School. (SA PH-S-13-C-2-24)

A view to the town from Shrewsbury School across the river and Kingsland Bridge. (Stephen de Saulles)

The view looking upstream past Shrewsbury School boathouse from Kingsland Bridge.
(Stephen de Saulles)

Another ferry plied between the Quarry and the Boat Inn. An old ferry crossing had been revived in 1834 between the Quarry and the Cann Office on Kingsland, and was used for carrying wagons from Burr's leadworks during its productive period, but ceased operation in 1893. (The Cann Office may be connected with a post route between Aberdyfi and Shrewsbury established by Henry VIII in the 16th century for the conveyance of mail. The posting inns on this route were ordered to display signs showing a symbol of three 'canns', or tankards.)

Yet another ferry from Smithfield Road to the cricket ground in the loop of the river in Frankwell was established in the 1860s.

The Railway Town

Throughout the country, the railway was the greatest agent of change in the 19th century. The physical impact was not as disastrous here as in some other towns, (and Shrewsbury was one of the last county towns to be linked to the national system), but railways brought enormous social, economic and topographical changes, some only temporary but some permanent.

The arrival of the railway in Shrewsbury meant that areas of housing were cleared away to make way for it. This housing was mostly rented out, and records taken of the tenants' occupations indicate the range of employment at the time. The area housed 107 men, 145 women, and 104 children aged under 15. A few under-15s worked in the thread and spinning mills, and most of the men worked in the shoemaking and tailoring trades. Others were engaged in baking and confectionery, with one on the canal and one elderly boatman. Other sources of employment were the mills, markets, laundries, stables and services such as the prison.

An illustration looking upstream captioned 'Viaduct across the Severn at Shrewsbury', from *The Illustrated London News* of 17 November 1849, shows a brick-built railway viaduct constructed for the Shrewsbury to Chester line that opened in 1848, and was extended to Wolverhampton and Birmingham soon after. Later bridges were added in steel on either side when the station was enlarged in 1900. (SA PH-S-13-R-4-1)

During the preparatory ground works for the construction of the station, mostly done by teams of itinerant navvies, the courts were kept busy dealing with the drinking and affrays involved. Recognisable by 'moleskin trousers, velveteen tail coats, felt hats turned up, and cheeky red handkerchiefs', the navvies got danger money for handling explosives, and spent it on drink. Two names familiar to modern ears passed through the courts: Mary Whitehouse, in connection with 'keeping a disorderly, and questionable, ale-house on Castle Hill', and John Humphrys, who was fined a shilling by the magistrates for 'creating a disturbance'.

The first stone of the initial railway bridge over the river was laid in 1847, by lowering it gently into a specially prepared large coffer dam. (Later, two further bridges were constructed, one on either side, to carry the additional lines.) The bridge was completed in 1848 and, unusually, carries part of the station over the river. The 'Shrewsbury and Chester' was the first line into the town in 1848. Other routes followed: to Birmingham in 1849, Hereford in 1853, Crewe in 1858, Worcester in 1862, and westwards into Wales in the same year. The Potteries route was envisaged as a route to Ireland but it was not sanctioned by Parliament or allowed to share the main companies' station, and its promoter, the Shrewsbury and North Wales Company, was obliged to create a separate terminus at Abbey Foregate, opposite the abbey. It opened in 1866, but soon closed due to lack of traffic, although it was to be revived again later.

In 1853 the Great Western Railway offered three trains a day to Paddington, via Oxford and Reading, the train leaving at 09:05 reaching London at 17:05 (by 1902, the time to Paddington had been reduced to 3½ hours). The 30-mile journey to Ludlow took 2¼ hours. Between 1849 and 1855 the new railway lines already going north to Chester came to the east side of Shrewsbury, all but surrounding the abbey church. A combination of geography and railway politics made Shrewsbury one of the most important junctions in the country, with several major routes intersecting at its station. As mail was moved by train, for several decades Shrewsbury enjoyed a range of services beyond what might have been expected for its size and population.

A busy outdoor market scene in the Square in the 1860s, before the construction of the Victorian covered market building. Growers brought their home-grown produce in from outlying farms. Traditionally, for centuries, the 'Green', or 'Apple' market was at the High Street end, and the 'Cornmarket', with sometimes intrusive livestock, at the other. The Plough Inn on the right of the picture is seen before the addition of its upper storey (see p.200).
(SA PH-S-13-5-28-20-1)

Markets

In the 1830s and '40s it was still common to see herds of animals being led through the town on their way to various open market places in the streets, and the Street Commissioners had been urged to provide a proper place 'where farmers can transact their business without interruption or danger' to themselves or to the surrounding crowds. The construction of a livestock market (by tradition always called a 'smithfield') eventually solved the problems created by the slaughter houses in Butcher Row. The best site available, Raven Meadows on the riverside, was subject to flooding, so the land levels were raised, the area drained, and links created between Mardol and the railway station. It was finally opened in 1850. It was then that the auction system was adopted, replacing the age-old custom of individual deals, sealed over a drink in the nearest public house.

The problem of how to accommodate the town's markets had still not been satisfactorily solved, despite the efforts of the Improvements Commission in the 1820s. The need for an indoor wholesale and retail market became an important issue, but the 'battle of the sites' went on for decades. There were strong differences of opinion as to whether the market was 'a commercial problem that should be solved by the traders' or 'a matter for the local corporation to provide'. The corporation eventually recognized that the investment required was beyond what the traders could afford, and that clearing the streets of market stalls and casual sellers would be of considerable social benefit to the whole community. They evidently set up committees, engaged successive outside consultants, and sought opinions, while they discussed, decided and re-decided which of the five alternative sites should be cleared and made available, a process that absorbed them for several years. Finally the matter was resolved, and around 50 properties were demolished and cleared between Mardol and Barker Street. A painting by Thomas Shotter Boys dated 1858 showed that six-storey jettied timber-framed buildings had existed in the area, reflecting the building density of the town centre at the time.

The new General Market, also known as the Indoor Market, was designed by Robert Griffiths of Stafford and built between 1867 and 1869. The two floors provided

Buildings in Mardol demolished in 1866 to make way for the Victorian General Market, from a painting by T.S. Boys, 1858. Five- and six-storey timber-framed buildings show the high density of development in the town centre. Casement windows indicate buildings that are pre-1680, and stone quoins those finished in c.1715. (Courtesy of Shropshire Museums)

The magnificent General Market building designed by Robert Griffiths of Stafford was lost in the 1960s' redevelopment massacre. It provided for trading previously conducted in the crowded streets on market days. Its replacement after 70 years, to yield lettable ground-floor shops, put the market up to first-floor level.
(Courtesy of Shropshire Museums SHYMS FA-1995-015)

The new General Market provided for the monthly wholesale Butter and Cheese Fairs held in Shrewsbury. (Shropshire Archives)

accommodation for the wholesale and retail markets for dairy produce which were able to move from their existing locations, and also the market at the Corn Exchange, the butchers from Fish Street and the green and apple markets from the Square. It also provided generous storage in the basement. Casual street selling thus disappeared, with some enterprises transferring to shops and many proprietors 'living over the shop'. The new market was a landmark building of strong design which came to be despised for its Victorian character, and then much missed once it was demolished some years later.

After the opening of the railways in 1848, the Howard Street Market (also known as the Butter Market), which had already been accessible to canal traffic, could be reached by more buyers, and goods were increasingly despatched by the more rapid rail services rather than by canal as hitherto. In 1857 it was taken over by the London & North Western Railway to be used as a goods warehouse. In 1851, the privately owned Circus Yard functioned as a wholesale depot for large quantities of Welsh dairy produce. The Circus Warehouse prospered, and was still in use in 1868.

Loaded carts c.1896 waiting in front of the old *Shrewsbury Chronicle* offices in St John's Hill for the wool sales held in the new General Market. The town's staple trade in Welsh cloth diminished when export markets were ruined by the American War in the 1770s, and by non-Drapers gaining direct access to the Welsh producers as a result of better roads. Until the Drapers abandoned the old Market House in 1803, each Thursday saw them, 'yard-measure' in hand, waiting until, at a set time, they went to the first-floor hall to do their buying. (Shropshire Archives)

Shopping, Commerce and Trade

Millard Harding in the Square provided for all the important niceties of Victorian social life, when ladies and their daughters still reflected the status of their husband and skilfully, though discreetly, displayed their class and breeding. Shrewsbury, as the county town, provided such specialist retailers who would be familiar with the conventions and rules of etiquette involved in a range of local, county and court occasions. (Shropshire Archives)

Royal Shrewsbury Cakes, 6 &7 Wyle Cop. 'Shrewsbury Cakes,' says Henry Pidgeon in 1837, 'appear to have been presented to distinguished personages on their visits to this town as early as the reign of Elizabeth I; and when their Royal Highnesses the Duchess of Kent and the Princess Victoria arrived here in 1832, they were graciously pleased to accept a box of them from the Mayor.' (Shropshire Archives)

A remarkable feature of the street scene would have been the number of carriers with their horse-drawn covered wagons entering the town from the surrounding areas. Goods, including dairy produce from the north Shropshire plain, were collected, sorted and despatched to customers in London and other destinations. A wide variety of goods, often purchased by the carrier on behalf of his customer, would be carried on the return journeys. Records show that in 1844, 87 carriers from 62 villages made 181 calls in the town in a week. Despite losing some business to the trains, they gained customers from villages not served by the railways, and by 1899, records show an increase to 91 carriers from 70 villages, making 135 calls in Shrewsbury.

The competition between shopkeepers was intense and led to long opening hours. In 1848, over 20,000 men were employed in Shropshire's shops, but only around 2,000 women. Female shop assistants were thought to be less acceptable to the public. The Early Closing Association met with little response in Shrewsbury until the 1850s. Employers' attitudes were that 'Temptations to evil were furnished by additional hours of leisure'. Accordingly, staff were expected to work for up to 95 hours a week. The Shop Hours Bill of 1886 provided for closing at 8pm on weekdays, and at 10pm on Saturdays, when most people shopped as a social activity. Its only concession to the demands

this placed on employees was to limit hours for those aged under 18 to 74 hours per week. Staff lived on the premises and could be expected to spend an hour or so arranging windows before opening time. The battle for a half-day holiday continued, but 'Thursday early closing' only became general, and still not universal, in the 1890s.

In the 1870s Adnitt and Naunton were based in the Square, above Hughes & Co's wine cellars under. They published books on local history. Eddowes' *Salopian Journal* was next door. The first local demonstration of the newly invented telephone took place in 1878, when a 30-yard line connected the shop to the Music Hall, where an audience was able to hear gentlemen in the shop singing a popular song. (Shropshire Archives)

Building Development and Suburban Growth

A few public buildings were built in this period, but the largest development must have been that concerned with the new railway service, involving lines, bridges and the station itself. The original station, a single-storey building of 1848, was

An example of a most unusual and successful feat in 'extension' and 'conservation'. In 1901 the station was enlarged by being extended downwards. Another floor was inserted beneath the original ground and forecourt level, and the subway access to the platforms was constructed at the same time. (Shropshire Archives)

The new head Post Office building built in the 'Modern Gothic' style in 1876 on the corner of Pride Hill and St Mary's Street. The Post Office took over providing telephone services in 1911, when a tall gantry was erected on the roof to carry overhead wires across the town on tall poles 80-90ft high right by the Watergate. The first telephone exchange had been opened by the Western Counties & South Wales Telephone Co at 2 Dogpole Court in 1887; the first telephone directory, published in 1895, included just nine subscribers.
(Shropshire Archives)

designed by Thomas Penson Jnr. It was built in grey stone and Tudor style with tall chimneys punctuating its high roofline. Pevsner found it disagreeable in several ways, but it has improved with keeping. Its later extension between 1899 and 1903, with the construction of a new floor underneath the original station building and a lowered forecourt, probably added the balance missing from the original design.

The new Shirehall in the Square was rebuilt by Sir Robert Smirke in the mid 1830s, this time with stronger foundations. Pevsner described it as 'large and dignified though cool rather than warm. Ashlar faced, nine bays.' It was extended in 1881, but has been demolished for redevelopment since. A Savings Bank, designed by Edward Haycock, was built in College Hill in 1839. The Music Hall in the Square was also designed by Edward Haycock in an imposing classical style in 1840. It incorporates the remains of the 14th-century medieval Vaughan's Mansion, which was used for smaller events and later as a bar facility.

A Post Office building in the High Street was built in red brick with Gothic details by the Office of Works in 1877. The Eye, Ear & Throat Hospital, also a prominent 'statement building' on Murivance, was designed in a hard-faced 'fiery red brick and red terra cotta', with an octagonal feature tower, by C.O. Ellison of Liverpool in 1880, and has now been converted into apartments.

The Jubilee Baths were erected in Priory Road to commemorate the queen's golden jubilee in 1887. The building contained two swimming pools – a first class and a second class – together with 13 slipper baths (the classic freestanding Victorian style bath) for use by people who had no bath at home. The first class pool had a balcony round three sides for spectators at swimming galas. Later, adaptations were made so that it could be boarded over for all-in wrestling on Saturday nights.

A few buildings were altered or converted to other uses. The old Shrewsbury School buildings were purchased by public subscription and remodelled to provide a public library and a natural history museum for the town in 1885. The Plough Inn in the Square, originally a two-storey 16th-century timber-framed and plaster building, had a top floor and gables added in about 1890, cleverly designed to blend in with the old.

The building of the new Shirehall, and then the Music Hall, would have disrupted the centre, followed by the new market building shortly after. It is not surprising that many were finding the town crowded and unhealthy, and probably uncomfortable with the additional noise and dust, and extra horse and cart traffic. The conditions probably encouraged the growth of the suburbs, and deepened the other 'class distinctions' common at the time. Traffic problems at the beginning of the Victorian period were caused by horses, but by the end, instead of horse droppings, the problems were created by the fumes, noise and speed of motor vehicles. Arthur Ward, writing in the mid 20th century, said that 'no fewer than 13 County Roads, (8 of them Class A Routes), converge on Shrewsbury, and the old streets in the town are rapidly becoming quite inadequate for the twentieth century traffic'.

Shrewsbury's Ear, Eye & Throat Hospital. Designed by C.O. Ellison of Liverpool and built in firery red Ruabon brick and terracotta, it opened in 1881. In 2004 it was converted to upmarket apartments which, being near the bridge, were given the name of Kingsland Bridge Mansions. (Stephen de Saulles)

This photograph of timber being hauled at the Smithfield Ironworks, near the cattle market, shows the local use of heavy horses. (Shropshire Archives)

Views of Shrewsbury in Victorian times. Clockwise from top left:
Royal Free Grammar School from Castle Foregate.
St Nicholas church and the gateway to Council House Court off Castle Gates,
where the Council in the Marches used to meet.
The Square and Old Market House, or Hall, built in 1595.
The two-storey Shrewsbury Station and forecourt, as originally built, with the castle behind.
The town centre, viewed across the river and the Quarry from Kingsland.
Quarry Walk, the main avenue in the Quarry with a statue of Hercules (now replaced by a
replica because of its valuable lead content) at the end, by the river.
(Shropshire Archives)

Suburban growth had taken place from the beginning of the 18th century, though only in a scattered form of ribbon development. Now, in the 19th century, the gaps were gradually filled in. On the outskirts, gardens were laid out like allotments, and were filled gradually, as at Castlefields and the Hermitages in Belle Vue. In the town, housing developments were on a small scale and piecemeal. Old burgage plots were filled with crowded developments, forming small courts. It had been traditional for shopkeepers and craftsmen to live above the shop but towards the end of the century, they were moving to separate homes, away from the centre. Brickyards and gravel pits were to be found on the outskirts of the town, and most suburban houses were built of locally quarried materials and by local craftsmen. Accordingly, they had local character and great variety.

Some suburban development was carried out from the 1850s by 'freehold land societies', which raised money from shareholders to buy land, then laid it out for housing, distributing the plots amongst their members. Housing was also built by speculators. Areas such Albert Street, Severn Street and Victoria Street in Castlefields, and later Bradford Street in Cherry Orchard, and Oakley Street in Belle Vue, were developed in this way. Cleveland Street and Tankerville Street in Cherry Orchard were developed in the 1880s, and the land around Whitehall was laid out and sold off in the 1890s. The majority of the houses are semi-detached, built of brick, with stone dressings and a variety of architectural details, such as gables and porches, and using building materials such as decorative tiles and stained glass. After the official ending of the Shrewsbury Show in 1878, Kingsland was developed with large and much-decorated villas for a separate social class. Bricks were supplied from yards off the Copthorne Road by a specially laid tramway.

The abbey or, more correctly, the parish church of Holy Cross had fallen into a dilapidated state, and its roof leaked. In 1859, George Gilbert Scott was approached

Between 1815 and 1836 the route to Holyhead and Ireland through Shropshire was improved under Thomas Telford's direction, until it was considered the best road in Europe. The work in Shrewsbury, seen to the left of the abbey, was executed after his death and he never saw the devastation it caused. (Shropshire Archives)

A photograph of the abbey, taken in late 1800s, shows the sweep of Telford's Holyhead Road to the right, cutting the abbey from its site and monastic buildings and, left, the old route to and from London, with sharp bends behind the abbey.
(Alfred Watkins, Hereford City Library)

about supervising restoration work, but his fees were deemed to be too high, so a local architect, Samuel Pountney Smith, was asked to submit his proposals. In summary, his report recommended 'restoring some kind of unity throughout', and he was appointed to carry out work to the existing nave. The first phase, to restore the nave to its pre-Dissolution appearance, involved bricking up the triforium (high) arches and inserting smaller windows with Gothic-style tracery and plain leaded-lights. By 1885, funds allowed for improvements to the east end, cleverly fusing the Norman and Gothic styles. Plans to restore the transepts had to be abandoned, but the infill walls were not bonded-in – in the hope of proceeding later. In 1890 the nave was re-roofed. The restored abbey church was then ready to serve the wealthy inhabitants of the Abbey Foregate and Wenlock Road areas, and also the artisans of the newly developed Cherry Orchard and Belle Vue areas who had come to the town to work on the railways and in other new industries.

Services

The Victorian era was one of great administrative improvements intended for the benefit of all. Change was ponderous in some areas but surprisingly rapid in others, and party politics was not yet the overriding factor in deciding controversial issues.

Policing, as such there was, was carried out by the watch (see p.136) until 1839, when the County Police Act was passed. Shropshire petitioned the Home Secretary for a chief constable, six superintendents and 43 petty constables, following reports suggesting that if such a police force was established, the average period for a criminal escaping punishment would be reduced by as much as half. A town police station was established on the ground floor of the old Talbot Inn in Swan Hill in 1854.

The source of river water was becoming insufficient for the growing population, so in 1836, the corporation had the conduit works at Broadwell thoroughly cleaned and overhauled to improve the supply from there. In 1842 a portion of lead piping was taken up and replaced with iron pipe at a cost of £46 4s 3d. During the hot summer of 1847, the river water supply almost ceased, and a letter to *Eddowe's Journal* commented that the town seemed 'to be relying entirely on two men filling the pipe to the reservoir with buckets'.

Cholera broke out in Shrewsbury in 1832, causing over 150 deaths, and then again in 1849, with 75 deaths. In between these outbreaks, the 1848 Public Health Acts provided powers to set up a local Public Health Board, but it was only after a third outbreak of cholera in 1853 that such a board set about the tasks of dealing with the existing squalor and improving health matters in Shrewsbury. From our 21st-century viewpoint, the resulting report by William Ranger makes surprising reading. He noted that J. Scarth Esq. of Wyle Cop had made a water closet that year, but was not permitted to connect it to the sewers, that single privies in courts served 100 persons or more, that pits were overflowing with sewage, and that there was a general lack of clean water – water pumped from the river, the only source for many, having a high pollution content. Then there was the problem of private wells being located near cemeteries. During periods of shortage, the report said, water was taken round by carriers, like milk. Ranger's report concluded that in an average year, 20% of deaths were caused by infectious diseases, helping to

A photograph of Frankwell taken in the late 1800s, with Fellmonger's Hall and workshops distant right. No.14, on the left, was probably originally one house, with a ground-floor business. From the close studs, no cross rail, and flat balusters, it was a pre-1550 'stately pile'. Oriel bays project 3ft (c.1m), providing shelter to the shop entrance, and more floor area above. (Alfred Watkins, Hereford City Library)

explain the low life expectancy in Shrewsbury, which ranged from 53 to 32 or only 30 years according to occupation: professional, tradesman or labourer respectively.

By the Shrewsbury Waterworks Act of 1856, the water company was authorised to erect a beam engine and housing at Coton Hill, and to construct an elevated brick water tank behind Butcher Row. This installation was to provide an intermittent supply of unfiltered water, piped to those houses that had cisterns with ball valves and stopcocks. In 1865 the reservoir for the Crowmeole spring water at Quarry Lodge was in poor condition, and was replaced by new reservoirs built in Kingsland. Additional conduits were provided in Frankwell, Castle Foregate and Castlefields, bringing the total up to ten by 1870. Meanwhile, in 1866 negotiations had begun with the water company to supply water for flushing toilets and washing streets.

The corporation bought the waterworks in 1878, and took on responsibility for supplying drinking water. By this time, filtering had become the general practice, but the Coton Hill site was not large enough to accommodate the necessary filter beds. The problem remained under discussion for nearly 30 years, during which the merits and disadvantages of alternative sites were considered.

The town's first sewers were built in 1848, but there was still no general acceptance of the link between cholera and contaminated water. In 1862, the Improvements Commission requested a report on the sewage disposal problems from Sir Joseph Bazalgette, the civil engineer who had recently designed and built London's revolutionary drainage system. However, action was not taken until towards the end of the century. Eventually, the sewage from existing outfalls was intercepted by a ring of new mains and then lifted from a pumping station in Coleham to a gravitational sewer that commenced in Whitehall Street and dropped over the course of one and a half miles to a treatment works at Monkmoor Farm.

At last this ended the practice of treating the Severn as a sewer, but the river remained a source of drinking water into the 1870s, and probably later. The work, started in 1899, suffered many delays, until it was said 'that the scaffold poles has been in the ground for so long that they had started to grow'. Work on the new pumping station also began, but then faced further problems caused by faults in the old system. When completed, many householders were reluctant to connect up to the new system, probably due to the cost – until a hot summer in 1904 caused them to feel otherwise.

One of the old cast iron conduits, used almost within living memory. The ones made for Shrewsbury included a drinking bowl for dogs, replenished by drips from the outlet, had provision for a gas heating jet in frosty weather, and bore the cautionary slogan 'Waste not, want not'. (Stephen de Saulles)

Floods, caused by snow-melt or heavy rains in Wales, have been a recurring problem in the low-lying areas of the town. In January 1899 the floods in Frankwell reached a depth of several feet, causing general inconvenience. The decorative urinal on the right, combining shelter, light and ventilation, was one of several, but probably the last. (Shropshire Archives)

In the early 1870s, a councillor advocated the provision of public toilets for men. One was installed in Fish Street, followed by a second near English Bridge. These were the first of many 'ironclads', which were to be a familiar feature of the town for nearly a century. Another modern device was introduced in the late 1870s – the public telephone.

A Shrewsbury gas company started to supply gas for street lighting from its works in St Michael's Street at the end of 1821. The town's electricity generating station was established at Roushill, in the town centre, in 1895. The corporation purchased the Electric Light Company two years later and it was a further two years before the first four arc lamps provided street lighting. A Bellis & Morcom engine and a Thomas Parker generator were installed in 1901, and the mains supply was extended to the Belle Vue area in 1902.

The Salop Fire Office was established in 1780 and housed in the 'Fire Office passage', which later became part of the Music Hall. Its horse-drawn fire-engine was housed nearby in Franklin's Livery Stables at Cross Hill. The firm enjoyed a privileged position locally until 1837 when a rival office, the Shropshire and North Wales Assurance Company was formed. These offices were united with the Alliance Assurance Co Ltd in 1890, and together they invested in a manual fire engine. In 1891, the Alliance built a new four-storey headquarters building in the High Street, facing the open end of the

Square. Designed by A.E Lloyd Oswell of Shrewsbury, it had a highly elaborate façade of Grinshill stone and polished Aberdeen granite. The County Fire Office Ltd became a part of the Alliance Assurance Company Ltd in 1906. The Alliance maintained the Salop Fire Brigade until it was taken over by Shrewsbury Corporation in 1918.

In 1885 there were several cases of smallpox. The Sanitary Committee suggested an isolation site in Underdale Road, but it was opposed. In 1888 the county council was set up, and it appointed its first, part-time, medical officer of health in 1890. More cases of smallpox occurred in 1893, but no decision had yet been made as regards an isolation hospital. Fears were expressed that milk coming from the area could carry the disease to the rest of the town, and in the following year, a 12-bed isolation hospital was finally built and remained in use until the disease disappeared, through vaccination, in the 1930s.

The Alliance Assurance Company offices building (left), on the High Street, facing into the main Square, was built in 1892. It was designed, with supreme confidence and competence, by A.E Lloyd Oswell, in brick and stone and with, as Pevsner says, 'a big gable in a kind of Northern Renaissance' style. Certainly a tour de force, and it maintains the town's natural vertical emphasis. (Stephen de Saulles)

The Royal Insurance Building, 1 Mardol Head, (right) is a splendid example of a corner building as handled in Victorian times. It established a tradition in the town, since lost, for its contribution to the street scene at street corners. (Shropshire Archives)

Industry

The amount of barley grown in the surrounding rural areas enabled Shrewsbury to boast 29 listed maltsters in 1851. William Jones enlarged his premises and built two new maltings, one in Bynner Street, the other in Castle Foregate, where he utilised the disused mills. Otherwise, there was a decline in some of the industries that had been important in the Georgian period. Many of the mills ceased production, finding it difficult to compete with the more heavily industrialized areas, or were gradually converted to other use, but several hundred people were still employed in the manufacture of linen thread and yarn until the 1860s. One of the Castlefields mills was demolished in 1830s; another was still engaged in linen weaving in 1871. Marshall's mill at Ditherington remained in use until 1886, when it was converted to a maltings.

After Hazledine's death in 1840, his ironworks went into gradual decline. It was replaced by Corbett's Perseverance Ironworks, which became the largest employer in the town, producing agricultural implements such as ploughs and harrows. Indeed, the company's motto was 'Speed the Plough'. As they expanded their works, they redeveloped areas previously occupied by some of the more crowded courts of 'slum' housing in the town.

A group of employees of the Midland Railway Carriage Works in Coleham grouped around their steam hammer. This is one of the few known photographs to show the town's factories and workshops in this period. (Shropshire Archives)

Thomas Burr's notorious lead-works opened in 1829, taking over Bage's weaving mill at the riverside on Kingsland. It was developed from 1836 by his two sons, Thomas and William Burr. They purchased further land on either side, and by 1847 the works included two steam engines, a rolling mill, a melting furnace and casting bed; also a hydraulic pipe-making machine, and ovens for producing both white lead and red lead. In 1853 they built a brick landmark, a circular shot tower, 150ft (46m) high, for the manufacture of shot. Molten lead dropped through a sieve from that height formed into perfect spheres, and cooled as it fell into the water below.

Although one of its chimneys was over 50 feet high, the poisonous fumes and white powder fell on the riverside pastures and were often carried on the wind towards the town, 'causing severe pollution'. There were numerous reports of grass

Mountford & Co, carriage-builders in Dogpole in 1888. (Shropshire Archives)

being destroyed, and the grazing sheep on Kingsland dying of poison. The works closed in 1894 and were demolished. A correspondent reminiscing in a local paper in 1959 recalled how, as a boy, he used to make deliveries of small items to the works and noticed how, in certain places, 'there were galvanised buckets containing cod liver oil and a tin cup attached to each bucket'. He said 'I saw men dip into the oil and drink it as I would drink water'. The manufacture of red lead was a particularly unhealthy process, and the men employed allegedly looked as white as ghosts.

Religion and Temperance

Religious observance remained important in the town. The census of 1851 showed that Shrewsbury, with a figure of 75%, had a higher church attendance than the 50% average for towns of a similar size. Just over half attended Church of England services, the other half being distributed across many churches and chapels: 12 forms of Methodists, four Congregational, two Baptists and one each of Plymouth Brethren, Quakers (or Friends), Unitarian, Roman Catholic and Mormon. Three new Church of England churches had already been built in the new suburbs to accommodate the increase in church attendance. When the pope restored dioceses in England, a Roman Catholic cathedral, designed by E.W. Pugin was built on Town Walls in 1856.

Mrs Julia Wightman, wife of the vicar of St Alkmund's, was nationally known as one of the leading figures in the Temperance Movement. While only partially successful in converting the pleasures of the local working class to the moral and social values of her own, she did succeed in establishing a working men's hall and dining room in Princess Street, and in restoring the balustrade and pinnacles on the church. She was probably less successful in restraining prostitution – which was the only means of support for many women and girls.

She took a prominent part in the great temperance crusade which had started in America in 1780, hoping to influence public opinion and stem the great tide of drunkenness through her writings and personal work. 'The pledge' (to abstain from all alcohol) started as a novelty, but she organised numerous meetings, and many were converted. The movement spread to Ireland in 1825, and by 1831 the British and Foreign Temperance Society had been formed. Later, when there were 150,000 abstainers, she had the support of Lord Shaftesbury and the bishop of Hereford, and Queen Victoria became a patron. As well as taking part in the movement's national progress, in Shrewsbury Mrs Wightman initiated ideas for occupying men's leisure-time in alternative pursuits. In 1859, for example, she organised sightseeing trips to the Wrekin, Llangollen, and Liverpool, to get people away from the drunken revels of Show Week. She also established many Sunday schools for children, which were highly valued by their parents if not always by the children themselves.

By 1858 she had succeeded in raising funds to provide initial premises beyond the St Alkmund's schoolroom, while the schoolroom itself was used to establish a night school for the 700 local men and 270 women who had joined. The foundation stone of the new permanent Working Men's Temperance Hall in the Market Square 'was laid in 1862 with great pomp and ceremony'. It opened in 1865, to provide Bible classes, religious services, a Ragged School, a sick club, a library, a brass band, lectures and meetings. By 1872, 4,500 people had signed the Pledge in her society, including many in Shrewsbury. To begin with, all the clergy in Shrewsbury were against her with the exception of the chaplain to the prison, who understood from his experience what her concerns were. By 1862, 10,000 copies of her book, *Haste the Rescue*, had been distributed among the clergy of the Established Church by the national Church Temperance Society.

Meanwhile, amongst the ladies afternoon tea came into being and was taking the place of their more usual cakes and wine.

Shrewsbury Shows

Having been in decline, there was a revival of the Shrewsbury Show in the 1840-50s, especially after the railways started to bring in crowds from outside the town. However, it began to change in character and become a nuisance, as feasting amongst the guilds was replaced by drinking for the profits of the publicans. It was noted after the 1860 procession round the abbey, that 'Queen Catherine seemed to have a permanent inclination to slip from her horse', and, of the departing multitudes at the station, that they 'perhaps have been more than satisfied with the pleasures of the day'. Crowds increased each year, and by 1862 over 30,000 people arrived. But the year 1875 saw the end of the Show on Kingsland, and it was abolished in 1878 after the corporation made this a precondition for the proposed development of Kingsland.

The first of the famous Shrewsbury Flower Shows was held in the Quarry in 1875, sharing the site with the first Shropshire & West Midlands Agricultural Show. The subsequent annual August Flower Show was staged by the Shropshire Horticultural

Society and became a fixed date in the horticultural calendar, quickly gaining a reputation for excellence. The attraction of the event was enhanced by its setting in nearly 30 acres of parkland, sloping gently down to the tree-lined riverside walk. Across the river was a steep grassy escarpment, soon topped by the elegant façade and skyline of buildings belonging to Shrewsbury School. In 1879 a bandstand was built in the Quarry, adding to its attraction.

Rising behind the showground itself was the Georgian edge of Shrewsbury town, dominated by the close presence and silhouette of the new St Chad's church with its gracious dome and unusual circular form. The Victorian bandstand and the Dingle, a tree-ringed sunken garden and pool hidden below ground level in part of the old quarry, added to the show's sense of occasion and spectacle. The floral exhibits were shown in canvas marquees, and over the years both exhibitors and visitors began to come from further afield.

'The Quarry' – likened to 'The Backs' at Cambridge – became the town's park even before the first avenue of trees were planted in 1719. Set between the town's Georgian edge, where new St Chad's provides a dominant but graceful backdrop, and the Severn, with Shrewsbury School above, this site provides the Shrewsbury Flower Show's annual home and, at other times, quiet leisure space. (Shropshire Archives)

Shrewsbury is in the centre of an important and varied farming area, having sheep country to the south and west, and dairy and arable farming to the north and east. The Shropshire & West Midlands Agricultural Show, based around agriculture, poultry and horticulture, was first staged in the Quarry in 1875, previously having wandered between locations in Wales, Wolverhampton and Wrexham. It moved to its present riverside site on the Berwick Estate in Shrewsbury in 1897, since when it has trebled in size. (In 1897 the livestock shown included 219 horses, 154 cattle, 197 sheep, and 74 pigs.) In its early years the show, which is still regarded as an important testing ground for stock breeders, was not attended by the townspeople; their interest was only captured later.

Sport
Working hours for many people gradually lessened during the Victorian era, allowing more leisure time, and organised sport began to emerge. In the mid-19th century sport was expected to be health-giving, and free of moral dangers such as drinking. Sporting

The Royal Agricultural Show was twice staged on the racecourse and in the Quarry.
This drawing of the second, 1845, event was published in *The Illustrated London News*.
(Shropshire Archives)

events such as archery, coursing, rifle shoots and regattas were organized, and clubs were formed, notably for football, whilst the Pengwern Boat Club, first formed in the 1830s, faded, but was reformed in 1870. Facilities were provided for sports such as golf, tennis, bowls, and indoor swimming.

The old racecourse at Bicton Heath having been returned to agricultural use, a new racecourse on the other side of the town, a part of the old 'Soldiers Piece' associated with King Charles I's visit, was purchased in 1838. It provided a course of over a mile in circumference with a straight run in of 500 yards (*c*.460m) and space for a grandstand. The plan was allegedly the first anywhere to allow for any distance from half a mile to four miles to be conveniently fixed and marked, and possessed 'the advantage of a sight of the horses throughout the race, combined with an extensive panoramic view of the adjacent richly diversified country; while the town, from so many points picturesque, has from hence a most pleasing appearance'.

The racecourse was also used by the Shropshire Yeomanry Cavalry for their training and reviews, and hosted a number of other events. The Royal Show, which was held at different locations around the country each year, used this site in 1845 and also the Quarry. That year it made a loss, but when it returned in 1884 it was recorded as a great success. In 1885, the Grand National Archery Meeting was held here, encouraged by Mr William Butler Lloyd, the mayor, who was a keen participant. Lunch for 400 was served in the 'Waterloo tent', so called as it had been used by Lord Hill in his Waterloo campaign. The Shropshire and West Midlands Show used the site in 1888.

Education

Several charity schools existed in Shrewsbury before the 1870-76 Education Act made schooling compulsory. Until then, schooling was ignored by many poorer parents who needed their children to earn money or mind the younger children in the family while their parents worked. Many of the children who did attend school tended to be absent at harvest time or at other times when their labour was required. Many 'bosses' too did not want their workforce to be too well educated, fearing that they would then become troublesome, or leave to find better paid work elsewhere. They also needed cheap and pliant child labour, in the case of factory work able to crawl under working looms to clear the waste. Small fingers could also do fiddly jobs.

Nevertheless, Thomas Bowdler's School, mentioned in chapter 10, was still providing for the instruction, clothing and apprenticing of poor children in the parish of St Julian's, with the aim of taking children off the streets and helping to make them employable, the instruction therefore including cooking, carpentry and shoe mending. Likewise John Millington's school in Frankwell was still educating 25 boys and an equal number of girls, seeking to provide them with apprenticeships when they reached the age of 14. Also still in operation were John Allat's school, which provided for 30 boys and 30 girls, the Lancasterian school and St Chad's Ladies' School.

Further education was provided as a result of the Poor Law Amendment Act of 1834, under which groups of parishes, six in Shrewsbury, became 'unions' responsible for the 'management of the poor'. The intention was the unions would provide workhouses so constructed and managed to act as a deterrent to anyone who might need them for assistance, but for those children who were placed there, a rudimentary education was provided. The Shrewsbury Union provided outdoor relief to many paupers, and actually treated those who entered the workhouse with a degree of humanity, whereas the Atcham Union was notorious for its pitiless severity to all who applied for assistance. After 1844, Poor Law Commissioners were empowered to appoint a schoolmaster for workhouse children. Shrewsbury had already established a House of Industry, or 'workhouse' as they were generally known, in 1784 on Kingsland. The 1840s also saw the building of a pauper lunatic asylum in Shelton. In 1871 the workhouse was closed (and subsequently bought by Shrewsbury School), and the inmates transferred to the gentler establishment of 'Cross Houses' in Shrewsbury.

Small schools were also attached to churches. Church-going was the norm amongst the middle classes, and members of each of the several congregations would generally run their Sunday School. A St Alkmund's schoolroom is mentioned as existing in 1858 when Mrs Wightman extended it to provide for the men's evening education she was pioneering as an alternative to drinking.

Special excursion trains were run to see the Great Exhibition of 1851, and Shrewsbury must have been one of the first provincial towns to set up its own School of Design. The school, which opened in 1855, has developed into the present College of Arts and Technology. The Public Schools Commission in the 1860s, reporting on Shrewsbury School, recommended a move to more spacious accommodation. Eventually, the Kingsland House of Industry site was chosen in 1875. As noted earlier, a bridge had been proposed across the river at this point in 1872, to give better access to Kingsland. Partly because of this proposed development, the Home Secretary banned the Shrewsbury Show from using the site. The bridge had been proposed to serve the upmarket properties being built on Kingsland, including masters' houses, and once it had been built, the old workhouse buildings were adapted and enlarged for the school by Sir Arthur Blomfield, or perhaps his son, later Sir Reginald Blomfield, who was working in his father's office at the time. The school moved to the new site in 1882.

Rejecting the notion of organised sport, Dr Butler, the headmaster from 1798 to 1836, expressed the view that 'football was fit only for butcher boys'. He made frequent efforts to stop boating, even on occasions flogging those caught in the act, although the school had taken part in a regatta in 1830. Cross-country running was also strongly disapproved of. His two fives courts can only have provided minimal facilities. But Dr Kennedy, his successor in 1836, understood that extra provision was necessary, and at once set about renting a playing ground of about one acre behind the school. For the first time, games were properly organised. A sport based on hunting was devised, which involved running and chasing, and used hunting terminology: there was a huntsman, a captain of running, senior and junior whips, gentlemen of the runs and hounds, or 'the pack'. Shrewsbury School became one of the first public schools to encourage the playing of football, in a very individual form called 'douling', which was referred to as 'slavery' because it was compulsory. The rules, dating from 1855, were idiosyncratic; even the numbers on each side could be unequal. Interest declined, and it was displaced by Association Football in the 1870s. Other sports were also introduced, a diary of one of the boys in 1844 mentioning running, rowing, cricket, swimming and 'rackets' – besides 'douling' with 'five a side'.

The school's tercentenary celebrations were held in 1851. The boys had to 'attend the dinner of portentous length – forty six dishes are named. Long, not because of the lavish provision of food but because of the surely interminable oratory – no fewer than forty-four speeches'.

Radbrook College was established in 1901 to provide formalised training for girls from rural areas in the subjects which they would be needing in their adult life; these were deemed to be domestic science and dairy work. Horizons for women had not broadened much since the founding of St Chad's Ladies' School in 1820. (It is now called the Radbrook College of Food Technology & Hospitality, an elaborate title, but it does reflect its greatly increased standards and status – including the status of employment anticipated, and achieved, by its students of both sexes.)

Societies and Pastimes

Many informal societies were formed amongst people sharing a common interest. The 1840s and '50s saw the infancy of photography, for example, and one of the earliest Daguerreotypes was of Lord Hill. It is interesting to see that in Kelly's 1856 *Directory for Shropshire* there are no entries under 'Photographers', but two listed under 'Artists (Photographic)', which reflects how they were first seen as successors to portrait painters. One of them was a Joseph Della Porta, an early member of the Shropshire Photographic

Society, formed in the 1870s. It appears that he was a native of Moltrasio, a village on the shores of Lake Como, who had come to England from Italy in about 1848. He had evidently first lived in Birmingham, amongst a colony of other Italians, where he met his wife. He moved his business to Shrewsbury in 1857, opening a small general store in Princess Street, where he lived over the shop. His enterprise grew at a steady pace, soon expanding into the old LLoyd's Mansion (since demolished), where he set up departments selling ironmongery, hardware, boots and shoes, sewing machines and bicycles. The boots and shoes were made on the premises under the name 'Deltada'. The business also dealt wholesale in furniture, upholstery, bedding and footwear. In 1869, a publication describing commercial services stated that 'all classes of the community flock to this establishment, for certainly not in the county, and hardly out of it, can be seen such a vast and multitudinous array of goods, while in regard to prices, advantages are offered that would be extremely difficult to duplicate'. His eldest daughter married a Mr Alfred Roberts, so the store became J. Della Porta & Son; the daughter ran a separate business in Mardol. Joseph's business later moved into larger premises built on the same site in Princess Street, where it still trades. Joseph was evidently a strong personality, brusque but warm-hearted, interested in the town and public-spirited. He was largely responsible for bringing electric light to Shrewsbury, and became a director of the original Electric Light Company. He was also the first in the town to use X-ray photography, to the benefit of patients at the new Infirmary.

The photographic society, like many others based on interests as opposed to occupations, was able to include a wide societal mix, and so began to create a new social pattern. The society went on expeditions all over the country, and made an invaluable pictorial survey of the town in 1888.

An Archaeological Society was also formed, and in 1898 the town mounted a display of interesting local treasures.

Leisure and Entertainment

Especially after the introduction of bank holidays in 1871, expeditions, by various forms of transport, were arranged, first by churches, and later by secular societies, and outings and picnics became an agreeable form of recreation and social mixing. Some leisure pursuits were intended to include women and children, and for men, there were more diverse leisure activities attached to suburban pubs and taverns. Areas of open land were allocated to football, cricket and other such informal games. Small spaces such as tavern yards were used for quoits and skittles, and a few rooms were set up for billiards. Free-ranging pursuits such as hunting, coursing and cycling appealed to certain groups, and there was a new interest in walking for pleasure. Cycling on the new penny-farthing bicycles became a social hobby for gentlemen, and there were said to be facilities for athletics and shooting. Bowling greens were attached to many public houses in the suburbs, and there was a cricket ground at Mountfields.

Of boating, Henry Pidgeon, writing in 1837, said, 'Much pleasant exercise and amusement is afforded on the Severn during the summer months. Several parties possess boats and an emulation of skill is frequently excited among the more experienced rowers.'

He said that boats could be hired, and that picnic parties took excursions up river and down (this was before the weir made excursions downstream impracticable). He also reported that 'an annual Gala is generally given by the young gentlemen of Shrewsbury School in the month of June'.

The Pengwern Boat Club provided for serious rowing for men, sculling and elementary competitive training. There were also facilities alongside the Boat House Inn for the hire of boats for pleasure, which provided agreeable opportunities for ladies to go out unchaperoned. When the river was low such trips became less attractive, however, due to the drains discharging into the water. It has been suggested that this was an underlying reason for the level of support given to the proposal to construct the weir.

There were a few other leisure activities in which women could join men; archery became popular, while lawn tennis and croquet were agreeable. Cricket was played on land in Frankwell which was liable to flooding in winter, so kept nicely level, and was pleasantly bordered by willows. The ladies would watch the matches and, of course, prepare the tea in the club house. A tea garden is mentioned in Underdale as 'a quiet rural retreat', and by contrast, a brass band provided a livelier form of entertainment.

Train excursions could be enjoyed by both sexes and by families. Then, in the 1890s, a new form of entertainment arrived, at least for the rich: the 'horse-less carriage' – the motor car. This, too, provided opportunities for outings, picnics and social activity, shared by both sexes.

Shrewsbury was large enough to attract professional entertainers of high calibre. The theatre, the Music Hall (the main assembly hall, erected in 1840) and the Lion saw many famous performers: Edmund Kean and other actors of the day; Jenny Lind, the singer; and 'General Tom Thumb', the diminutive performer promoted by P.T. Barnum. In 1838 Charles Dickens stayed at the Lion with 'Phiz' (Hablot K. Browne), his illustrator, when on a tour reading his writings. He wrote to his daughter, saying 'We have the strangest little rooms, the ceilings of which I can touch with my hand. The windows bulge out over the street as if they were little storm windows in a ship, and a door opens out of the sitting-room on to a little open gallery with plants in it, where one leans over a queer old rail.'

Part of Sanger's Circus in Murivance on its way from the Quarry where performances were held, with the front of new St Chad's (1792), in the background. (Shropshire Archives)

191

The circus was an annual event, and excitements such as hot air balloon displays provided entertainment for all. Then there were the preachers, and speakers such as the American Temperance advocate J.B. Gough, who came to the town in 1858, probably invited by Mrs Julia Wightman.

Personalities

Charles Darwin was born in 1809 and educated in Shrewsbury. As a boy at Shrewsbury School, he was not the best of scholars, preferring to talk with Mr Cotton, 'who knew a good deal about rocks' and who aroused his interest in geology, and also to study the unacknowledged work of worms in the natural meadows of Frankwell rather than preparing Latin verse. After his voyages in the *Beagle*, and while gathering material for his large-scale work on natural selection, a letter from Alfred Wallace, who had similar ideas, precipitated him into producing an abstract of his own ideas, published in 1859, and now known as the *Origin of Species*. As Britain's greatest biologist, Darwin will be remembered not only for his Theory of Evolution – a word he rarely used – but also for the outstanding contributions he made to geology, soil science, the study of animal behaviour, and experimental botany.

Charles Darwin (1809-1882), one of Shrewsbury's most famous pupils, is commemorated in the statue by H. Montfort erected outside his old school.
(Stephen de Saulles)

Benjamin Disraeli, later Lord Beaconsfield, stayed at the Lion in 1841 just before the election at which he was returned to Parliament as a Member for Shrewsbury. Until 1858, practitioners of Judaism were excluded from Parliament, but Disraeli had been baptised as a Christian at the age of 12. His father had articled him to a solicitor, but Benjamin gained a reputation as a philanderer, gambler and dandy. He published a daily paper which failed and in 1827, aged 23, also published a novel. Humiliated by his failures, he had a nervous breakdown and travelled around Europe, returning in 1831. Deciding to stand for Parliament, he failed four times to gain a seat before being successful at Maidstone in 1837. His maiden speech was a disaster, his theatrical form of delivery being greeted with derision and his dress (in a time of sober fashions) ridiculed, and he soon loss the support of his constituency in Maidstone. With the election of 1841 looming, Lord Forrester, of Broseley, suggested that he should stand in Shrewsbury, where both Parliamentary seats had become vacant. The election proved ugly. Each side accused the other of encouraging physical violence and intimidation; when Disraeli was addressing the electorate outside the Lion hotel there was heckling and rotten egg-throwing, and stones were thrown during a meeting in the Square. Anti-Semitism was also involved in the taunts and demonstrations. Disraeli wrote a letter in which he said 'The canvassing is more severe from eight in the morn to sunset'; part of this letter is displayed in the Lion to this day. In the event, the Conservatives won both the Shrewsbury seats, and Disraeli was duly elected, remaining the town's MP until 1847. The local Conservative Club building still bears his name.

The 'Father of the Council', Thomas Southam, born in Shropshire in 1818, was the son of a corn merchant in Shrewsbury. As a lad he worked as a counter clerk, and he set up his own business as a wine and ale merchant in Wyle Cop in 1842. Having acquired the necessary knowledge, in 1886 he established his Southam's Brewery alongside the river in Chester Street, and soon owned 20 public houses in the area, as well as shipping beers from Mardol Quay. He also imported wines from France and developed several of his own secret recipes, including one for a version of champagne and another for a Shropshire liqueur.

He was also intensely interested in the welfare of the town. He was first elected councillor for the Stone Ward in 1851, and was made a life-long alderman in 1869. Following the formation of the Salop County Council in 1889, he was elected councillor for Shrewsbury Abbey & Stone Ward. He was a member of Shrewsbury Council for nearly 45 years, and was mayor three times. He was also a long serving magistrate in the borough and the county courts, a director of the Shrewsbury House of Industry (the workhouse) until it closed in 1872, and vice-chairman of the Atcham Poor Law Union.

He played an active part in pushing for improvements in the town, including schemes for improving the water supply and health such as the 'dead meat' market at Smithfield, increasing electric street lighting, promoting safety for the increased rail traffic, advocating high design standards for the station building, and arguing for new indoor market facilities, to which he donated the clock tower despite not approving of the building's ornate design. As chairman of the Estates Committee he initiated the improvements to the Quarry area as the town park, replacing the old borough's common at Kingsland, and supported the conversion of the old Shrewsbury School buildings to the town library and museum, which he 'opened' in their new role in 1885. The top floor of the library was soon furnished with large glass show-cases full of stuffed animals, fish and birds. In one of his last mayoral addresses, in 1885, he referred to 'our old friend, the sewerage', and added 'it may force itself upon us at any time ... I look upon it as a still unsolved problem' ... and he never saw it solved. A 'vigorous, patriarchal-looking man', one of his last public acts, only a few days before he died, was to sign, on Boxing Day 1895, the report for building the footbridge across the Severn at Monkmoor to improve access to the station and town centre. He is now remembered on an inn sign for the Proud Salopian in Smithfield Road, which stands quite close to the site of his Southam's Brewery – where the Gateway Education and Arts Centre now stands.

Outings were a popular pastime in Edwardian England. Destination, means of transport, food and company were selected, and separated, according to subtle grades of social standing. It was natural for the Raven, the hotel behind the coach, to be associated with 'the better class of gatherings of this kind. (Shropshire Archives)

The high sheriff's coach waiting outside St Chad's church. In Edwardian times a coach and coachman was part of his equipment. (Shropshire Archives)

12   EDWARDIAN INTERLUDE

'As we send our messages far and wide by telegraph or telephone – as we steam
from one end of the kingdom to the other in our express trains, or drive our motor
cars along the broad roads which are one of the few good heritages which were
the dying bequest of the period (previously) under consideration – as, in fact, we
try to contrast our modern life in all its fullness of knowledge and political and
social freedom, with the time when beaux in their full-bottomed wigs, and belles
in their hoops, slowly moved from place to place in their coaches and four – when
coarseness and unreality abounded on every side – we feel that the interval is one
that cannot be measured by years.'

Prebendary Thomas Auden, Shrewsbury, 1905

The Edwardian period marked the beginning of new conditions, attitudes, horizons and
changes in the social structure of the country; also of technological advances beyond
anything that could have been envisaged earlier. The effect of motor traffic, for example,
was first noticed in the 1900s. In 1903, when there were only about 125 cars on the
Shropshire roads, complaints of 'dust clouds' created by 'speeding vehicles' began to
reach the council, and the first signs of deteriorating road surfaces appeared. The answer
was known – tarmac – but it was expensive, and the council refused to lay it, until 1911
when government grants had been made available. Even then, the work was carried out
so slowly that it failed to keep pace with the growth of motor traffic.

As the county and borough councils took over greater responsibilities, the role of the
gentry and of the clergy became less prominent.

Until 1897 the county council had refused to appoint a full-time county medical
officer. They had seen their role as limited to supervising the inspectors of nuisances
appointed by the lesser authorities. (An inspector of nuisances was a person employed
to inspect for breaches of law, e.g. bad sanitary conditions, obstruction to footpaths and
roads etc. Refuse heaps, smells and insanitary conditions of all kinds were known as
'nuisances'.) One councillor of the day attacked this unsatisfactory situation, claiming
that the part-time inspectors were often men who had failed in other walks of life.
When Dr James, reputedly 'a man with a long view', was appointed as county medical
officer in 1902, the council began contributing to many improvements in public health,
particularly in child welfare, midwifery, dentistry, and the treatment of the common

Above: A smithy in the town. The volume of horse traffic still kept smithies busy in Edwardian times. Each horse would be individually fitted with its shoes and regular customers would have their set of patterns hanging up, for reference. Headgear of various kinds, or its absence, distinguished rank and status at this time.
(Shropshire Archives)

Left: Fire, a constant hazard in the town, has dictated changes in building materials and design since early times: window frames, shown flush on one building in the picture, are set behind the brickwork on adjoining later buildings, while overhanging timber eaves have been replaced by safer parapets. This picture appears to show a fire practice underway.
(Shropshire Archives)

complaint of the time – tuberculosis. A nurses' home was built in 1908 alongside the Salop Infirmary in St Mary's Place for the benefit of nurses working at the hospital. It was a large building with a stepped frontage, all in Edwardian red brick with bold stone dressings and a mansard roof.

At the end of the century the police had come under the control of a joint committee of 'Justices of the Peace' and council members. Captain Williams-Freeman, the chief constable from 1890-1905, reorganised the force on military lines. He introduced merit badges, sports, drill, and ambulance training, and also the use of bicycles. A new headquarters was opened in Shrewsbury in 1903, and in 1907 a car was first provided for the chief constable.

After nearly 30 years spent considering various alternative 'upland' and 'river water' schemes, and being advised by many experts, a decision was finally made in 1906 on the vexed subject of the general water supply. As a result, Shrewsbury was one of the first towns in the country to adopt a new system of pressure

The nurses' home in St Mary's Place. Revival stone quoins came back, no longer for supposed strength but for status and preference. (Stephen de Saulles)

filtering. (It lasted well, and only needed to be replaced in 1935, when the town had greatly increased in size, and population.) In consequence, water charges were reduced to almost the lowest in the country. To improve the quality of water at the intake, the sewage system was linked to a pumping station built in Coleham. The beam engines, built by W.R. Renshaw and Company of Stoke on Trent, used to pump sewage to the 1905 works at Monkmoor, are no longer in operation, but are occasionally on view.

By the time the weir was built, in 1910, river trade had finished, and the weir was merely for the benefit of pleasure craft and residents. With the increase in population, and the number of sewers emptying into the river, boating had become unpleasant in the summer, and in dry weather, almost unbearable. The weir raised the level all round the town by over three feet (about a metre). The first Castle Footbridge, a suspension bridge, described as 'picturesque', was constructed at the same time, making the old Underdale ferry redundant.

Boating on the river was a pleasant social recreation, the more so after the construction of the weir had raised the water level. The Boat House Inn is probably much older than the 18th-century print on which it first appears, and is still a favourite drinking place. The building on the left was first used as a tea room, later as a boat house, and subsequently as a room for private bookings. The ferry operated until the Porthill Footbridge was erected with the help of the Horticultural Society in 1923. (Shropshire Archives)

The Castle Footbridge was erected, to give access to the town centre from the Cherry Orchard and Underdale Road areas, at the same time as the weir was built, in 1910, to raise the water level around the town. It was later replaced. (Shropshire Archives)

The Priory School for Boys, the first grammar school established in the town since that founded by Edward VI in 1552, which had become Shrewsbury School, was designed for the new county council by F.H. Shayler & J.A. Swan, and opened in 1911. The site had been granted to the Austin friars in 1254 by Henry III, who allegedly rated the site as 'marshy, waste and liable to flood'. Pevsner rated the school building as not much better: 'Large, two storeyed building in William & Mary style, though in the detail a little inflated, as the Edwardian revival of William & Mary tends to be. Pale brick and generous stone dressings.' Despite these two handicaps, the school flourished, contributing to the higher than national average university admissions that Shropshire had attained by 1920. Although named as being for boys, it started as a mixed sex school. Boys, on one side of the school, were taught Greek, Latin and manual work. Girls, on the other, were prepared for home, cooking and needlework, as was usual for the time.

Under the 1902 Education Act, the county council became responsible for the general education of both sexes, and between 1909 and 1914 13 new secondary schools were established in Shropshire.

Shrewsbury Town Football Club had been formed, like many other societies, in the 1880s. Originally, the club had used the old Racecourse ground, but in 1910, they started playing at Gaye Meadow, their new riverside site in the centre of the town. A man with a coracle was employed to retrieve the ball from the river when necessary.

By this time, the *Shrewsbury Chronicle* was owned by Mr (later Sir) Beville Stanier. He introduced a political emphasis, which was unusual amongst local newspapers, and not popular with the Shrewsbury public. He was also interested in agriculture, and

A tailor's workshop in Chester Street. Before the days of ready-made suits, men's suits were made by hand. The craft was learned by long apprenticeship, a trainee only graduating from weeks of 'button-holing' when proficient in the art. The paper pattern sections, specially cut or marked to fit the client, are lying on the table and hanging up. (Shropshire Archives)

Above: The Salop Steam Laundry vehicle c.1912. (Shropshire Archives)

Left: The Castle Restaurant and Tea Rooms, established in 1760 on the corner of Castle Street and School Gardens. It specialised in Pailin's Shrewsbury Cakes, originally made on the site by Mr Pailin to a secret recipe. (Shropshire Archives)

The Square in Edwardian times after a fall of snow. The 1860 statue of Robert Clive is by Marochetti. Smirke's Shirehall is on the left, while the Plough Inn to the right of the statue has had another floor discreetly added (compare with the illustration on p.168). Markets have been removed, and the area provides a cab rank. (The cabbies' shelter is now used as the kiosk at the entrance to the castle.) (Shropshire Archives)

commended the merits of sugar beet in advance of the accepted wisdom of the day. On seeing one year's accounts, he is reputed to have said that he 'would sooner keep two packs of hounds than one damned newspaper'. This was presumably in either 1908 or 1909 when the newspaper made a loss, but evidently 1910 saw improvement.

During this period there was a terrible railway accident just outside the station on the Crewe line, which lived on in people's memories for many years. On the night of 14/15 October 1907, the night sleeper was travelling from Manchester to the west of England via Crewe and Shrewsbury. At Crewe, extra carriages had been added on, originating from Glasgow, York and Liverpool, making the train up to 15 carriages. The train left Crewe at 1.20am. The derailment occurred on the downhill gradient of the sharply curved approach to Shrewsbury station, where the speed limit was 10mph – but the train was going at an estimated speed of 60mph. The death toll of 18 included the driver and fireman and two other railway staff, three postal workers, and 11 passengers, one of whom lived in Shrewsbury. As a report later said, 'Nearly four hundred tons travelling at 60 miles an hour is a very powerful missile'.

The official Board of Trade Enquiry, held at the Raven Hotel and led by a Colonel Yorke, opened the day after the accident and lasted three days, its report being published on 12 February 1908. Representing the board was David Lloyd George, the future Prime Minister. On the first day, apparently satisfactory evidence was given on the known capacity and reliability of the engine's braking power, one of the possible causes of the

The Unicorn Hotel (altered and now Tanners) on Wyle Cop was one of the inns used by carriers as a regular collecting point for goods and passengers. (Stephen de Saulles)

accident. During the second day's hearing, a theme developed questioning the health and sobriety of the driver, and his employment record. The latter was shown to be not as exemplary as had been suggested on the first day. A bottle had been found in the driver's basket – but it had been carefully cleaned before it was replaced for inclusion in the enquiry. The Coroner ordered a post mortem. However, the report noted that 'despite probing cross examination of witnesses with regard to the driver's character, the enquiry concluded that all the evidence, including the post mortem chemical analysis of the driver's stomach contents, indicated that alcohol and drugs were not present and that the driver did not suffer a seizure'. The report was to conclude that the likely cause of the accident was that the driver had dozed off, missing the signal and failing to brake in time. Subsequent scheduling bore that in mind.

This was the third derailment in the country within 12 months. Although each was different, enquiries suggested that there was probably a common cause: the susceptibility of drivers on intermittent night-time duties to drowsiness. The conclusion was that regular working schedules, as well as alarms and signals, could play an important part in future safety.

Transport issues were also causing concern in another part of town. As previously mentioned, the 18th-century English Bridge was crowded with pedestrians morning and evening, a crush added to by the increased population in the suburbs entering and leaving the town by bicycle. Some relief had been given by the construction of the Greyfriars Footbridge, but the case for improvements to the English Bridge was raised again in 1904, as congestion was being increased by the motor car. Consequently, the borough set up a committee in December 1904 'to consider the feasibility of widening and improving the English Bridge', but an application to the county council produced no help with meeting the costs, and the borough's dejected reaction (it was deeply involved in trying to solve the water-supply problem at the same time) was a resolution to defer the project to a later date, interpreted as indefinitely. However, the problem of motorised traffic became insistent, and then urgent. In June 1909, and again in February 1911, the borough raised the idea of improving the bridge, and they got as far as deciding on a design and inviting tenders in November 1912. (Pressure was on, because they hoped to resolve the bridge problem in time for George V's visit to the Royal Agricultural Society's Show, planned for July 1914.) Another application was made to the county council for 'a substantial contribution to the cost', but again it was refused, and there the record goes silent. It can only be assumed that the war intervened – but the bridge survived all the proposals intact.

The old 'Potts' railway was left derelict for many years until it was revived by an enthusiast, Col H.F. Stephens, who cleared the line of undergrowth, repaired stations, restored engines and carriages, and built new where necessary. Renamed the Shropshire and Montgomery Railway, it opened in 1911 and ran from Shrewsbury Abbey to Llanymynech, where it linked with the Cambrian line from Whitchurch to Welshpool. A Criggion branch, opened in 1912, was used by market-day traffic, but its most memorable use was for the many specially chartered specials – for Sunday school, and choir, picnic outings, and occasions such as birthday parties. Many must have taken these memories of Edwardian days into the next, less agreeable chapter of their lives.

13   THE FIRST WORLD WAR

> War broke; and now the Winter of the world
> With perishing, great darkness closes in.
> The foul tornado, centred in Berlin,
> Is over all the width of Europe whirled,
> Rending the sails of progress ...
>
> Wilfred Owen in his poem *1914*

The First World War broke the peace of Edwardian Shrewsbury and drew heavily on the patriotism built up in previous decades. It was not merely a duty; men were proud to fight for King and Country. In this war, the 'pressing' came from the volunteers, rather than being in the style of the over-persuasive Lieutenant George Farquhar, the recruiting officer of the 18th century.

Shrewsbury once more took on a role that had become familiar over centuries: assembling, quartering, and training in barracks in and out of town, and then sending

Prisoners-of-war on the same site as the Welsh Prince David nearly 700 years before. The faint image of the abbey can just be seen behind the trees. (Shropshire Archives)

Report on Shrewsbury Prisoner of War Camp, September 1916

Committees
Workshop, canteen, educational, recreation. Run by the prisoners themselves.

Sleeping Accommodation
Concrete has been laid in sleeping quarters since last visit.
Everything found neat clean, well-lighted, well-ventilated, well-warmed.
Beds are regulation army pattern.

Sanitary Arrangements
22 Water closets, self-flushing. 6 hot & cold showers.
A drying room & an ablution shed installed.
All found neat, clean and odourless.

Infirmary
1 Doctor, & 3 British Attendants.
8 patients were in the wards, 6 of whom suffering from wounds.
1 case of kidney trouble, 1 indigestion.
All patients seemed to be recovering and were in good spirits.

Kitchen
1 kitchen & a head cook with 11 helpers, all German.

Work
Prisoners were engaged in tailoring, carpentry, and making articles for sale by the
Emergency Committee for the Assistance of Germans, Austrians & Hungarians in
Distress, such as boxes and chessmen. Also undertaking boot making and repairs.

Exercise
Prisoners are allowed to have route marches 4 days a week, 2 companies going each day.
Opportunity for gymnasium and exercise with horizontal and parallel bars, dumb-bells,
'sandow-development' [not explained] and boxing.

Also noted
Good opportunities for classes, a piano they were playing while the inspectors were there.
A field 90 yards (27.5m) square. Compound 50 by 40 yards (46m by 36.5m) where the
prisoners play football and hockey.

Complaints
No serious complaints, but evidently the bread ration had been reduced by half a pound,
and there was some problem with the flour, for 'Difficulty of baking made it almost
impossible to use this flour.' Action: Taken up with the War Office.
There were requests for a gym which, given the materials, the prisoners would build for
themselves.
Also a request for the compound to be surfaced, to avoid mud. A terse note was added
that it had been raining during the inspection, but no mud was observed.

Summary
There were no men in cells, and the general feeling was excellent.

men off to battle. The record of Shropshire's volunteers in this, and other wars, is now displayed in the military museum in Shrewsbury Castle, which replaced the variety of small museums in the Copthorne Barracks and other places. The county regiment, the King's Shropshire Light Infantry, had been formed under Edward Cardwell's army reforms at the end of the previous century. In the war, the regiment was much enlarged. The 6th Battalion was one of the 'Pals' battalions, consisting entirely of men from Shrewsbury. It spent most of the war on the Western Front.

A camp for German prisoners-of-war was established in Abbey Foregate. In the early years of the war it was inspected regularly by officials from the United States Embassy and reports made on comprehensive pro formas. The details opposite are taken from the report for September 1916, by which time there were evidently 464 prisoners: 411 military, 46 naval and 7 civilians. Unfortunately the report does not deal with the prisoners' origin or stories; it covers their welfare only. A report on a camp in Abergele, north Wales, carried out at roughly the same date was attached which showed that there the prisoners also had a committee for amusements, together with wine, cigars and cigarettes, and even a postmaster-general. Clearly camps were allowed a large degree of autonomy when it came to decisions about provision for prisoners.

Early in 1918, a flying field was laid out and used as an aircraft acceptance park (where aircraft were initially delivered from the factory where they had been made), a repair depot, and a school of reconnaissance and aerial photography.

In 1915 the firm of Alley and Maclellan established a factory on the north side of Shrewsbury to build Simpson-Bibby steam engines, the firm becoming the Sentinel Waggon Works Ltd in 1918. On the opposite side of the Whitchurch Road, the company built an estate for their workforce, the houses being unusually supplied with central heating, hot water and electric power from the factory.

Apart from these new activities for the town, Shrewsbury took on two new responsibilities: the establishment of a hostel for Belgian refugees, and the provision of hospital and convalescent services for those wounded in the war. Injured military personnel were brought to the town by train, usually under cover of darkness so that the general public would not see the seriousness of the injuries being suffered. Besides using the existing hospitals, other buildings were converted. Oakley Manor, later the local authority offices but then privately owned, was adapted by voluntary effort into a St John Auxiliary Military Hospital. It was run with the assistance of the British Red Cross, and the Voluntary Aid Detachment, better known as 'the VADs'. All the cleaning and handyman work was also done by voluntary labour. The first patients were accepted in December 1914, and by April 1915 Oakley Manor had received a total of 91 wounded and sick, and they continued to arrive. The gardens and lawns provided restful outdoor surroundings for wheelchair and ambulant patients, and a large greenhouse was converted into an open-air ward. In March 1917, the temporary hospital facilities transferred from Oakley Manor to Prestefelde, the present prep school, which remained in action until March 1919. A thousand servicemen were treated in these two establishments alone. King George V granted the prefix 'Royal' to the Infirmary in 1914, in recognition of its services in caring for the wounded.

Shrewsbury took on new roles in caring for refugees and wounded from far afield.
This photo shows the living accommodation of a hostel established for Belgian refugees.
The floral decorations were painted on the walls; it was wartime! (Shropshire Archives)

Voluntary female helpers in nursing and caring services who converted the Armoury into
use as a hostel for Belgian refugees. Many of these women were highly educated, and had
often been trained in one of the few professions open to them but which normally they
were obliged to leave on marriage. Few ladies took employment at this time for social
reasons, (it would have reflected on their husband's status and 'ability to provide for his
wife and family'), but voluntary work was acceptable, indeed expected. (Shropshire Archives)

Wilfred Owen became one of the best known of the English poets who wrote during, and about, the First World War. His poetic manifesto includes the statement that 'My subject is War, and the pity of War. The Poetry is in the Pity'. He was born in Oswestry, the son of a railway employee, and moved with his parents to Monkmoor Road, Shrewsbury in 1907. Having attended the Technical College when it was at the English Bridge (now the Wakeman School) site, and passed the matriculation examination, he was teaching at the Berlitz School of Language in Biarritz when war was declared. Returning home, he enlisted in the Artists' Rifles, and was commissioned in the Manchester Regiment. In 1916 he was posted to France, and spent the worst winter of the war on the Western Front. He suffered shell shock and, while recovering in an army hospital in Scotland, made the acquaintance of the poet Siegfried Sassoon.

Owen wrote technically experimental poems expressing his hatred of war, savagely and ironically describing the cruelty, horror and waste he saw about him at the battle front. When he returned to France, he was made a full Lieutenant, and was later awarded the Military Cross for 'conspicuous gallantry and devotion to duty'. He was killed in action on 4 November, and the news of his death reached Shrewsbury on Armistice Day, November 1918. His parents received the news of their son's death as the abbey's church bells were ringing their victory peal. Only five of his poems were published during his lifetime, and it was not until 1920, when a collection of his poetry was published under the editorship of Siegfried Sassoon and Edith Sitwell, and Edmund Blunden's enlarged 1931 edition, that his work became more widely known.

The generation of the First World War talking with that of the Second, yet to come.
(Shropshire Archives)

All through the war he kept up a frequent correspondence with his family, and a collection of letters was published in 1931. It was learned then that when writing to his mother, he had used a secret code, evidently undiscovered by the censors, to tell her of his whereabouts in France. After he used a previously agreed keyword she was to look at the second letter in the succeeding lines. The word in January 1917 was 'mistletoe', and the following lines revealed that he was at first in the Somme, and then at Serre. A later letter from his mother asked when she might hear more about parasitic shrubs on oak and apple trees. In another letter, he wrote: 'Shells made by women in Birmingham are at this moment burying little children alive not far from here', and he ended his 'Anthem for Doomed Youth' with appropriate words for the impact of the war: 'Each slow dusk a drawing down of blinds' – in those days, an action symbolic of bereavement and respect.

Wilfred Owen, MC
(1893- 4 Nov. 1918)

Perhaps the greatest change that happened to society as a result of the war was the increased role it gave to women, who took up occupations which had previously been regarded as purely male preserves. With the ending of the war this process was only partially reversed, while pressure grew to give women the vote.

The Wilfred Owen memorial erected in the shadow of the abbey in 1993. The inscription includes a line from his poem 'Strange Meeting': 'I am the enemy you killed, my friend'.
(Stephen de Saulles)

14   THE INTER-WAR PERIOD

> 'I set out to explore a town which for unaffected charm would be hard to beat in all England. Shrewsbury is delightful because here are more lovely half-timbered houses standing together than it has been my lot to see ... In ancient streets, where houses overhang the pavement, nodding forward in the sun like tired professors of history, the rich stream of English country life flows on unaltered since Elizabethan times ...'
>
> H.V. Morton, 1927, *In Search of England*

The first few years after the First World War were a period of recovery and adjustment to a number of changes – among them new inventions, new social and physical mobility, the enlarging role of local authorities in everyday affairs and, not least, the place of women in society, although they were not yet allowed to vote or to own property. Then came the General Strike, the years of depression in the '30s, followed by news of 'storm clouds gathering over Europe'.

Perhaps the nature of the town's business best illustrates the times and gives us clues as to where, with hindsight, we can see indications of later trends. Broadcasting – as it began to be called, to emphasise the development from one-to-one communication – was one of these businesses. A young Shropshire man from Wem, A.R. Mitchell, after demobilisation, took a certificate in advanced telegraphy and telephony in London. He was familiar with the triode valve, developed by the French at the Eiffel Tower during the war, and in 1923 he moved to Shrewsbury where he developed, made, and sold his 'Albertross' (Albert Ross) receivers. His small experimental workshop could be described as the centre for technological advance, and chat, in Shrewsbury at that time. A brother joined him and the firm spread into the adjoining premises, No. 1 Mardol, developing the maintenance side of radio, and preparing for the technicalities of television, dealt with later by his son. This was an almost typical example of the 'Shrewsbury family firm'.

Plumbing and central heating were comparatively new. The Scull brothers established themselves in Shrewsbury in 1919, engaging two assistants. One earned 1s 6d a day and the other, as an improver, the princely sum of 1s 6d an hour. One of the firm's many jobs was to modernise the Raven. This included the installation of central heating, and bathrooms with hot and cold running water, in place of the traditional water cans brought to the bedroom washstand every morning. Another firm, A.T. Marston, had been founded by great-grandfather Richard Marston when decorating Shropshire mansions in 1840. Grandfather Tom took over, and then, when father Alfred took control in 1900, he expanded the firm to include plumbing and, with his sons Richard and George, the installation of central heating. They modernised many large country house and public buildings' systems. Sometimes this was in houses where the firm had already installed elaborate drainage systems, sufficient to receive the necessary 'London Approved Certificate' in Edward VII's time – all in hopeful anticipation of a possible royal visit. (They knew that 'searching official enquiries about the drains' were always made beforehand by 'the Palace', notoriously worried by a property's elevation, fresh air, and the effect of poor drains on 'the chest'.) Between them, these two firms were bringing Shropshire's buildings up to 20th-century standards.

Despite these improvements to many of the larger private properties, the shift of power and influence was moving away from the landed gentry to the elected representatives and their officers. In the 1920s and '30s local government was not yet run on party political lines, but councils were naturally conservative and usually reluctant to take any positive action which involved expenditure, except that forced on them by legislation. Luckily, approval was given to a new water scheme in time for it to meet the greatly increased demands of the following decades.

In the 1920s, the smaller railway companies were grouped together and as a result Shrewsbury was served by the London, Midland and Scottish (LMS) and Great Western (GWR) railways. The coats of arms of the two companies remain carved in stone on each side of the main entrance to the station. Shrewsbury continued to occupy a key position in the railway network, being on the GWR line from Paddington to Birkenhead, and a changing point for locos on the important Manchester and Liverpool route to the west of England. It was a railway enthusiast's dream. Trains of five different companies passed through Shrewsbury where all the great locomotives could be seen, including the Castles, Kings, Stars and Saints of the Great Western, and the Princess Royals and Coronations of the LMS. It was a time of strong railway loyalties, which bred a tightly knit railway sub-culture. Top drivers and firemen were the gentry of the

The Abbey Foregate Signal Box was constructed in 1903, housing a 180-lever frame and controlling at least five lines, and is situated in the centre of the junction triangle. It is now a 'listed building', and can claim to be the largest remaining mechanical signal box on the British railway network.

(Stephen de Saulles)

Originally a two-storey, symmetrical building with a central tower, designed in a 'gothic' style by T.M. Penson, the station building was constructed in 1848 for the new Shrewsbury-Chester line. In 1904 it was extended to the left in a matching style. Upper floors were left vacant for many years, until the Civic Society's scheme for restoring them for staff use was produced in the 1980s, and acted on ten years later. (Stephen de Saulles)

railway world. Their pride was beyond what is understood as job satisfaction today, and they served, but were much respected by, their public.

At the same time, road transport was increasing. By the 1920s, 13 county roads converged on Shrewsbury, eight of them classified as Class A routes. Increased motor traffic, including motor buses after 1916 as well as a growing number of private cars, was causing congestion in the town and at its approaches. When designed by John Gwynn in the 18th century, the English (East or Stone) Bridge had been planned to accommodate the horse and carriage. The problem had been discussed for years, but a possible solution had last been shelved because of the war.

Proposals for an entirely new structure were now made by the mayor, supported by various 'practical men whom he had consulted'. Fortunately, Shrewsbury's borough surveyor, himself an architect, was able to persuade the committee to postpone a decision 'to enable the matter to be considered more fully'; there was at least a glimmer of reluctance to interfere with the architecture of 'one of the most beautiful bridges in the kingdom'. The proposals which Arthur Ward then put forward were ingenious. He showed that it was possible to increase the bridge's width and lower its crown, which until then had always been a problem, 'while at the same time, ensuring the preservation of the dignity and beauty of the design as far as possible'. The scheme was supported by Sir Henry Maybury of the Ministry of Transport, and a substantial grant was offered, provided the overall width was increased even a little more, to 50ft (*c*.15m), which was more than double its original width of 23½ft (*c*.7m). The brief specification – 'Take down, alter and re-erect the bridge' – was enlarged upon, and work eventually began. The bridge was carefully dismantled, and the stones re-shaped to form the slightly lowered arches. The blocks of stone were taken to a site on the old abbey ground, except for the

Widening English Bridge in 1925-7 with the temporary bridge alongside. (Shropshire Archives)

two huge centre keystone effigies of Sabrina and Neptune, separated for a century and a half, which were stored on a downstream island.

Despite the inscription on the bridge's parapet, it was never officially opened. The Prince of Wales was to have performed the ceremony, but there was a death in the royal family, and it had to be cancelled. However, Queen Mary, while staying nearby with her brother, the Marquis of Cambridge, was the first lady to cross the bridge when it was nearly finished in 1927, and she suggested the wording on the plaque. Incidentally, the police escort, provided on this and other occasions when she visited her brother, comprised three police constables mounted on their own motorcycles which they had to insure 'against all risks'.

One other bridge was constructed in this period. The Porthill suspension footbridge, dated 1922, in a pleasing decorative Victorian design, was a gift to the town from the Shropshire Horticultural Society in 1923. It connected the Quarry with the Porthill Road area and Copthorne, its western end met the road alongside the New Street Boat Inn, overlooking the river. It replaced a 300-year-old ferry service. The original chains have been replaced by steel cables, but its simple elegance has been retained.

In 1924 the castle was purchased by the Horticultural Societyed and presented to the town corporation. All Telford's partitioning was demolished, and the main entrance was restored to its original Edward I position, in the east tower at the main floor level.

The Dingle's sunken garden was created from a worked-out quarry that had provided local building stone. It is concealed from view by a circling belt of trees, so creating that delightful townscape element, 'surprise'. (Shropshire Archives)

The main hall was furnished, and used, as the town's council chamber until 1983. The bailey wall and its crenellated parapet were probably rebuilt as part of Telford's work, or in work done in 1887.

The original Norman ramparts on which the present walls stand can be seen from inside the bailey – but they are disguised by the higher level of the ground, which has been raised to about 13ft (4m) above the interior ground level (now creating an apparent 'basement' level). The rampart on the town side is also disguised by raised levels. The sloping courses of the sandstone walls which once connected the castle to the upper town gate (which cut across the Castlegate roadway, to the library buildings), show how the ground levels have been changed. The wall and ditch of the original outer bailey, crossing just north of Windsor Place, have long ago been filled in. Traces of the timber bridge which crossed the early outer ditch, (perhaps demolished when the area was being cleared for the Norman building work), were found by workman laying a new water main in recent years. The timber was tested and carbon dated to about 1030.

The General Strike of 1926 affected even rural counties. For some people it was probably the most memorable event between the wars. Ellen Wilkinson, one of the first female Members of Parliament, spoke at a meeting in support of the strikers held in the Quarry, while, to counter the effects of the strike, 1,500 people enrolled as volunteer workers in Shrewsbury alone, although practically nothing is recorded of their activities. The National Citizens Union organised lifts, and a co-operative of parents drove boys

The *Shrewsbury Chronicle*, founded in 1772, was originally based in 38-41 St John's Hill, but had to move to temporary premises in Swan Hill when the building developed structural defects during the First World War. In 1920s they acquired 'Corset House' (the central property of the three shown in the left-hand photograph). The drawing on the right above was their architect's scheme for the conversion and extension to the offices and printing works in Castle Foregate to which they moved in 1927. They only moved out a couple of years ago when the business came under new management. (Shropshire Archives)

The everyday street scene on Pride Hill in 1923 showing the mix of cars, horse-drawn vehicles and bicycles that was usual. The Victorian market is seen beyond. The ladies demonstrate a freedom not appropriate before the First World War. (Shropshire Archives)

Morris's Restaurant on Pride Hill was a period piece and a commendable contribution to both the street scene and the town's social life, providing genteel teas accompanied by violin music. It was designed by W.J. Harris. (SA PH-S-13-P-4-69)

to Shrewsbury School for the beginning of term. Work stopped on the widening of English Bridge. The railwaymen attended prayer meetings each morning, held in the Primitive Methodist Chapel. BBC broadcasts were relayed by loudspeakers, set up at police stations, to counter rumours. No national newspapers were printed, so the *Shrewsbury Chronicle* was issued as a 'daily' for almost a fortnight, conveying information based on the BBC bulletins. The strike came to an end without any violence in Shropshire, and people were soon able to return to their normal occupations.

In the following year, 1927, the *Shrewsbury Chronicle* opened new works and offices in Castle Foregate, and the printing works was able to return from its wartime location in Newport. Printing had been handled there for a few years because its property in Swan Hill could not be repaired during the war. In the late '30s, greater coverage of local news began, and leading articles were based on local subjects. One of the junior reporters around this time was a Scot named, not unusually, Robertson – Fyfe Robertson, later to make his name as a television reporter.

Business was becoming more formalised, with increasing requirements for records, storage and banking. In 1928 the Chatwood Safe Company, which later became Hall Engineering, took a 325 acre (over 130ha) site on the outskirts of the town. They created new products, making safes and locks, and added ranges of fireproof cabinets and strongroom doors.

The business of another family firm, Cooper and Green, started by Geoffrey Cooper and Bruce Green in 1930, was in auctions, shipping and travel. Over the next few years they focussed more on property auctions and sales, and by 1933 expansion enabled them to move into larger premises and open branches. In 1932 they advertised semi-detached houses at Copthorne for £595, or '£30 down' and 14s 8d per week. Detached, four-bedroomed houses at Porthill were offered at between £850 and £1,000. Now trading as Cooper Green, the firm remains a Shrewsbury-based estate agents.

Prior to 1930, Shrewsbury's 20th-century growth was mainly northward, but the building of the bypass to the south-west of the town in the '30s led to new building on that side. The suburbs of Monkmoor, Underdale, Sundorne and Meole Brace, which had all started to grow before 1930, developed considerably in the next two decades. In the 20 years 1911-31 Shrewsbury's population grew by just over 10%; thereafter the growth accelerated and the next 20 years showed an increase of 38%.

A good deal of rebuilding took place in the town centre. Apart from individual buildings, certain street improvement schemes were carried out, largely under Arthur Ward's guidance. Ways needed to be made through the medieval town to allow the passage of motor traffic and Barker Street was widened in the 1930s, while buildings were demolished in Castle Gates to allow for the new Granada Cinema. As part of the Barker Street works, the Exchange Hotel was demolished, and rebuilt, to provide a wider corner. The old inn had specialised in stout and oysters, once the poor man's fare, and had been on the site since 1868. The original façade was left standing while the new construction went on behind. A number of other Georgian façades were carefully taken down and rebuilt to a set-back building line, with considerable success.

The Reform Act of 1832 and the Municipal Corporations Act of 1835 had provided for an elected town council, and separated local government from the administration of justice. County councils and county boroughs were formed in 1888, then the 1933 Local Government Act established the clear allocation of responsibilities between the county and boroughs. Shrewsbury was the one municipal borough in Shropshire. While the county was responsible for education, social and welfare services, and the fire brigade, amongst other services, the borough was responsible for libraries, museums, open spaces and recreational facilities, the collection and disposal of refuse, traffic management and car parking, markets, abattoirs, the burial of the dead, and certain planning powers. Both tiers of local authority had responsibility for public housing – the houses promised by Lloyd George in the 1918 general election under the cry 'Homes fit for heroes'. Shrewsbury's first council housing estates were in Longden Green and Hill Crescent, south of the river.

The growth in population and the extension of the suburb areas made it necessary to replace the water treatment works at Coton Hill, whose service had already been extended, and it was decided to establish the new treatment works at Shelton. A new pump house was built near the river edge at Shelton Rough, and the remainder of the works, including the now familiar tower landmark, on the high land bordering the west side of the London to Holyhead road. The necessary Parliamentary powers were sought, and the works started in 1933. Shrewsbury continued to operate its unusual two-source supply, from the river, and from the wells at Conduit Head.

The firm of Tanners could be taken as the measure of the region's growing sophisti-cation. William Tanner, a retired sea-captain, founded the wine business in 1872. He had offices in the old Victorian market building, and had used the cellars below until they were requisitioned for air-raid shelters during the Second World War. In 1936 they took over Thos Southam & Co, which had been founded in Wyle Cop in 1842, and traded as Tanners & Southam in this period. The business acquired a national reputation in the wine trade, and it is still a family business, now employing about a hundred staff.

This was the age of the cinema, a weekly event for many families. The theatre was also functioning and the Shrewsbury Amateur Operatic Society was founded in 1923. It used to give performances in the Theatre Royal before moving to the Granada in 1936. One of the highlights of the early years was when it presented the comic opera *Tom Jones* in 1930 in the presence of its composer, Sir Edward German, a Shropshire man.

When clearing areas of slums in Barker Street in the 1930s, Rowley's House was revealed
(on the left in the upper, and centre of the lower, photographs) and described as 'terribly
dilapidated; almost ruinous'. With patience the building was rescued, made structurally
sound and repaired using timbers from adjoining buildings. From 1934 until recently the
building housed the town's principal museum. (Shropshire Archives)

The Shropshire & West Midlands Agricultural Show, the great social event for farmers and their families, survived the depression of the 1930s. It not only gave opportunity for exchange of information, experience and ideas amongst the farming community, but stimulated constructive competition, and provided entertainment and interest for the townspeople.

The Co-op, the first of our chain stores, appeared in Castle Street. To make way for more modern 'chains', and the financial benefits it was hoped they would bring, many of Shrewsbury's most delightful buildings, the town's greatest assets, were sacrificed. This was the beginning of the disastrous imposition of 'company drawing-office' schemes, in the form of what Pevsner has called, with some restraint, 'bland neo-Georgian'. It was also the beginning of the factory production, and application, of crude building elements and workmanship, alien to the quality of Shrewsbury's existing buildings.

Most fortunately for the town, the professional influence of Arthur Ward, architect and civil engineer to the borough, prevented worse alterations. Before the existence of any conservation legislation, he was negotiating on a personal basis, making suggestions, offering advice, and persuading many developers and building owners to adopt higher standards of design and more sympathetic treatments when making alterations and 'modernising' premises. Perhaps, though for unfortunate reasons, Shrewsbury benefited from the enforced halt to building work caused by the Second World War. Manpower, materials and concentration were diverted before they could cause further damage. It was a case of 'All change'. History, again, was intervening.

Edward Prince of Wales, the future Edward VIII, inspecting Shrewsbury School cadets on their 50th year at Kingsland in 1934. (Shropshire Archives)

15 SHREWSBURY IN THE SECOND WORLD WAR

'HOME GUARD NOTES - Exercises and Parade at Shrewsbury.
The salute was taken in the Square by the earl of Bradford, chairman of the
Shropshire Territorial Army Association, who afterwards addressed the men in the
Quarry. He said that to repel invasion was the main object of the Home Guard.
The battalion had the task of defending their home town, and it was up to them to
see that they were properly fitted in every way to carry out that duty should that
occasion arise.'

Shrewsbury Chronicle, 1 November 1940

In September 1939, Shrewsbury became embroiled in the Second World War, which was
to be so different in scale and nature from the first, only a generation earlier. This time
there were immediate, and constant, fears of bombing, and also of invasion from the
west (via Ireland), and preparations were made accordingly.

The local authority took on responsibility for civil defence under the supervision of
the borough engineer. An air raid shelter was built under the old Market House, and
others underground in the Quarry. Buildings were commandeered for official uses; Air
Raid Precautions (ARP) posts and first aid casualty stations were set up and manned;
and fuel and food controllers were appointed to supervise rationing. Evacuees arrived;
gasmasks were issued; sinister, whining air-raid sirens were installed; pillboxes were built;
signposts were removed 'for the duration' – an endlessly repeated phrase – (to confuse
the enemy when they landed); and 'the blackout' was imposed. 'Put that light out!' was a
constant cry from the voluntary, but official, patrolling air raid wardens, whenever they
spotted a crack of light between the curtains.

In the surrounding countryside, War Agricultural Committees directed new
regulations, including the ploughing up of grassland, and this often caused tension with
farmers, who felt they knew what their land was best suited to producing. The following
example comes from *The Farmer, the Plough, and the Devil - The story of Fordhall Farm* by
Arthur Hollins; Fordhall Farm lies a few miles to the north-east of Shrewsbury.

'Every word he uttered seemed backed by quiet menace, "I'm afraid you have no
choice Mr X. We want every possible acre ploughed." After only three visits, the 'Man
from the War Ag' had already established a harsh reputation at Z-Z.Farm. One of the
men charged with maximising farm production by the government, he was no respecter

of land quality, and his answer was to plough everything, even soil which would have produced more food if it remained in pasture and carried livestock. But when I tried to outline our bitter cropping experience decade and my belief that it would be better if we continued to try to improve the land by carrying more stock, he became very impatient. "You are a lowland farmer, Mr X. It's crops we want from you – leave meat production to the men in the hills who can't do anything else. I'll be round again shortly and I'll want to see your complete cropping plan." That was at the end of his first visit, and he left me feeling very miserable as, without any attempt at a formal goodbye, he strode to his car and drove away. Anyone less equipped to obtain the collaboration of farmers by humane and gentle persuasion it would be difficult to discover. ... "and if the Committee doesn't feel you are obtaining the best from your land, it's entitled to put in someone else who can." Realising how poor our yields were, compared with those on richer soils, I knew that it wouldn't be long before his threat could become a reality.'

Buildings' Changing Roles

Many buildings were commandeered or acquired for new uses, taking advantage of Shrewsbury's existing administrative structures and contacts as the county town, its geographically central position in a rural county, and its likely low priority as a German bombing target. It also had good communication routes in all directions by road and rail.

An Air Raid Warden's Post in Perche's Mansion, Windsor Place. (Shropshire Archives)

The principal hotel, the Raven on Castle Street, was taken for the Ministry of Supply with their 150 civil servants until 1943, when it became an American services club. The Crown, a few yards away, was used by the Pearl Insurance Company, who also took over part of Attingham Park. Radbrook Hall, later a hotel, was converted into a rest home for sick factory workers, some probably suffering from long hours and perhaps stress, their city homes having been bombed. The Royal Infirmary and Copthorne Hospital were prepared as base hospitals, where casualties were first received.

The Music Hall 'filled up with furniture as the Army Pay Corps moved in'. The Ditherington maltings, the previous flaxmill, was turned into an army training barracks for recruits, with a large war map displayed on an outside wall. Shrewsbury School took in 500 scholars from Cheltenham College, their red-tasselled mortar boards providing an unusual sight in the town. The old Wyle Cop Schools were commandeered as a recruiting office and a citizens' advice bureau was set up in Princess Street, both of these in the town centre, whereas the British Restaurant, established to serve basic inexpensive meals, was set up in Dithering on the outskirts of the town, and was subject to criticism accordingly. Metal railings were removed from around churches and several other buildings, to be melted down and used in munitions, although it was rumoured that some were used for prestige purposes in London. Shrewsbury once again mustered troops, trained them and sent them overseas and, as D-Day approached, military vehicles were marshalled on the Shrewsbury by-pass.

A reinforced brick air raid shelter was built under the old Market House.
It also served as a central posting site for war-time information. (SA PH-S-13-S-30-34)

As before in the history of this part of the country, attack was expected from the west, but in this war, attack from the air was also feared. In plans to defend Shrewsbury against capture, emphasis was placed on the defence of the Welsh Bridge entry to the town as part of an overall intention to delay invaders' progress from any west coast landings by creating a network of sequential 'stop lines'. In Shropshire these were formed along natural hindrances such as the rivers Severn and Teme, brick and concrete pillboxes being sited at vulnerable crossing points. Airfields were also prepared against possible enemy landings in order to counteract the German tactic of seizing airfields by airborne assault and using them to bring in troops.

To man some of these defences, and to provide a force familiar with the local terrain and able to watch a wide area for enemy paratroop landings, the Home Guard was formed from those not called-up for active service due to age or health or because they were working in 'reserved' occupations which needed to retain their skills. The organisation's structure and hierarchy reflected the still rigid class system of the time: battalion and company commanders were invariably recruited from the ranks of those who lived in the local 'big house', though many of them did have valuable First World War experience of leadership and administration. Members were expected to give their time on at least one evening a week, after their normal day's work, and to spend their Sundays on training courses, exercises or parades. They were also expected to acquire new or specialised skills, such as map reading, fieldcraft, battlecraft, signalling, aircraft recognition and weapons training, although weapons were often in short supply. While invasion threatened, the Home Guard had to roster parachute watch patrols from dusk to dawn, and provide a constant lookout for saboteurs and possible spies.

Social Life

Shrewsbury Station was important to many troop movements, and many individuals. A night canteen and hostel for travelling and stranded servicemen was opened at 4 Chester Street, opposite the station, just before Christmas 1939, and it operated throughout the war. The town became a social centre for service people from all parts of Britain, the Commonwealth and occupied countries of Europe and, after 1942, for American and Canadian servicemen stationed in Shropshire. A special Red Cross Leave Club was established at the Raven Hotel for the Americans and Canadians in 1943. In 1944, there was an American football match at Gaye Meadow in aid of the Red Cross. Nylon stockings became a form of local currency, at least among young people.

The population of Shrewsbury was swollen by troops, evacuee children from Liverpool, whole firms moving out from London, and servicemen and women, who were accommodated in the existing and converted barracks, such as the Ditherington maltings, and the larger houses, in which precious fireplaces and other historical features were boarded up. Everything was rationed, although less strictly than in London.

Silhouette Corset Ltd was incorporated in London in 1936 by Otto Lobbenberg and Hans Blunenau. They had fled from Germany, where they feared for their future, with the kernel of their established factory business, first to France, and then on to England, where they established themselves in Islington, producing good quality ladies' corsets. In the late 1930s there had been a craze for health and fitness, and for lightweight 'girdles' guaranteed not to split, peel or crack. From a Paris partner came the offer of rights for a new garment – the radioactive corset, 'Radiante'. It was advertised as being made with radioactive elements, and was said to 'give a feeling of energy, fitness and a resistance to chills'. It had been an immediate success.

When war broke out there were restrictions on all forms of production. Unable to produce its normal high quality products, the company was ordered to produce 'Utility' goods. After Germany invaded France, the British became very suspicious of all foreigners, especially German-born, interning all German refugees. Fortunately, Otto Lobbenberg was out on ARP (Air Raid Precautions) blackout duty when the police came for him, so they could not take him in. It happened to be the day the government changed policy, recognising that Jewish Germans should not be included, so they did not return for him. Hans, however, was interned for many months. Production carried on at Angel House in Islington well into the Blitz, even diversifying into making gas mask carriers, but when their East end employees' homes began to be bombed, Otto and Hans decided to move to somewhere safer, and chose Shropshire. Within 48 hours of arriving they had found a disused pub for offices and a cutting room, a small church hall for manufacturing, and three private buildings for housing their staff and their own families. Their records show that the factory played an important part in Shrewsbury's life and economy, then and in their later larger premises.

The old 'Potts', the Shropshire and Montgomery Railway, had the distinction of being requisitioned by the War Department in 1941. The old line increased its mileage fourfold as it became the vital transport link with the 2,000-acre central ammunition storage depot, near Nesscliff, where over a thousand different types of munitions were stored underground by the Royal Engineers.

A feature of this war was the number of voluntary organisations, most already established, which extended their numbers and the range of their activities. Their county headquarters were generally in Shrewsbury, well placed in the centre of the county for meetings and liaison. Within 48 hours of mobilisation orders, nearly 50 Voluntary Aid Detachment (VAD) nurses had departed by rail, for duty at military hospitals all over the country. There were Auxiliary Nurses helping in civilian hospitals, and the Women's Voluntary Services (WVS), undertook a range of duties. The Soldiers', Sailors' and Airmen's Families Association paid special attention to the families of servicemen and their needs. As so often at this time, it was a case of 'noblesse oblige', and the Dowager Lady Harlech was their President.

Many women served in the armed forces, or alternatives such as the Women's Land Army, whose Shropshire headquarters were in Shrewsbury, under the chairmanship of Viscountess Boyne. The Federation of Women's Institutes (WIs) were strong in Shropshire, and had their headquarters in Shrewsbury's Claremont Buildings. Shrewsbury WI organised an Emergency Food Production Committee, a War Agricultural Sub-committee, and 55 fruit preservation depots throughout the county. Special courses were held at Radbrook College for WI members to teach food production and preparation, Shropshire winning the inter-county fruit preservation competition for the final three years of the war.

By the end of the war, Shrewsbury men and women were scattered in many parts of the world. The threatened invasion had not taken place, and Shrewsbury had been spared the bombing suffered by many urban areas. Victory was achieved in Europe in May 1945. Austerity still prevailed, but was relaxed for V-E Day, 8 May. The borough provided a gramophone, and there was dancing in the Square. Celebrations for the final victory in Japan on V-J Day on 15 August brought out the flags and bunting, and brought in the Land Girls from outlying farms, who were seen dancing with policemen. At the same time, with no explanation, a little way out of the town centre, on top of his column in Abbey Foregate, Lord Hill's arm unexpectedly fell off. (It was later replaced by the council with a wooden one.)

Readjustment and return to normality began. The Civil Defence organisation held a farewell parade on the playing fields of Shrewsbury School, German prisoners-of-war were set to laying sewers for a new council estate at Crowmoor, and parts of the Sentinel Works were adapted to the production of steel bathroom and kitchen units for the new prefabricated houses being developed.

Shrewsbury's Second World War Memorial, built in 1922 in the Quarry, is the focus for Remembrance Sunday. The bronze statue of the Archangel Michael, patron saint of warriors, is by Jeremy Bolwell & A.G. Wyon. County and Regimental arms are shown in the gold mosaic floor; the seals or arms of the six boroughs of the county are embossed on the inside frieze.
(Stephen de Saulles)

Despite the darker side of war, there were certain compensations. Anyone living through it experienced a camaraderie, a sense of common purpose, and of achievement which has never been recaptured.

16   THE POST-WAR YEARS

'Site and buildings have combined here to give one of the greatest townscape experiences of Britain. A hill in a horseshoe loop of the Severn, the riverside mostly a lush park, the town on top a continually changing sequence – from shopping bustle to quiet churchyards and from alleyways to calm Georgian streets which still have people living in them. This is a kind of Haydn among towns, inexhaustibly full of surprises; and Shrewsbury could have a great future by developing and intensifying these deceptively quiet contrasts. Instead, it seems to be headed for mediocrity, purely and simply because the local councillors, officers and townspeople don't realise the value of what they have got ... Shrewsbury is sitting on a townscape treasure-chest and doesn't know it.'

Observer 19 September 1965, Ian Nairn's Britain: 'Shrewsbury, a town going downhill'

The early post-war years was still an age of austerity. Some goods were unobtainable, rationing continued for several years, and there were shortages of everything from bedding plants to building materials. But slowly, the evidence of wartime disappeared. The lights came on, wardens' posts were removed, the incongruous brick shelter under the old Market House was demolished, and offices returned to normal ownerships and uses. Eventually this even included the part of the *Chronicle* offices which had been commandeered for use as a hairdressing establishment for the women members of the forces: the WAAFS, WRAFS and WRENS.

The first post-war West Midlands Agricultural Show (known locally as the West Mid Show, and organized by the Shropshire and West Midlands Agricultural Society) was held in 1946. It was organised with great ingenuity, using make-shift equipment, but suffered a disastrous flood during a late stage of the preparations. With yet more improvisation, well learned during the war, it proved a great success to the show-starved farming community of the time. Livestock exhibits came from as far away as the Isle of Wight and, despite petrol rationing, over 30,000 people attended. This was many more than expected, and it created unprecedented traffic jams in the town – a problem foreseen and solved for later shows.

At the end of the war the *Shrewsbury Chronicle* initiated the annual Town of Flowers competition. One of the little known judges, Percy Thrower, then Shrewsbury's parks superintendent responsible for the plant displays in the Dingle, was asked afterwards to take part in a radio programme, and as a result he became one of the first radio and television 'personalities'. Retired from his municipal duties, he attracted visitors from all over the country to his own nurseries (one of several around the town). He exhibited at the Shrewsbury Flower Show every year in the same Quarry park he had cared for in his earlier years. His work and memory was kept alive by his daughter Margaret Thrower, who used to manage and give lively demonstrations at the garden centre that bears his name. The centre is now under new management, and she retired a few years ago.

In 1950 the Shrewsbury police became part of the Shropshire constabulary and Shrewsbury Town Football Club was elected to the Football League. The following year, after all the delays related in chapter 11, the new main sewer was finally completed, with a tunnel under the river connecting the Monkmoor plant with Harlescott. Also in 1951 the old 'picturesque' Castle Footbridge was replaced with what was reputed to be the first prefabricated, pre-stressed concrete bridge in the country. In 1956 the conversion of electrical supply from DC, direct current to AC, alternating current, was completed, and the Roushill power station was closed. Other works included a new and enlarged Shrewsbury College of Arts and Technology built in 1961 on an open site on the outskirts of the town along the London Road, and a new footbridge of modern design constructed in 1979, to link the town centre's Riverside Shopping

The War Memorial was given to the town by Shrewsbury School in 1952 to mark the 400th anniversary of their founding in 1552. It took the place of the old market cross, at the highest point of the town. (Shropshire Archives)

Centre with the Frankwell car park, relieving the old Welsh Bridge of much of its pedestrian traffic.

Many clubs and societies were formed during these decades, covering cultural and entertainment interests of all kinds, and Shrewsbury was still fulfilling its role as headquarters for many regional organisations, official and informal. From the mid-1940s Shrewsbury had, besides three cinemas, its own professional repertory theatre company called the Beacon Players. The theatre, which seated about 150, replaced the Wightmans' Working Men's Club on the site of the present Dyas premises. Despite the lack of heating, and spartan decor, it attracted good and regular audiences, this being before the days of television. It put on a new play every week right up to 1954.

During the Suez Crisis in the 1950s the old 'Potts' railway line came into active service again, operated by the Royal Engineers with civilian support, moving thousands of tons of ammunition. But within five years the ammunition stores were abandoned, and the Criggion branch became redundant when the quarry closed. The last scheduled train ran in 1960. A few weeks later the Stephenson Locomotive Society went on a sentimental farewell outing. The much loved 'Gazelle' engine used on the line had remained under War Department control after the end of the Second World War until included in the 1948 railways nationalisation. It was exhibited at the York Railway Museum, representing

The building of the new Castle Footbridge of 1951 which replaced the original one built in 1910. It is an interesting structure, being the first pre-stressed, post-tensioned, reinforced concrete, counter-balanced cantilever bridge in the country. (SA PH-S-13-C-2-24)

the Shropshire and Montgomery Railway, from 1971 until it was moved to its rightful place in Colonel Stephens' museum at Tenterden. Colonel Stephens was an engineer eccentric, and his railways were renowned for their motley collection of adapted ancient and non-standard locomotives and his ingenious restoration work.

Newspapers to the Fore

In 1947 the *Shrewsbury Chronicle* celebrated its 175th anniversary with a lunch limited by the Ministry of Food, as was usual in those days, to 100 guests, and strict control of the courses served.

When Mr Morley Tonkin took control of the paper in 1945, the works at Castle Foregate were limited to six 'No. 1' Linotypes, which could only produce one size and style of typeface, and one 'No. 4' which could set three different sizes and styles. An array of trunking carried the fumes away. The battery of typesetting machines was driven by pulleys off one shaft driven by a direct current motor. (Shrewsbury then still had a diesel engined DC generating station.) At one end of the top floor they processed half-tone blocks for the pictures. The large flat bed press on the middle level shook the floor, while on the ground floor was a vintage rotary press that had been used for printing the *Daily Tribune* in London in the 1890s, plus a gas-heated pot keeping a ton of metal liquid for casting the curved plates of pages for the rotary press.

Mr Tonkin bought two more papers, the *Bridgnorth Journal* and the *Salford City Reporter*, and realised that they could be produced more economically using just one plant, and that the volume of work would justify more modern equipment. Accordingly, adjustments were made to the layout of the premises, a 'Foster' rotary press was bought second-hand from Blackburn, and the whole top floor was devoted to composing. That section was probably the best equipped of any weekly in the country.

Then, in 1957, he travelled across Canada, visiting the works of several newspapers and seeing the pioneer Photon photo-setting machine, which, he realised, coupled with a rotary lithographic press, could greatly improve the printing process and the clarity of illustrations. He knew that rotary lithographic ('web-offset') presses were being produced, but they were only used for magazines, because exposing the paper to open gas jets to dry the ink was far too dangerous and costly for newspaper work. However, he also knew that ink manufacturers were experimenting with quick-drying inks that could be suitable if a slightly different method was used. Tonkin and one or two of his production staff made several study trips, and he also went to work on an early press himself.

By 1962 the *Chronicle* was able to produce a 16-page paper on the first broad-sheet web-offset press in Britain. Soon they were producing 20 pages, then up to 24, and also including spot colour, followed by full colour. The press comprised eight units, and was then the largest newspaper press to be built. Later in the year they were setting headlines on two Japanese photo-setting machines found in California, and in 1963, they began photo-setting text. They had eliminated the use of metal entirely.

The *Shrewsbury Chronicle* sparked one of the most significant national revolutions in newspaper printing since the invention of Linotype in 1889 did away with individual letters. The *Shropshire Star*, founded in 1964, bravely adopted the same method. It was the first used in Britain by an evening paper, which has to keep so strictly to its press times. Others gradually followed. Morley Tonkin was rewarded by being made President of the Institute of Journalists in 1965 in the presence of the then Prime Minister, Harold Wilson. The 1965 conference of the institute was held in Shrewsbury, and the pioneering works was visited by journalists from all over the world.

Schools and wider education

Rab Butler's 1944 Education Act revolutionised state education. Sir Offley Wakeman, chairman of the County Council Education Committee, strongly supported the Act, seeing it as 'a very far reaching measure' giving 'new opportunities to the great mass of children of this country such as they never had before'. He urged the committee and the county 'to create educational facilities in Shropshire as great as those of any county in the kingdom'. They succeeded. For the next two decades he, and his chief officer, headed a team which enjoyed an international reputation in the field of progressive education. Many new primary schools were built by the local authority in the 1940s, followed by secondary schools in the 1950 and '60s.

As a result of the school building programme, the county architect, Ralph Crowe, had been able to attract well-qualified architects from London to join his progressive department. Geoffrey Hamlyn, who trained as a furniture designer as well as an architect, along with furniture designer Douglas Webb, joined the department in 1965. Geoff Hamlyn was appointed county architect when Ralph Crowe retired, and was responsible for initiating and developing the Second Consortium of Local Authorities (the SCOLA system), a pre-fabricated building system used especially for schools. In the 1960s, the Shrewsbury department was designing buildings, furniture and equipment not only for Shropshire, but also for a consortium of several other counties.

Led by these Shrewsbury-based architects and furniture designers, Shropshire established a high reputation for design generally. Apart from the extensive post-war school building programme, they designed other creditable buildings in the town, for example, the new Shirehall, opened in 1966, the new police station at Monkmoor (using the same SCOLA prefabricated system as originally devised for schools), and the new riverside leisure-learning 'Gateway' building in Chester Street. They also skilfully restored and extended the historic local library building, opened by Princess Margaret. The tall roadside block that later housed the town's natural history collection, and the other parts of the old school group, all became the public library, expertly repaired and imaginatively converted and extended in the 1970-80s by the county architects' department. This local professional expertise also influenced the furniture design department of the Shrewsbury College of Arts and Technology, whose students gained national recognition and several awards, and places in specialist workshops outside the county.

Soon after Geoffrey Hamlyn left the county, the architects' department came under a new regime, dominated by administrators, and as staff left, the department finally disappeared, leaving the county and the borough without the level of the professional expertise that the architectural heritage requires. During the 'enlightened' period, several schools, under the same influence, taught visual as well as other forms of literacy, enabling young children to produce surprisingly mature work, which was featured in several exhibitions and in the national press. When Lord Asa Briggs, chairman of the Civic Trust's heritage education group, came to view the work done by the schools taking part in Shrewsbury Civic Society's 'Project, Our Town' in the '70s, he declared that the work done by one of the town's primary schools was 'the best he had seen anywhere in the country'.

Town Planning and Development

Arthur Ward had been unusually conscious of the town's exceptional legacy of old buildings. He was equally aware of the problems of adapting a unique, historic town to the needs of the 20th century – as he showed in his book *Shrewsbury, A Rich Heritage*, published just after his retirement in 1946. Shrewsbury owes him a great debt of gratitude. He 'held the bridge', it could be said, literally as well as metaphorically, pending the support and authority given, at least in some measure, by two Town and Country Planning Acts. The 1944 Act introduced the concept of listing certain properties, and the 1947 Act instituted formal 'Listing' and grading, according to age and degree of historic or architectural interest. Thus it was that the town's attention was first drawn seriously to the interest, and even potential commercial (tourism) value, of its building heritage.

The last auction at the old Smithfield livestock market on the Raven Meadows site, recorded in the *Wellington Journal*. (Shropshire Archives)

In the early 1950s there was a growing interest in Shrewsbury's past, stimulated largely by the Shropshire Archaeological Society. Shortly after Arthur Ward's historical summary of the architecture and buildings of the town, Miss Lily Chitty, a well-known character respected for her knowledge of local history and archaeology, wrote her *Prehistoric and Other Early Finds in the Borough*. It has since been subject to many revisions in the light of further research. Nevertheless, her lively personality and wisdom live on in the wealth of papers and material she passed to the Local Studies Library.

In 1953 J.T. Smith prepared an MA Thesis on the subject of the old houses of Shrewsbury which, although it has remained unpublished, has been used as a work of reference in the borough since he left it in the library's care. It was used as the basis for listing the earlier buildings of architectural and historic interest in the town as directed by the 1947 Planning Act. In

The demolition of the Raven Hotel in Castle Street will never be forgiven by many. It was replaced by a clone town frontage for a Woolworths store (closed in 2009) and others. (Shropshire Archives)

the following year J.L. Hobbs compiled his fascinating book of Shrewsbury street names. This gave the earliest forms, changes and possible origins of many of the street names that are such an interesting feature of the town – Dogpole, Mardol, Belmont, Murivance, Wyle Cop and so on (see Appendix) – together with snippets of history.

All these works described interesting history, individual buildings, and streets and shuts. It was an article by Gordon Cullen (an honorary Fellow of the RIBA and one of only 200 Royal Designers for Industry) in the May 1954 *Architectural Review* that first analysed Shrewsbury's townscape features. In a series of studies on four West Midlands towns, he drew particular attention to Shrewsbury's 'secret town' behind, and interlocking with, the traffic routes. Shrewsbury had been spared the destruction caused by bombing suffered by other towns and cities, but despite the two Planning Acts and the nascent interest in its older buildings and townscape, it lay open to business interests and a local government whose patronage had shifted from those seeking excellence to those engaged in producing a short-term commercial return, often for distant shareholders as opposed to local interests, allowing them to siphon money out of the town in return for some recompense by way of payment of rates. They were not brought up to consider visual matters and long-term amenity.

Between 1956 and 1970 no less than 52 of the town's then listed buildings were destroyed, 27 of them in the town centre, all for the purpose of redevelopment. Commercial development had grown in scale, and 'building' was now out of the hands of the earlier local owners, architects, designers and craftsmen, with their natural sense of the pleasing and appropriate. It had passed to companies' 'head offices' located elsewhere, who were dictating their gross, wide-span, horizontal frontages, with draughtsmen specifying details and materials alien to Shrewsbury's traditional shopfronts and street façades. Many fine buildings and street scenes, which would have been retained at all costs in the following two decades, were sacrificed. The national companies and developers wrought havoc while Shrewsbury slept, lulled by the illusion that change meant progress.

Contrary to expectations, the planning legislation had no adequate means of stopping this legalised vandalism, or of assessing the quality of design submitted in planning applications. These were assessed by the local authorities 'responsible' only on practical criteria, such as heights of buildings, and ideals thought at the time to be desirable, such as 'uniformity of roof-lines', 'comprehensive development', and the use of 'modern materials', none of which were advantageous in historic towns. Subsequent protective legislation came too late to prevent much damage to the existing fabric and character of the town. The Raven Hotel was one of the largest demolitions, and its loss has proved iconic, its mention now representing the total losses Shrewsbury suffered at the hands of officialdom. Several of the other old hotels and coaching inns were also demolished, together with large 'black and white' town houses, and what could now be described as 'charming old terraces' of houses, some because they lacked amenities such as indoor

For many years one of 'sights of the town', the secondhand furniture store of 'Wappy' Phillips finally collapsed into the river in the 1980s, and was promptly cleared away to prevent any obstruction to the river's flow. (Shropshire Archives)

toilets and hot water systems, others because their sites appealed to developers who saw them as sources of profit-making building investment and activity.

There were honourable exceptions. One, by John Colliers in 1962 (now Bank Fashions), was one of the first to show that it was possible not only to save old features in new work, but also to incorporate them imaginatively. They retained, and incorporated in their interior design, the remains of the 13th-century Bennet's Hall, (traditionally called the old mint), which was discovered while clearing the site for their premises on Pride Hill. A few doors uphill, the lower floor of McDonalds occupies the original stone-built medieval undercroft. This would have been a basement warehouse of a medieval hall, of around 1400, demolished above ground level a long time ago.

In redesigning Lloyd's Bank, adjoining the west side of Bennet's Hall, the designer also made a conscious effort to create a frontage design to suit the context, knowing that, terminating the view at the end of the High Street, it would be seen with nearby Ireland's Mansion in the High Street. It received one of the first Civic Trust Awards. Although not universally liked, it is at least excellent of its type, and has a vertical emphasis, characteristic of so many buildings in Shrewsbury. It shines with classic elegance when compared with the newer monster General Market Hall building, within sight nearby, inflicted on the town by a

The General Market Hall & Shopping Centre built in 1965 (known as 'The New Market Hall' to distinguish it from 'The Old Market Hall' of 1596 in the Square.) The largest of the 1960s 'developer-schemes', it was designed by David Aberdeen for the Second Covent Garden Property Company to replace the old Victorian market and provide lettable retail units at ground-floor level. Ian Nairn, in *The Observer* for 19 September 1965), asked whether the white walling and black ribs 'God forbid, have been a concession to Shrewsbury's half-timbered buildings?' John Cornforth, in *Country Life* for 6 October 1977 noted that it was 'a successor that repels one ... and thrusts up a tower that contributes nothing positive to its silhouette'.
(Stephen de Saulles)

property development company based in London. It was described as 'Developer's floor space … reached by lifts or grim loveless stairs' by Ian Nairn in an article on Shrewsbury in 1965 appropriately titled 'A Town Going Downhill'. It was an unforgivable mistake, and unfortunately a big one, to allow such a block to be sited in Shrewsbury's historic town centre.

There followed a number of other regrettable blocks of building in pseudo-Georgian or 'contemporary' cladding, creating scars which will take many years to mask or heal, or ultimately, one hopes, replace. Ian Nairn, who had collaborated with Nikolaus Pevsner on his *Buildings of England* series, wrote in his *Observer* article: 'Shrewsbury could have a great future by developing and intensifying [its] quiet contrasts. Instead, it seems to be headed for mediocrity, purely and simply because … the local townspeople don't realise the value of what they have got'.

The subsequent change in opinion amongst many is reflected in the number of more recent national articles and local publications concerned specifically with mourning these various losses to our heritage, and in preserving them at least in photographic and recording terms. There are none, so far as I know, which support the destruction and the 'blocks of building' which replaced them.

With increasing post-war legislation and the intrusion of politics in local affairs, the Shirehall in the Square, shared with the borough, was cramped. Back in 1912 'the clerk of the council had refused to unlock the Grand Jury Room for a borough committee, and the borough's men broke open the door'. A few days later, 'a final and legal settlement of the Shirehall question' was resolved, but it took time to implement. The new Shirehall, seen here beyond Lord Hill's Column, was designed by the county architect's department. The ground-breaking interior furnishings were designed by their qualified furniture designers led by Geoffrey Hamlyn, by then the county architect. It was opened by the Queen in 1967.

(Stephen de Saulles)

17 'Exceptional Heritage', Leads to the Future

'Undoubtedly Shrewsbury's architectural heritage is exceptional. It was recognised by the Department of the Environment some time ago as being one of the 21 priority towns in England and Wales ... The Conservation Area contains more than 1,100 listed buildings, of which nearly 700 are in the old town centre. The town is particularly rich in buildings of the 13th-15th Centuries and of the early 18th Century, although fine buildings from almost every period can be found. This alone would make Shrewsbury outstanding. But the significance of the town lies not only in its listed buildings, but in the overall impact of the Townscape and its surroundings.'

Michael Quinion Associates in their *Study for the Case for Establishing a Heritage Centre in Shrewsbury* (1984) for the Shrewsbury Civic Society

Every good story should have a happy ending, and a fortunate change of attitude towards the future character of the town has indeed been the most conspicuous, and probably the most important, theme in Shrewsbury's development during recent decades. In February 1986, *Country Life* published a follow-up to previous articles. In it John Cornforth wrote that, when he visited the town in 1977, it had seemed 'quite on the cards that Shrewsbury would make another series of demolition and redevelopment decisions as regrettable as those taken in the previous 15 years. Fortunately, however, there has been a major change of heart …'.

Historians of the last millennium – or even this – will see the period with a different perspective, but it is possible now to pick out some of the threads which had been drawing together, beginning to recreate a town fitting for the 'proud Salopians' we have claimed to be, and a source of revenue to the town and a pleasure to our visitors.

In 1965 Ian Nairn, in his scathing *Observer* article, was able to say 'Shrewsbury is sitting on a townscape treasure-chest and does not know it'. But, fortunately, there were some citizens who did, and who were already taking action behind the scenes. The demolitions of the 1950s had caused great concern. The loss of the Crown, George and Raven hotels, all within a short space of time, alerted many people to the consequences of post-war redevelopment in a town like Shrewsbury. Other areas of the town were under threat, including the group of picturesque cottages on the Bear Steps in St Alkmund's Square, often referred to as 'the heart of Shrewsbury'.

'The Heart of Shrewsbury' – the area around St Alkmund's Square, the original market place, Fish Street at the lower level with St Julian's at the end, and Bear Steps. (Stephen de Saulles)

236

In 1957 Duncan Sandys, Minister of Housing and Local Government, sponsored by powerful sections of British industry including ICI, Unilever and Shell, had formed the Civic Trust, which he then led and inspired as its president. In 1963 a public meeting held in Shrewsbury Castle saw the formation of the Shrewsbury Civic Society as a branch of the Civic Trust. The founder-members included not only architects, but also townspeople from nearly a dozen other professions, including masters from Shrewsbury School. It represented a cross-section of the more articulate public and was chaired by Sir George Trevelyan, its president for several years. One of its first tasks was to repair and restore the Bear Steps group of properties.

In 1966 Duncan Sandys won first place in the House of Commons' ballot for introducing private members' bills and used the opportunity to bring forward a bill to strengthen the law regarding historic buildings and, most importantly, to provide for the designation of what he called Conservation Areas to protect whole areas of towns and villages and not just individual buildings. The resulting Civic Amenities Act received Royal Assent in 1967.

In 1966 the Shropshire Society of Architects mounted an exhibition called 'A Town Like Shrewsbury' in the Square. It was designed to show how it could be possible to combine new and old buildings in a town like Shrewsbury, as long as it was done with care and sympathy.

By 1969 the council had prepared, in response to the Civic Amenities Act, a report and illustrated booklet called *The Challenge of Conservation*. Imaginatively produced, it succeeded in demonstrating some of the attractions and benefits of conservation and townscape work to the councillors of the day. Due in particular to the efforts of two planning officers, central Shrewsbury was officially designated as a Conservation Area in 1970, neatly coinciding with the first of the Council of Europe's three environmental campaigns, 'European Conservation Year 1970'. Gradually the borough council was responding to public pressure and beginning to play its part, and also to gain confidence in its officers' advice. In 1971 a system of Townscheme Grants was instituted under which scheme the government agreed to match whatever repair grants a local authority was prepared to commit to aiding the repair of buildings in a conservation area.

A major step in creating the necessary confidence in conservation was the completion of the Bear Steps project by the Shrewsbury Civic Society in 1972. It showed dramatically, and in practical form, what could be done with semi-derelict old buildings which, to the layman's eye, looked beyond repair. It was a daring venture. The society had started with faith and determination, but only £50 in the bank. Somehow they managed to raise the thousands required from grants and many generous donations. Then, and for some years later, it was the largest project undertaken by any society in the country.

During the early stages of the surveying work there was an unexpected find. Some of the old cottages had concealed part of a 14th-century medieval hall, a large double-height room but open to the roof and with exposed timber trusses. This old 'hall' was restored to provide a space still in constant use for meetings and exhibitions of all kinds. The small room over the old flight of steps, between Fish Street and St Alkmund's Square above, became a miniature office for the Civic Society, extended in 1986 and shared

The restored 'Bear Steps' L-shaped 'group of old cottages' rescued and converted by the Civic Society in 1968. This wing straddles the change of level from St Alkmund's Square, the original market area, down steps, to the present Fish Street below. Amenity society offices are above a café at Square level, with a shop underneath. A tree hides the Hall.
(Stephen de Saulles)

with other societies. The Bear Steps group has been the most visited and photographed tourist attraction in the town, welcoming nearly 100,000 visitors a year; and the hall has provided the focus and venue for conservation and townscape matters generally – and for much of the public participation envisaged in the 1968 Planning Act.

Local Government reorganisation in 1974 established Shrewsbury as its own planning authority, (i.e. no longer under the more remote county council). Significantly, a Chartered Architect (now dealing with parts of the restoration of York Minster) was appointed 'to assist the new department on architecture and conservation matters'. The town owes a debt to this conservation officer, Andrew Arrol, and to his successor, Michael (Micky) King, also a highly qualified and experienced architect (now retired). They made possible a quite unusual degree of cooperation between everyone involved in the following period of improvements, from government departments to archaeologists. Harold Berry, the Chief Planning Officer, initiated regular confidential meetings to which were invited representatives of amenity groups, specialists such as archaeologists and the police, to discuss any controversial planning applications and proposals. The informal interchange of views led to many ideas and suggestions that were later adopted, such as how to provide a fire escape to Rowley's House without 'vandalizing' the building. The system was continued, uniquely in Shrewsbury in that form (even with some reluctant successors), for nearly 30 years.

The principal of the Technical College Art School also broke new ground in 1974, by inviting a panel of local architects to conduct a series of talks and walks on the urban environment of Shrewsbury. Since that time there have been several 'Townscape' courses, also the Tape Trails cassette guides (at both general interest and academic levels), all aimed at helping people to see the town with greater understanding and pleasure, guided 'through the eyes of an architect'. Interest in the history of the town was heightened by the then repeated, and always fully booked, winter series 'The History of Shrewsbury' organised by Dr Barrie Trinder, the county council's adult education tutor for historical studies.

The Council of Europe designated 1975 as European Architectural Heritage Year. The BBC, then still wary of the visual arts, especially buildings, nevertheless showed the Civic Trust's internationally award-winning film on conservation. That year also saw Shrewsbury Civic Society win the Heritage Year Award for its successful restoration of the Bear Steps property. The society also saved the 1835 Howard Street Warehouse, originally the Shrewsbury Canal terminus, by the case they put to the Department of the Environment at a public enquiry. European Architectural Heritage Year also appropriately saw the first of a growing list of restorations, which prompted the Civic Society to set up its own local awards scheme the following year, awards being made over a number of years to restorations of No. 1 High Street, Dogpole Court, the Summer House on Town Walls and the old Union Wharf buildings, along with letters of appreciation to several other smaller projects. The tide had seemed to turn; there was a noticeable return to the re-use and adaptation not only of old buildings, but also local and natural building materials.

In 1977 *Country Life* published a series of three long articles by John Cornforth on the history of Shrewsbury buildings, the *Shrewsbury Chronicle* brought out the first of their collections of comparative photographs, *The Changing Face of Shrewsbury*, based on the popular weekly series by Patrick Smith, and old Shrewsbury was displayed in an exhibition – 'The Living Past' – at the Bear Steps. This was followed by A.M. Carr's evocative booklet *Shrewsbury As It Was*. At about this time the local planning department published the first of their series of discussion booklets concerning the different aspects of planning which were to be incorporated in the Local Plan. In clear layman's language they explained the issues and invited comment, so involving amenity societies and the general public to an extent which had never before been possible.

In 1981 the President of the Royal Institute of British Architects (RIBA) visited Shrewsbury to present an award for the restoration and conversion of the old Union Wharf buildings to a pair of riverside town-houses, a project already commended by the Civic Society. This was the first such award in Shrewsbury, and quite an honour for the town, as these awards are normally reserved for new buildings and larger schemes. It was described in the RIBA report as 'an example of conservation at its best'.

The RIBA's national Festival of Architecture 1984 was designed to draw attention to the best of buildings, past and future. By this time Shrewsbury had a number of schemes to celebrate. They included the dramatic repairs to and commendable extension of the library buildings (old Shrewsbury School); the restoration of the unique Tudor-style station building; the conversion of Allat's School on Murivance to offices; and the conversion of the abandoned Greek revival Infirmary to 'The Parade', with residential use above, attractive specialist shopping arcades on two lower levels, and a spacious outdoor terrace at the rear, high above the river and with views of English Bridge; the Victorian Arcade and Mardol Gardens shopping arcades (both altered and lost since) created out of almost derelict central areas; and the 16th-century Fellmongers' building

in Frankwell, restored and converted by the Civic Society. In addition, a number of restaurants of character were created out of existing buildings, among them the Old Police House, the Cornhouse and Traitor's Gate. The riverside Gateway Education and Arts Centre was one of the few new buildings. A benefactor's gift to the town, designed by the county architect's department, it replaced the old College Hill House premises, and now provides a venue for a myriad activities and courses. The traditional materials used, and design detailing, convey a sense of quality strikingly different from the semi-industrial structures of the '60s.

Over 150 of the now about 750 listed buildings in the town centre were repaired and restored to useful life, and more than 40 new residential units were created out of mostly unused upper floor space. With this level of success, the town was put in a stronger and apparently more determined position to start the second phase of conserving our heritage. This should have dealt with the remaining 100 or so buildings which needed attention and have enabled still more people to live within the river loop, giving life to inner areas once again, but cuts in grants and changes in personnel at the council meant that the impetus was lost.

'Darwin Gate public art installation', erected in 2004, is a controversial piece of public art that replaced a well-loved tree at the top of Mardol. It is not near any of the 'gates' to Shrewsbury, and connection with Darwin is not clear. Despite its mixed reception, it has been represented in some 'official quarters', and even some publications, as a 'symbol' of the town. The surrounding sandstone blocks are used as seats by young and old for relaxing, but how many notice that one the 'stones' is in fact an electrical sub-box disguised, found to be too expensive to move elsewhere?
(Stephen de Saulles)

Apart from the visual improvement enjoyed by everyone working, shopping or living in the town, increased prosperity was reflected in a survey carried out in 1984, which showed Shrewsbury to be rising twice as fast as Chester in the league of regional shopping centres. It was being found that 'conservation pays'. It was also noted that Shrewsbury was attracting an increasing number of appreciative visitors, contributing to its economic

Mock Tudor showing on the Darwin and Pride Hill centres built in 1988/9. The design was in response to the local authority's request for a scheme more suited to Shrewsbury than the developments of the 1960s, and one that was required 'to echo details of a number of properties in the vicinity such as the Abbot's House in Butcher Row and the Confectioners on Pride Hill.' The scheme's frontage to Raven Meadows is over 140m (450ft) long, whilst The Confectioners is under 4m (about 14ft), and the Abbot's House was built in about 1450 – creating problems for any architect, even Harry Wilson of Eaton Manning Wilson. *Building Design* observed at the time: 'the shopping citizen of Shrewsbury will come because of the convenience rather than the sensual experience'. (Stephen de Saulles)

In 2007, Shrewsbury Town Football Club, formed in 1888, moved from its town-centre Gaye Meadow site by the river to its new four-stand, 9,500 seater stadium on the outskirts of the town, in Ottley Road, Meole Brace. It includes conference and various other facilities. The club played at the 'Gaye' from 1910-2007, where a stand-by coracle was used to retrieve the ball from the river. The club was promoted to the Third Division in 1958-59, remaining there for 15 years, and reached the 2nd Division in 1978-79. The 1980s were their golden years. After a time in the doldrums, 'Town' fought their way back into the League in 2004. (Stephen de Saulles)

growth. Visitor surveys consistently showed that visitors were coming primarily for our 'History' and 'Buildings'. 'Shopping' was the good supporting feature.

However, the battle for Shrewsbury's future was (and still is) by no means over. In the early 1980s there were proposals for building another bridge across the river below the old Infirmary; the plan depended on Parliamentary consent as it spanned the river. *Country Life* expressed the view of many, including the Shropshire Society of Architects, when John Cornforth wrote in an article 'Happily that was turned down ... the link road below the Infirmary and the bridge would have surely dealt a fatal blow to one of the classic views of English towns'. Shrewsbury's future attractiveness and prosperity depends on finding ways of preserving such unique characteristics by pursuing more ingenious and professional design solutions.

Shrewsbury's new 650 seat theatre, with a 250 seat studio theatre, opened in Frankwell in 2009 overlooking the river. (Stephen de Saulles)

Leads to the Future

A cause for recent hope is the rising concern for the environment in what has come to be known as the third, or charitable, sector. Their concern has permeated much recent activity in Shrewsbury.

In 1981 the abbey church's administration realised that the then future nona-centenary was perhaps something that should be celebrated and could act as a focus for carrying out necessary repair work. A structural study was made by English Heritage, and a surveyor's report prepared. A local architect, David Morris, was engaged, and a new vicar, Rev. Ian Ross, (with relevant teaching and 'youth organisations' experience), was appointed, accompanied by a similarly experienced and active wife, Jean. He was given an onerous two-fold brief: to get the already commenced urgent and extensive repair work completed, and to get the church opened up and used for arts activities as well as worship.

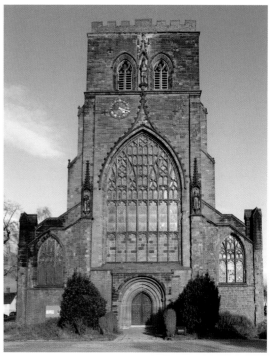

The west front of the abbey, in which a Perpendicular style window was inserted in 1387. It measures 46ft x 23ft (14m x 7m) and its glass contains heraldic shields.
(Stephen de Saulles)

With the involvement of the church parishioners, forming first the Abbey Restoration Committee and then a Nona-centenary Trust, a programme of celebrations involving exhibitions, schools events and historical music concerts was put in hand.

When I wrote the first version of this book in 1985, there were proposals for constructing a new supermarket over part of the site of the abbey buildings and precinct area, which could otherwise have been retained, free of development. It could have been landscaped with the help of available grants as an important tourist attraction and educational site related to the 900-year-old abbey. This, I argued, would be especially appropriate in view of the abbey's possible future broader function as a venue for the arts and educational activity. It could renew one of its original purposes, whilst including the story of the monks' industrial work in their milling activities as well as their building techniques and scientific knowledge. As a rare survival of an urban monastic site, such a combination would probably be unique. In the event the supermarket was pushed back off the abbey site, but the land was then acquired by the local authority and turned into a car park. In 1993 the Wilfred Owen Society commissioned a piece of modern sculpture and placed it in the abbey grounds. (The alternative suggestion for panels of quotations from Owen's anti-war poems to be placed inside the church was rejected.)

Another feature of the town is the canal. Closed by Parliament in 1944, the Shropshire and Newport Canal was left to decay, but then the Shrewsbury and Newport Canals Trust was formed in 2000 in the belief that the canal could be restored to use. Only a part of it had been built over and no insuperable engineering problems lie in the way of restoration. The ultimate aim is to restore a continuous navigable waterway linking Shrewsbury, through Newport, to Norbury Junction and so to the national network. Voluntary working parties are currently engaged in clearing parts of the canal and restoring the canalside buildings. Being the reason for the original siting of the famous iron-frame Ditherington Flaxmill, it is now a vital component of the mill's restoration scheme, with the potential of being grouped with the two other nearby pioneering masterpieces of engineering at Ironbridge and Pontcysyllte Aqueduct, both World Heritage Sites. The Shrewsbury & Newport Canals Restoration Scheme has been evaluated by government as the third most important such scheme in the country.

The conversion c.1990 of the Cornhouse, a former corn merchant's warehouse built c.1850 at bottom of the Cop near the river, by local architect Andrew Arrol has been generally acknowledged as a highly successful example of rehabilitation. External features include arches with blue brick dressings and French doors replacing loading doors on the first floor. Internally, exposed brick walls, new wrought ironwork stair and decor items conserve and add character, all matched by good local food that has been enjoyed by patrons of Grant Pennington's Cornhouse Restaurant for more than 20 years. (Stephen de Saulles)

In the spirit of conservation, the old riverside Pump House, built in the 1850s as part of Shrewsbury's early municipal water supply, has been converted into an 'Eco-cluster' of offices and serves as a model for appropriate energy-saving devices. One of the businesses based here is the Marches Energy Agency (MEA), founded in 1998 as a registered charity and social enterprise, which specialises 'in the delivery of practical, effective and creative ways of promoting energy reduction and renewable energy solutions'. Friends of the Earth started the recycling centre in the town, and regularly publish and distribute a Green Guide which lists local 'environmental' suppliers and services.

The Field Studies Council, an educational charity committed to bringing environmental understanding to all, was established in 1943. Seeking to expand its activities, the charity decided to move its headquarters out of London in the 1980s and chose Shrewsbury as an attractive and central location from which to liaise with their UK network of what is now 17 education centres. One of these had already been established at Preston Montford, some 12 miles west of Shrewsbury. Environmental concerns have also started to affect proposed actions to counter the prospect of flooding. The serious floods of 2000 and subsequent years initially brought forth suggestions for high protective walls round the town. Since then there has been more careful thought, with consideration being given to the whole Severn catchment area upstream and more natural preventative measures such as tree planting, restoring wetlands, and modifying farming methods to delay 'run-off'.

Recent floods have also brought the matter of flood prevention and defences to the fore. As a result, a partial flood alleviation scheme was installed in two stages. The first, completed in 2003, protected the riverside area at Frankwell. Permanent reinforced concrete walls were built alongside the towpath, constructed to permit access at intervals where barriers could be inserted in times of flood. This system protects the western route into Shrewsbury, the council offices, and a number of properties and businesses, although not the adjoining public car park. A smaller section, protecting the Coleham Head area, the abbey and nearby historic properties, was installed in 2010.

Meanwhile, the Shropshire Wildlife Trust was able to purchase, in 2006, about 50 acres of floodplain land, already designated an SSSI (Site of Special Scientific interest), upstream at Melverley. They will preserve and manage the site as a demonstration of effective flood alleviation to other landowners – by

Rehabilitation of 63 Mardol c.1981 included renewing the 'dragon beam', which was done with a bit of humour at street level. (When a timber-framed building is on a corner, and the first floor is projecting on both faces, the important diagonal first-floor beam at the corner is called a 'dragon-beam'.) Architect Andrew Arrol made the visible projecting end in an amusing carved and painted dragon's head when he supervised the restoration of this old building. (Stephen de Saulles)

keeping the ground wet through spring and summer, allowing it to seep away in autumn, but be ready to soak up and store the following winter's floodwater.

Transition Town Shrewsbury, allied to the growing community-led national Transition Network, was formed in 2009 in response to global warming and 'peak-oil' thinking. Their locally devised scheme, Shrewsbury Hydro, a proposal for generating electricity at the old Castlefields Weir, was one of the four selected out of over 600 entries in the national Energyshare competition in 2010, winning £15,000. In 2011, this community-based scheme, including technical and film-making involvement from students at the Sixth Form College, won a further grant of over £40,000 from the government's Local Energy Assessment Fund (LEAF), to finalize the plans for the hydro scheme and fish pass.

The enterprising Battlefield 1403 visitor attraction on the northern side of the town, which could be the first of several other such facilities in the town, was opened as part of a family-run farm in 2003. It includes interpretation of the battle site and church, walks, a small visitor centre, a permanent 'farmers market' shop, and an attached bistro-café serving good food based on local produce. Long-bow archery demonstrations and try-it sessions are held at intervals.

Shrewsbury was chosen to be the West Midland's first – and 'flagship' – Food Enterprise Centre as the hub for regional food. This was due not just to the county's long history of food and drink production combined with good transport links, but also because food, linked with tourism, had been identified as Shrewsbury's two 'industries' with best potential for growth. Jointly funded by Shropshire County Council and

The scene of the battle of Shrewsbury (1403) by Vandyke Brown c.1830. The name Battlefield is still retained, and the church built by Henry IV as a chantry commemorates the great number killed, including Hotspur. Young prince Henry, later Henry V, fought in the battle alongside his father. (SA 6001-5558-60)

Advantage West Midlands, the services building was opened in 2009 on the 24-acre dedicated site in north Shrewsbury. The centre's facilities include training, advice and technical support, lecture and meeting room facilities, test kitchens, available by the day or week, and 12 business-start-up units, all of which are now occupied and operating successfully.

There have also been two important recent studies on Shrewsbury. One, a Visitor Economy Strategy commissioned by the new Shropshire Council unitary authority, was published in 2011. It confirmed several earlier reports by saying that 'Shrewsbury has the potential to draw visitors from further afield and for longer stays,' and that 'it has a strong portfolio of tangible assets that have the potential to deliver a rich visitor experience to a wide audience'. They commented on the 'limited amount of information on the current visitors,' and advised that 'The town needs to embrace delivery of its assets in a visitor orientated manner'. They advised Shrewsbury, as a 'Historic and Quintessentially English Town', to develop as a town that delivers a 'rich visitor experience'. (However, the authority's present policy is to concentrate on new big-name retail development.)

The other, *Shrewsbury, An archaeological assessment of an English border town*, was published in association with English Heritage in 2007. This was the first attempt to describe the whole range of physical remains, both below and above ground, for one of one of the best preserved medieval and ancient towns in England, and to set up an associated data base of information. In the introduction, Dr Nigel Baker referred to 'the growing realisation that the urban archaeological resource was not a dead issue, but that

Gordon and Mrs Manser and four adult children, each an expert in a different specialty, established an internationally-known antiques business in the High Street, before moving to premises with on-site parking at the bottom of the Cop. Then, just before retiring, Gordon Manser commissioned new premises, across the river, in Coleham. The scheme, designed by Paul Harries of Baart Harries Newall of Shrewsbury solved problems of awkward site, a new traffic island and ground floor flooding, producing what many think of as the best modern building in Shrewsbury. The planning department even needed urging by the Civic Society and other amenity groups to 'recommend it for approval'. The scheme subsequently received several awards. Gordon and Mrs Manser retired in about 2003. (Stephen de Saulles)

the streets, properties and buildings of modern town centres are often a direct reflection of patterns and structures established centuries ago, and it is these factors which help mould the individual identity of an urban place, give it its special character and impart, to those who live, work or visit there, the feeling of a 'sense of place'. When launching his book, he declared able to affirm his conviction, that 'Shrewsbury is unique'.

Still, the conflict is between long term values – social, educational and the economic value of 'heritage' – which cannot be measured, and the short term pressures of developers or financial expediency. In a town like Shrewsbury a balance is needed between retaining the irreplaceable features and character of the past, while still encouraging lively innovation, demanding the highest qualities of practical and visual excellence in any changes made. Decisions left to the short-term dictates of finance, expediency, or traffic engineers and councillors will continue to produce Ian Nairn's predicted 'mediocrity', to be regretted later as judgments mature, as happened after the short-sighted '60s. One of the uses of history should be to learn from past mistakes.

As we reach this point, everyone who reads this story becomes a part of Shrewsbury's history and someone who can influence its future – a privilege, responsibility, but great delight. We are only the trustees of our English heritage. It is ours not to destroy but to use, care for and enjoy, and then pass on to future generations, having awakened in them the interest, and the will, to do the same. As the pioneer of heritage interpretation, Freeman Tielden, adviser on their National Parks to the United States, said in *Interpreting our Heritage* in 1957, 'Through interpretation, understanding; through understanding, appreciation; through appreciation, protection.'

The dramatic castle silhouette, especially at night, rising high above the forecourt of the historic station below, makes one of Shrewsbury's memorable points of
entry and departure.
(Stephen de Saulles)

APPENDIX: SOME SHREWSBURY STREET NAMES

Belmont
This is a modern name, first adopted by the Shrewsbury Street Act Trustees in 1795, and is derived from the French for 'handsome hill'.

Dogpole
Spelt variously Doghepol (*c*.1270-80), Doggepol (1319) and Dogpoll (1538), the origin of this unusual street name seems obscure. The customary derivation of the suffix, 'pole' from the O.E. 'pol', a deep place in a river, hardly seems applicable here, although the bank on the north side descends steeply to the river. A more plausible explanation is that it derives from a variant of the word 'poll' meaning a head or summit. There is a possibility that the first syllable is from 'ducken', to stoop or duck, and perhaps signifies a low gate in the wall here at some time when the supposed inner wall of the town crossed the Wyle Cop end of the street. Several references to the 'upper part of Dogpole' in mediaeval deeds suggests that the street formerly extended further than it does today, perhaps to the High Cross.

Fish Street
Known as Ffyschestrete in 1377, Ffyschestrete in 1379, New Fish Street in 1649 and Old Fish Street in 1657, it has been suggested that the name derives from the emblem of the Abbot of Lilleshall, which was three fishes, but it is more likely that it arose from the fact that fish was commonly sold from the stalls or 'fish-boards' which stood here at least as early as the 15th century, and as late as 1857.

Frankwell
The main street leading from the Welsh Bridge was called Frankevile in mediaeval times. The Elizabethan poet Thomas Churchyard called it Franckwell. The origin of the name is obscure, but Thomas Auden, in his *History of Shrewsbury*, suggests that this suburb grew up as a centre for 'free' (hence 'Frank Ville') traders who were outside the jurisdiction of the lord of the castle, and who were subsequently encouraged by reason of the trade and commercial prosperity which they brought to the town. If this was the origin, one would expect to find remnants of Norman names in the fields and properties of the area, but this is not the case.

Gullet Passage

Known as The Gullet in 1577 and Gullet Sutt in 1696, this passage, leading from the Square to Mardol Head, is, strictly speaking, a 'shut'. At the head of the passage stood the famous Gullet Inn, on the site of the present Market Vaults. The inn was here in the 16th century, but it is not clear whether it took its name from the passage or vice versa. In the Middle Ages, however, a stream ran down the shut to the river at the Mudholes, draining the pool which stood on the site of the present Shirehall, and the name probably derives from the Middle English word, 'golate', meaning a stream, channel or ditch.

Gumblestolestrete

Known as the Street of Gomesall c.1278, Gumstalstrete in 1324 and Gumbalstalstrete in 1390, this was the medieval name for the High Street, part of which was also known as Cooks' Row or Bakers' Row. The name derives from Gumstol, or Gumble stool, the cucking stool for the punishment of scolds, and it is known that Shrewsbury possessed this instrument as early as 1292. In addition to its customary use for scolds, an Act of 1266 ordered this form of punishment for the drenching of defaulting bakers and brewers, and this perhaps accounts for the proximity of Gumblestolestreet to Bakers' Row. After the 14th century the name disappears, giving way to the modern High Street. It had, in any case, lost its relevance, since the cucking stool had been removed to St John's Hill, probably because of the drying up of the pond.

Mardol

Spelt variously Mardeval, Mardevol (c.1270), Mardefole (1295), Mardall (1596) and Mardowell (c.1710), this is another street where the derivation and meaning is obscure. A frequent attribution is from Marlesford, which the historian, Thomas Phillips, interprets as 'the ford at the marly pastures', but nothing resembling this form can be found in early records. The first syllable is always 'marde', not 'marle'; nor is there any trace of the 'ford' ending. The pseudymous 'Boileau' in Shropshire Notes and Queries (20 November 1885) gives 'dol' as the Welsh word for a riverside meadow, and 'maer' as the lord's steward or mayor. Others have suggested the Welsh 'mawr', great, or 'mur', a wall, linked with 'dol', a meadow. None of these, however, is convincing, chiefly because they all ignore the three syllables of the early forms. Joseph Morris gives the meaning as 'the dairy house fold'. Another possibility is suggested from the Anglo-Saxon words 'maere', a boundary, and 'deofol', the devil – the meaning being the devil's boundary, perhaps an illusion to local legend. Certainly in early times Mardol was divided from the settlement of Romaldesham by a small stream which ran from the bog near the High Street down the Gullet Passage and to the west of Mardol to the river.

Milk Street

Recorded as Milke Street in 1621, Mill Street in 1664 and Milk Street in 1757, this street was anciently part of St Chad's Lane or Stury Close Lane (see below) and extended past St Chad's church to the town walls. In the Poll-Tax Roll (1377) it is referred to as 'parva venella tendente ed ecclesiam sancte ceddi' (St. Chad). The Corporation Orders for 1792 mention the 'town walls at the bottom of Milk Street', and Roque's plan of 1746 confirms this. The record of it as Mill Street in 1664 may simply be a scribe's error, for both before and afterwards it is Milk(e) Street. The connection with either Milk or Mill remains obscure.

Murivance
This street has had various spellings over time: Murywans in 1353, Meryvans in 1608, Merivans in 1672, and Murivance or Swan Hill in 1771. It had become St John's Row in 1828. Murivance was originally a general term for the open space between Belmont and St John's Hill and from Princess Street to the town walls. The name derives from two French words 'mur' and 'avant', meaning 'before or within the walls,', and it has been suggested that the area was the customary parade ground for troops. As this area was built up the various streets across it were called Murivance, and the name applied at various times to St John's Hill, Swan Hill, College Hill and Belmont. From the 16th to the 18th centuries, however, it applied particularly to Swan Hill, and appears thus on the maps of Speed and Rocque.

Stury Close Lane
Recorded initially as Seynt Chaddestret in 1306 and Seynt Chaddis lane in 1459, it had become Sterry Close Lane on Speed's map of 1610. Stury Close Lane is one of the old names for the modern Belmont, which has been known successively as St. Chad's Street or Lane; Stury Close Lane (from about 1350 to 1600); Milk Street (*c.*1600-1800) and Belmont (*c.*1800 onwards). It was named after the medieval family of Stury whose name appears nine times in the lists of bailiffs from 1308 onwards. In 1305 the bailiffs granted Richard Stury 'all that place behind the walls from the gate of St Chad's college to the convent of the Friars' Minors ... for faithful services rendered'. It was this land which became known as Stury's Close and which gave its name to the street to it from the town. Richard Stury, described as 'mayor of the merchants of this realm', was Edward II's emissary to the Court of Flanders in 1313,

Wyle Cop
Recorded as De Wila: Sub Wila in 1219-20, Sub vico de Wila *c.*1350, La Wile strete in 1356 and Wile Copp in 1621, this area, particularly the top of the Cop, was perhaps the ancient part of the town originally settled by the Saxons, and the name probably dates back to pre-Conquest times. It has been suggested that Wyle is the old Welsh 'hwylfa', a road leading up a hillside, and that Cop is the Welsh 'coppa', top or head. Professor Ekwall alternatively suggests that the name may come from the O.E. 'wil' (Welsh 'gwil') meaning 'trick', and denotes the existence of some mechanical contrivance such as a windmill. There are really three parts to the thoroughfare, Under the Wyle or Sub Wila, the lower portion from the English Bridge to the foot of the hill; the Wyle, the rise itself; and Wyle Cop, or Super Wilam, the summit portion from Dogpole to High Street, but the whole is often called simply the Wile or Wyle Cop, and there is no consistency in the use of these terms, as far as records are concerned. The Shrewsbury Street Act trustees

in January, 1825, tried to introduce some uniformity by deciding that from the English Bridge to the turning into Dogpole be called the Wyle, and from Dogpole to St Julian's steps the Wyle Cop, but this does not seem to have had general acceptance.

With thanks to *Shrewsbury Street Names* by John L. Hobbs

Index

Abbedesle, Roger de 69
Abbey 20-5, *21, 23*, 27-8, 32, 41-2,
    44-6, 48, 65-9, 134, *148, 177*
    buildings 54, *68*, 76
    Church of the Holy Cross/ St
        Peter & St Paul 67, 177
            alterations 144
    cloisters 148
    damage to during Civil War
        105-6
    and Dissolution 67-9
    fishponds 143
    gardens, destruction of 148
    income 45-6, 54, 66
    mill *22*
    nona-centenary 243
    refectory reading pulpit *50*
    relations with the town 44-5
    restoration in late 1800s 177-8
    St Winefride's shrine, *see under*
        St Winefride
    scholastic reputation 48
    state of affairs in 1322 48
    west front *243*
    west tower, building of 46
Abbey House *118*
Abbot's House *59*, 241
abbots
    election 24, 45
    London residence 45
Aberdeen, David 233
Act of Union, 1800 156
Acton Burnell 38
Adam, Abbot 32
Adnitt and Naunton *173*
Aedric 14
Aelfrith of Bernicia 4, 6
Aethelred, Earl 10
    King, 'the Unready' 14
Albright Hussey manor house 102
aldermen 58
Aldersley, Robert 111
Alley and Maclellan 205
Alfred the Great 9
Alison, Archibald 151
Alliance Assurance Co Ltd 181-2,
    182
almshouses *55*
    Drapers' *55*, 56, 57, 130, *130*
    Millington's 127-8, *128*
Anarchy, The 28-9, 31

Aragon, Katherine of 111
archaeological assessment 247-8
archery 187, 191
Arrol, Andrew 238, 244, 245
Arthur, Prince 65
Ash, Richard 163
Ashby, John 123, 151
Ashton, Thomas 65, 70
Assembly Room 123
Assizes 120, 123
Atcham 138
Athelstan, King 11
Attingham Park 221
Auden, Thomas 70, 126t

Bage, Charles 129, 139-40, 141,
    151
bailiffs 58, 87, 96
    dispute with abbot 65
Baker, Nigel 7, 8, 247
    Abbot Richard (also Richard
        Marshall) 66
Bank Fashions 233
'Bank's Horse' 87
barge owners 95
Barnard, Lord 83
Basingwerk Abbey 28
Bayston Hill 7
Bazalgette, Sir Joseph 180
Bear Steps 235-8, *236*, 238, *238*,
    239
Bear Steps Hall 48
Belesme, Mabel de 19
    Robert de 26
Belle Vue 7, 177
    Oakley Street 177
Belmont 161, *162*
Benbow, Admiral John 114-5, *114*
    Lieutenant, later Captain John
        103, 106, 114
Benedictine Rule 23
Bennett, Mr 126
Bennet's Hall 40, 233
Benyon, Benjamin 139, 141
    Thomas 139
Berry, Harold 238
    Colonel James 106
Berth, The *5, 7*
Berwick 7, 53, 186
Betton, John 142
Bicton Heath 125, 187

Black Death 48-9, 58
Black Prince, the 62
Blakeway, Rev. John Brickdale 134
Blomfield, Sir Arthur 189
    Sir Reginald 189
Blount, Edward 72
Blunden, Edmund 207
Blunenau, Hans 222-3
Boat House Inn, The 191, 198
boatbuilding 138
boating 190-1
Boteler (or Butler), Abbot Thomas
    66, 67
Bowdler, Thomas 127, 188
Boys, Thomas Shotter 107, 169
Bradford, earl of 83
Braun & Hogenberg 91
Breteuil, Laws of 57-8
breweries 142
    Coleham 142
    Salopian 142
    Southam's 193, 216
    Trouncer's 142
brick buildings 91
brickmaking 142
bridges
    Castle Footbridge 197, *198*,
        226, *227*
    English Bridge/ Stone (East)
        Bridge *15*, 27, *43*, 65, 69,
            148-50, *149*, 211-2, *212*
            widening 202, 211-2, 215
            new bridge 148, *149*
    Greyfriars Footbridge 202
    Kingsland Bridge 164-5, 189
    Porthill Footbridge 212
    railway 167
    St George's Bridge/ Welsh
        Bridge 36, *42*, 43, 62, 150,
            153
            replaced in 1796 150
Bridgnorth 26
Briggs, Lord Asa 230
Britannia, The 158
Broadwell 137, 179
Brochmael 5
Brockwell Ysgythrog 15
Bromfield, Joseph 150
Bronze Age 7
Brooke, Lord 71
Brown, Vandyke 246

Browne, Hablot K. ('Phiz') 191
Buck, S. & N. *viii-ix*
burgesses 19-20, 34, 58, 120, 121
Burgh, Hubert de 35
Burghley, Lord
    map 84, *85*, 86
Burnell, Robert 39
Burr, Thomas 141, 183
Burr's leadworks 141, 166, 183-4
business 215
Butler, Dr Samuel 126, 151, 189
Byron, Lord 102

Cadwallon 6
Calton, Prior Thomas de 48
Cambrensis, Giraldus 31
canals 154-5, 163-4, 244; *see also*
    under Shrewsbury
    Shropshire and Newport 244
Cann Office 166
Canute 10, 14
Capel, Lord 100-2
Caradoc 27-8
Caratacus 1
Carline, John I 143
    John II 21, 55, 130, 132, 140,
        141, 143, 151
    John III 143
Carline and Tilley 151
Carr, A.M. 239
castle 10, 18, 26, 31-2, 39, 42,
        43-4, *44*, 69, 84-5, 107,
        121, *176, 248*
    alterations by Telford 124-5
    besieged by King Stephen 29
    Laura's Tower 10, 44, *124*, 125
    military museum 205
    purchased by Horticultural
        Society 212-3
Castle Gates House 83, *83*
Castle Restaurant *200*
Castlefields 141, 160, 246
    Albert Street 177
    Severn Street 177
    Victoria Street 177
celebrations, royal 159
Chaloner, Thomas 99
Chambre, Esther 113
Charles I, King 96, 97
    charter 89, 96
Charles II, King 107
Charlton, Sir John de 47
    mansion of *47*

charters 26, 32-3, 34, 50, 57-8, 68,
    89, 107
Chatwood Safe Company 215
Cheney Longville 20
Cherry Orchard 160
    Bradford Street 177
    Cleveland Street 177
    Tankerville Street 177
Chitty, Miss Lily 231
Christmas Carol, A 82
churches
    Battlefield *246*
    Holy Cross 67, 177
    Roman Catholic cathedral 184
    St Alkmund's 12, 13, 60, *132*,
        144, *145*, 188
    New St Chad's 137, 146, *147,*
        186, 191
    Old St Chad's 8, 12, *12*, 15, 57,
        106, 114, *145, 146*
        collapse 144-6
    St George's 142
    St Giles's 142
    St Julian's 12, 55, 73, *132*, 142,
        163, *236*
    St Mary's 7, 8, 12, *14, 36, 47*,
        55, 60, *60*, 73, 114, 142
    St Nicholas *176*
    St Peter 13, 20
cinema 216, 227
circus 192
Circus Yard 134, 171
Civic Trust 230, 233
Civil War, The 97-105
Claremont Buildings 223
Clive, Lord Robert (of India) 121,
    121, 123, *200*
cloth trade 73-5, 77, 109
Clowes, Josiah 154
Cluny 20, 25
coaches, *see under* roads
'coade stone' 158
Coade, Mrs 158
Coalbrookdale 152
Cobbett, William 117
Coleham 95, 140, 160, 180, 197,
    247
    Midland Railway Carriage
        Works *183*
Coleridge, Samuel Taylor 131
    Rime of the Ancient Mariner
        131
Colliers, John 233

commercial activity 109, 143,
    172-3
Commonwealth, The 105-6
Confectioners, The 241
Conservation Areas 237
Cooper, Geoffrey 215
Cooper and Green 215
Copthorne 160
    Barracks 160, 205
Corbet, Sir Andrew 70
Corbett's Perseverance Ironworks
    183
Cornforth, John 235, 239, 242
Cornhouse, The 244
Cornovii 1, 2, 5, 6
'Corset House' *214*
cotton works 140-1
    Hulbert's *141*
Council Gates 103
Council House 70, 98, *98, 99*, 112
    Court *176*
    gatehouse *84*, 89
council housing 216, 224
Council in the Marches 62, 70, 71,
    89, 108
County Hall 150
craftsmen 143
Crew, Randolph 71
cricket 191
Cromwell, Oliver 105, 106
    Thomas 68
'Cross Houses' 188
Crowe, Ralph 229
Crowmeole 86
Crowmoor 224
Crown Hotel 221
Cullen, Gordon 231
Cunorix 3-4
Cynddylan 5, 6, 12
Cyndrwyn 6

Danegeld 14
Danelaw 9
Danes 9-11, 14-5
Darwin, Charles 151, 191, 192, *192*
    Robert Waring 151
Darwin centre *241*
'Darwin Gate' *240*
David ap Gruffydd 38-9
    ap Llewelyn 37
Della Porta, Joseph 189-90
Devereux, Richard 67
de Quincy, Thomas 123

Dickens, Charles 123
Disraeli, Benjamin 192-3
Dissolution, The 23, 67-9
Ditherington 160; *see also under* mills
Domesday survey 15, 18, 19, *19*
Downes, Andrew 71
Drapers 55, 56-7, 69, 73, 74, 160, 171
  Almshouses, *see under* almshouses
Drapers Hall 74
ducking-stool mere 88
Dun Cow 143

Eccleston, William 137
Eddowes' *Salopian Journal 173*
Edgar the Peaceable, King 8, 10, 11-2, 14
Edmund 'Ironside' 14
  earl of Rutland 56
Edric Sylvaticus 18
Edric the Wild 18
education 49, 67, 69-72, 126, 127, 188-9, 199, 229-30; *see also* schools and colleges
  SCOLA system 229
Edward I, King 37-9, *38*, 41, 43-4, 45
Edward III, King
Edward IV, King 56, 61
Edward V, King 62
Edward VI, King 70, 72
Edward VII, King
Edward VIII, King 218
Edward the Confessor, King 10, 15
Edward the Elder, King 11
Edward the Martyr, King 14
Edwin of Northumbria 6
Egbert of Wessex 7, 8, 9
elections of 1774 121
electricity 181, 226, 246
  Castlefields Weir 246
  generating station 181
Elizabeth I, Queen 84
Ellison, C.O. 174, 175
Emma of Normandy 14, 15
entertainment 87, 113, 124, 125, 227
  dancing 113
  gardens 113
Erneley, Sir Michael 103
Ethelfleda 10, 11
Evans, David 142

Exchange Hotel 216
Eyton, Thomas 151

fairs 22, 46
  Butter and Cheese Fair 170
Fallows & Hart 136
Farquhar, Lieutenant George 107, 113-4, 124
Feast of Corpus Christi 56-7
fellmongering 142
Fellmonger's Hall *179*, 240
Field Studies Council 244-5
Fiennes, Celia 112-3, 124
Fillilode, Thomas 69
fire precautions 132, 137, 181-2, *196*
  Salop Fire Office 181
First World War 203-8, *206, 207*
  hospital 205
  hostel for Belgian refugees 205, *206*
  POW camp *203*, 204, 205
Fitzalan, John 42
  Richard 58
  William 29
floods 153, *181*
  prevention 245-6
Food Enterprise Centre 246-7
football 187, 189, 199
Fordhall Farm 219-20
forges 138
Foundling Hospital, *see under* hospitals
Fowler, Mr 155
Franklin's Livery Stables 181
Frankwell 31, 59, 60, 79, 134, 142, *179, 181*, 188, 240, *242*, 245
  Cadogan fort 101, 103
  origin of name 249
  Quay 95
'freehold land societies' 177
friars 67
  Austin 41, 68, 199
  Black
  Dominican 35, 40-1, 45, 67-8, 154
  Franciscan (Grey) 41, 68, *69*
Friends of the Earth 244
Fulchred, Abbot 23

Gaol, County *120*
gardens 109, *110*, 124; *see also* The Quarry
  Underdale tea garden 191
Gardiner, Mr 126
gas supply 181
gates
  Mardol Gate 42
  Watergate/'Traitors Gate 36, 97, *104*, 154
  Welsh Gate 42
Gaye Meadow 98
General Strike 213-4
German, Sir Edward 216
Gibbon, Richard 99
Gibbon's Mansion 142
Giraldus Cambrensis 31
glass-stainers 142
Glen, The 143
Glyn Dwr, Owain 51, 53, 55
Godefred, Abbot 28
Godfrey, Abbot 27
Gough, J.B. 192
Grand National Archery Society 187
Green, Bruce 215
Greenfields 7
Greville, Sir Fulke 70, 91
Griffiths, Robert 169, 170
Gruffyd ap Llewelyn 15
Guildhalls 74-5, *74, 112*
guilds 39, 55, 115; *see also* Drapers, Merchants, Shearmen
  Whitsuntide theatrical productions 65
Gumblestolemore 88
Gwynedd, Owain 18
Gwynn, John 148, 151

Hadrian, Emperor 2, 3
Hale, Sir Matthew 159
Hall Engineering 215
Hamlyn, Geoffrey 229, 234
Hampton, Mary 142
Hancock, Walter 87-8, 92
Hanmer, Sir David 51
  Margaret 51
Hardicanute, King 15
Harries, Paul 247
Harwood, Edward 138
  John 138
Hawise 47

Haycock, Edward 130, 131, 158, 174
   John Hiram 88, 128, 129, 150, 151
Hayward, Sam 158
Hazledine family 139-40
Hazledine, William 139-40, 151, 183
health 86, 87
   cholera 179
   developments in public health 86, 195-7
   inspector of nuisances 195
   medical officer 182, 195-7
   smallpox 182
Hearth Tax (1672) 109
Henry I, King 26-7
   siege of Shrewsbury 26
Henry II, King 29, 31
   charter 58
Henry III, King 35, 37, 45, 69
Henry IV, King 50, 51-3
Henry V, King 51, 54, 62
Henry VI, King 60
Henry VII, King 62-4, 65
Henry VIII, King 66
   charter 68
Henry, duke of Buckingham 63
Henry Tudor House 63, *63, 64*
Herbert, Abbot 28
Heseltine, Lord 72
Heylyn, Rowland 71
Hill, Captain 105
   John 114
   Sir Rowland, later Lord 123, 157, 189
Hill Crescent 216
Hitchcock, A. 160
Hobbs, J.L. 231
Holland, Thomas 109
Hollins, Arthur 219-20
Holywell, Flintshire 27, *30*, 54
Hopton, Arthur 71
horses 175, 196
hospitals
   asylum 188
   Copthorne 221
   Eye, Ear & Throat Hospital 174, *175*
   in First World War 205
   Foundling Hospital 122, 128-9, *131*
   isolation 182

Millington's Hospital 127-8
   nurses' home 197, *197*
   St George's 42
   St John the Baptist 42
   Salop Infirmary 124, 128, 130, 221
   conversion to 'The Parade' 240
House of Industry, *see* workhouse
Howard, John 120
Howard Street Warehouse 164, 239
Hulbert, Charles 140, 151, 158, 164
Hulme, Alfred J. 63
Humane Society 131
Humphrys, John 167
Hunckes, Sir Fulke 103
Hunt, Rowland 151
Hunt Ball 124, 125

Improvements Commission 134, 180
industry 138-41, 183-4, 209
Ireland, Robert 74, 75, 80
Ireland's Mansion 80-1, *80, 108*
Iron Age 7
Isocrates 92

Jacobite Rebellions 118
James II, King
   charter 107
   visit to Shrewsbury 107
James, Dr 195
Jenkins, Thomas 118
Joan, Princess 34, 37
John, King 34-5, 58
   charters 26, 34, 57
Johnson, Dr 124
Johnson Marshall & Son 140
Jones, Thomas 75
   William (Draper) 75
   William (maltster) 183
Jones's Mansion 75

Kean, Edmund 191
Kennedy, Dr 189
Kenyon, Hon Thomas 163
King, Michael (Micky) 238
King's Head *64*
King's Shropshire Light Infantry 205
Kingsland 115, 116, *123*, 128, 141, 160, 177, 185, 189
   Bridge Mansions 175

Lancaster, Joseph 129
Laura's Tower, *see under* castle
Lawrence, Robert 155-6
leather trade 31, 73, 109
Leigh, George 74
Leighton, Sir Charlton 120-1
Leland, John 65, 69, 151
Liberal Club *144*
library 131, 136, 174, 193, 239
Lichfield 6, 8, 12, 20
life expectancy 180
lighting 136, 181
Lind, Jenny 191
Linnel, Henry 143
Lion and Pheasant, The 201
Lion Hotel 123, 125, 155-6, 158, 162, 191, 193
listed buildings 230-2, 240
Llewellyn ap Gruffydd 37
Llewellyn ap Iorworth (the Great) 34-35, 37
Lloyd, Mr William Butler 187
Lloyd's Bank 233
Lloyd's Mansion 78, *78*, 190
Llywarch Hen 5, 12
Lobbenberg, Otto 222-3
lodes 32
Loggerheads, The 105
Longden Coleham 56
Longden Green 216
Lord Hill's Column *157*, 158, 224, *234*
Ludlow, John de 39
   Nicholas de 40
Lye, Abbot Richard 67
   dispute with bailiffs 65
Lyster, Richard 143

Mackworth, Humphrey 105
Magonsaete 6
malting 142-3
Manser 247, *247*
maps, *see under* Shrewsbury
Marches, laws of 18
Marches Energy Agency (MEA) 244
Mardol Gardens shopping arcade 240
Mardol Quay 95, 101
markets 132, 133, 134, 168-71
   butter 136, 164
   butter and poultry 134
   General (Indoor) Market 135, 169, *170*, 171, 233, *233*

livestock ('smithfield') 132, 168, *230*
New Market Hall 233-4, *233*
'pannier' 133
Saxon 11
street 171
Victorian *214*
Market Cross 111, 113
Market Hall/House 87-8, *88,* 133, 171, *176,* 219
Marlowe, Christopher 72
Marochetti 200
Marshall, John 139-40
Richard, *see* Baker, Abbot
Marston, A.T. 210
Richard 210
Mary, Queen
as a child in Shrewsbury 111
Massey, Edward 151
Matilda 29
Maurice, Prince 102, 103
mayor 58, 96
McDonalds 233
Meighen, John 92
Richard 94
mental illness 87
Meole Brace 7, 143, 215, 241
Mercers 74
Mercia 5, 6, 7, 8, 10, 11, 14
Merivale House 83
militia 100, 118, *119*
mills 21, 42, 45, 46, 49, 140
Benyon Bage and Marshall Flax Spinning Mill, Ditherington 139, 155, 183, 221, 244
linen and flax spinning 141
windmills 45
Millington, James 127
Mitchell, A.R. 209
Moleleye, William de 46
Monkmoor 125, 215, 229
Farm 180
Montfort, Eleanor de 38
H. 192
Simon de 37, 42, 46
Montgomery, Hugh de 26
Roger de 18-20, 23, 24-5
tomb of 25, *25*
Morris, David 243
Morris's Restaurant *215*
Mortimer, Edmund 53
Mortimer's Cross, battle of 62
Morton, H.V. 209

Mountford & Co, carriage-builders 184
Much Wenlock 10
Municipal Corporations Act, 1835 160
museums 193
military museum 205
natural history museum 93, 131, 174
Music Hall 174, 181, 191, 221
Mynde, Abbot Thomas 53-4, 65, 67
Mytton, John 'Mad Jack' 123
Thomas 61, 63
Colonel Thomas 102, 104, 105
Mytton's Mansion *61*

Nairn, Ian 233, 234, 235
navvies 167
Nesscliff 223, 227
Newport, Sir Francis 83, 107
Richard 97, 99
Newport House *112*
newspapers 138, 228; *see also under* individual titles
Newton, Henry 134
New Chronicle 138
Norman period 17-30

Oakley Manor 205
Odelerius 18, 20
Offa 6-7
Ogilby, John, maps of *30, 116*
Old Cross Keys 76, 78-9, *78*
'Old House' *110, 111*
Onslow, Richard 84-5
Ordericus Vitalis 17, 18
Oswell, A.E. Lloyd 182
Otley, Adam 74
Ottley, Sir Francis 99-100, 102, 103, *100*
Richard 106
Owain ap Gruffydd 37
Owain Gwynedd 34
Owen, Rev Hugh 151
Nick 72
Richard 75
Tudor 62
Sir William 84, 90, 103
Wilfred 203, 207-8, *208*
memorial *208*, 243

Pailin, Mr (Shrewsbury Cakes) 200
Palin, Michael 72

Palmer, John 156
Panzetta, Joseph 158
Parade, the 240
parishes
St Chad's 8
St Mary's 8
Parliament 192, 213
of 1283 38
of 1398 50
Pearl Insurance Company 221
Peel, John 72
Penda 5
Pengwern 5, 6, 7, 12
Pengwern Boat Club 187, 191
Penson, T.M. 211
Penson, Thomas Jnr 174
Perche, John 81
Perche's Mansion 81-2, *81, 220*
Percy, Henry ('Hotspur') 51-3
Thomas, earl of Worcester 51-3
Pevsner, Nikolaus 174, 182, 199, 218, 234
Phillips, James 143
Thomas 164
'Wappy' 232
photography 189-90
Pidgeon, Henry 130, 131, 148, 172, 190
Pitchford Hall 74, 77
plague 128
planning regulations 134-5
Pleyley, Sir John 69
Plough Inn 168, 174, *200*
Plough Vaults 79
Plymley, Archbishop Joseph 151
police 178, 197, 226
station 178, 229
Poor Law Amendment Act, 1834 188
population 109, 120, 132, 160
Porch House 94
Post Office building *174*
Powis & Hodges 140
Prestefelde 205
Preston Montford 245
Prince Rupert Hotel 75, 102, *102*
prison 90, 131
Pritchard, Thomas Farnolls 119, 128, 132, 151
Proud Salopian 193
provosts 58
Pugin, E.W. 184
Puiset, Adeliza de 19, 26

Pulteney, Miss 125
 Sir William 121, 124
Pump House 244
Puritan clergy 72

Quakers 108
Quarry, The 36, 65, 84, 123, *176,*
 186, 187, 191, 226
 bandstand 186
 Dingle, The 186, *213*, 225
Quarter Sessions 58, 120, 123
Quatford 19

racecourse 125, 187
Radbrook Hall 221
railways
 Abbey Foregate Signal Box
 210
 accident, 1907 201-2
 arrival in Shrewsbury 162, 163,
 164, 166-8
 bridge 167, *167*
 companies grouped together
 210-1
 'Gazelle' engine 227
 Great Western 210
 London, Midland and Scottish
 210
 Midland Railway Carriage
 Works *183*
 Shropshire and Montgomery
 202, 223, 227-8
 station 167, 173-4, *173, 176,*
 211
 in Second World War 222
Ralph, bishop of Bath and Wells 53
Ranger, William 179
Raven Hotel 113, 114, 155, 158,
 194, 222
 demolition *231*, 232
 modernisation 209-10
 in Second World War 221
Rea Brook 45, 54
Recruiting Officer, The 107, 113-4,
 124
recycling centre 244
Red Lion 155; *see also* Lion
Rees, John 154, 164
Reinking, Colonel William 103,
 104
religion 106, 108, 131
 Sunday School 188
 and Temperance 184-5, 192

Renaissance 88, 89-92, 110
Reynolds, William 139, 151
Richard, duke of York 56, 60, 61
Richard, son of Edward IV 62
Richard I, King
 charter 57
Richard II, King 49-50
 charter 50
Richard III, King 62-3
river
 accidents 131
 ferries 164-6, *165*, 197
 Frankwell Quay 95
 Mardol Quay 95
 navigation 85-6, 133-4, 163
 towpath construction 133
 trade 95, 109, 152-4, *153,*
 163-4
 weir 197
roads
 coach travel 118, 155-8, 162-3
 mail coaches 156-7
 'posting' 162
 coaching road ('A5', London-
 Holyhead) 148, 155-7, *177,*
 178
Robert, duke of Normandy 26
Roberts, Alfred 190
Robertson, Fyfe 215
 Henry 164-5
Rocke, Anthony 111
 Mr 126
Rocque, John 133
Romans 1-3, 7
ropemaking 143
Ross, Rev Ian 243
 Jean 243
Roushill
 power station 226
 Wall 101
Rowley, Roger 91, 114
 William 75, 82-3, 90-1, 96
Rowley's House 82-3, *82*, 91, *217,*
 238
Rowley's House Museum 83
Rowley's Mansion *82*, 91
Royal Agricultural Show 187, *187*
Royal Baths 126
Royal Insurance Building *182*
Rupert, Prince 101, 102-3
Rushton, 'Willie' 72

St Bueno 27, 49
St Chad 12
St Dunstan 11-2
St Samson 6
St Thomas à Becket 32
St Winefride 27-8
 Guild of 65, 67
 shrine 25, 28, 43, 45, 49, 53,
 54, 67
St Wulfstan 13
Salopian Journal 138, 173
Salop Steam Laundry *200*
Sandford, Adam 74
 John 77
Sandys, Lord Duncan 237
Sanger's Circus *191*
Sassoon, Siegfried 207
Saxfield, Barbara 113
Saxons 3-16
Say, Picot de 19, 20
schools and colleges
 Allat's School 129, *129*, 188,
 240
 Bowdler's (the Blue) School
 127, *127*, 188
 Chambre-Saxfield Academy
 113
 charity schools 127
 College of Arts and Technology
 188, 226, 229
 Design, School of 156, 163,
 188
 Gateway Education and Arts
 Centre 193, 229, 240
 Grammar School (Shrewsbury
 School) 65, 70-2, 91-2,
 92, 123, 126, *128*, 165,
 165, 166, 174, *176*, 192,
 221, 226
 figures at main entrance 92,
 93
 headmasters 189
 new site (Kingsland House
 of Industry) 188-9
 Rigg's Hall 94
 Top Schools 93, *94*
 Mrs Gwynn's 'Boarding School
 for young ladies' 126
 Mrs Jaquet's school 126
 Lancasterian Schools 129, 188
 Mechanics Institute 131
 Millington's School 188
 Prestefelde 205

Priory School for Boys 199
Radbrook College 189, 223
St Chad's College 67, 70
St Chad's Ladies' School 129,
188
St Mary's College 67, 70
secondary schools 199
Wakeman School 83
Scoltock, Samuel 156
Scott, George Gilbert 177-8
Scull brothers 209
Second World War 219-24
air raid precautions 219
ammunition storage depot 223
British Restaurant 221
Home Guard 219, 222
Memorial *224, 226*
'stop lines' 222
V-E Day 224
V-J Day 224
War Agricultural Committees
219-20
Séez 20, 23, 24
Sentinel Waggon Works Ltd 205,
224
Severn, River, *see under* river
sewers and drainage 137, 179-80,
197
Shayler, F.H. 199
Shearmen 55, 74, 77
Shearmen's Hall *77*
Shelton 188, 216
Shirehall 78, 88, 150, *150*, 151,
174, *200*, 229
new 234, *234*
shops 218
working conditions 172-3
Shrewsbury
Archaeological Society 190
& Atcham Borough Council
Amateur Operatic Society 216
battle of 51-3, 154, *246*
Battlefield visitor centre
246
Cakes 172, 200
Canal 136, 139, 140, 142, 152,
155, 163, 239
Carpenters, School of 77-85
Choral Society 131
Chronicle 199-200, 214, 215,
225, 228, 239
Civic Society 48, 142, 230,
237-8, 239, 240, 247

coach travel, pioneer 118
Corporation 58
seal *54*
county town 95-6, 117, 124
diocese 67
Flower Show 56, 185-6
government of the town 57-9,
160-1, 210, 216, 238
historic centre
conservation of 233, 237-42
threat to post WWII 231-4
Hydro 246
maps of 13, 32, 40, 52, 84, 85,
90, 91, 104, 122, 133, 158,
160, 161
Mint 10, 11, 98
Parliament of 1283 held in 38
School, *see under* schools and
colleges
'Season' 124
Show 115-6, 185, 189
siege of 26
Station, *see under* railway
street names 249-52; *see also
under* streets
Town Football Club 199, 226,
241, *241*
Town of Flowers competition
225
Transition Town 246
Waterworks Act, 1856 180
Waterworks Company 137
Shropshire
Archaeological Society 231
'Enlightenment' 151
Horticultural Society 131, 212
Photographic Society 189-90
Regiment 118
shiring of 12
Society in London 94
Star 228-9
and West Midlands Agricultural
Show 185, 186, 187, 218,
225
Wildlife Trust 245
Yeomanry Cavalry 187
Sidney, Sir Henry 70, 71
Sir Philip 70, 71
Silhouette Corset Ltd 222-3
Sitwell, Edith 207
Siward 20
Smirke, Sir Robert 150, 151, 174,
200

Smith, J.T. 231
Samuel Pountney 178
Smithfield Ironworks *175*
smithy *196*
Southam, Thomas 193, 216
Speed, John 90, 91
sport 186-7
Stanier, Sir Beville 199-200
Stephen, King 29
Stephens, Col H.F. 202, 228
Steuart, George 145-6, *147*
Stevens, Abbot Nicholas 49
stonemasons 143
street names 32
streets, Shrewsbury
Abbey Foregate 44, 83, *118*,
134, 137, 143, 205, *210*
Back Lane 154
Barker Street 82, 216, *217*
Beeches Lane 127
Belmont 249, 251
Butcher Row *59*, 168, 241
Bynner Street 183
Castle Foregate 95, 183, 214
Castle Gates 131, 136, 216
Castle Street 154, 218, *231*
Chester Street 199
Claremont Hill 134, 137
Coleham Head 132
College Hill 174
Corvisors Row 73
Coton Hill 115, 137, 180, 216
Dogpole 16, 83, *110, 111, 112*,
134, 184
origin of name 249
Dogpole Court 239
Fish Street *236*, 249
Frankwell, *see under* Frankwell
Gullet Passage 250
Gumblestolestrete 250
High Cross 134
High Pavement 94
High Street 76, *78*, 82, *108*
No.1 239
Hill's Lane 114
Howard Street 136, 164
Mardol 16, 42, *64*, 95, 135,
135, 169, 182
No.63 *245*
origin of name 250
Milk Street 250-1
Monks Foregate 44, 65
Murivance 174, *191*, 240
origin of name 251

259

Ox Lane 134, 136
Pig Hill 136
Pride Hill 94, *108*, 134, 135, *214*
  centre *241*
Priory Road 174
Quarry Walk *176*
Racecourse Lane 125
Raven Street 154
St Alkmund's Square *236*
St John's Hill 134, 136, 161, *171*, 214
St Mary's Place 197
St Mary's Street 134, 136
St Mary's Water Lane 40, *152*
St Mary's Well 40-1
School Gardens 144
Shoplatch 126, 135
Square, The *121, 168*, 174, *176, 200*, 234
Stury Close Lane 251
Swan Hill 94, 161, 214
Swine Market Hill 134, 136
Town Walls 36, 129, 184
  Summer House 239
Union Wharf 239
Wenlock Road 142
Wyle Cop 15, 16, 27, *61*, 63, *63*, 132, 201, *201*, 244
  origin of name 251-2
Street Improvement Acts 132, 134
String of Horses 79, *79*
Strutt, William 139
Stury, Richard 251
Stuttard, Sir John 72
suburban development 160-1, 177, 215
Suez Crisis 227
Sundorne 215
Swan, J.A. 199
Swan Hill Court *119*
Sweyn, King of Denmark 14
swimming pools
  Jubilee Bath 174

tailors *199*
Talbot Hotel *156*, 158, 163, 178
Tanner, William 216
tannery 45, 143
Tanners 201, 216
Tarbuck, John 117
Taylor family 142-3
Taylor, Isaac 162-3
  William 142

telephone 173
  exchange 174
Telford, Thomas 2, 10, 118, 124-5, *125*, 135, 139, 145-6, 148, 151, 153, 154, 157, 177
Temperance Movement, *see under* religion
tennis 126
theatre 126, 191, 227
  Beacon Players 227
  new (2009) *242*
  Theatre Royal 126, *126*
Thomas de Prestbury, Abbot 42, 45, 52, 53
Thrower, Margaret 226
  Percy 225-6
Tilley, John 132, 151
timber-framed buildings 58-60, 76-85, *108, 179*
'Tom Thumb, General' 191
Tomkys, John 72
  Thomas 71-2
Tonkin, Mr Morley 228, 229
town planning 230-4
town walls 32, 35-7, *35*, 43, 96, 101, 122
traffic congestion 175, 202, 211
transport 152-8, 162-8; *see also* canals, railways, river, roads
Trevelyan, Sir George 237
Trinder, Dr Barrie 239
tub-boats 154-5
Turneur, Timothy 81
Turnpike Trusts 118, 156, 157
Tussaud, Madame 123

Underdale 191, 215
  ferry 197
Unicorn Hotel *201*
Union Wharf Company 154, 164
Upton, Abbot William de 45
Urien of Reged 4
urinals, public ('ironclads') 181, *181*

Vaughan's Mansion *46*, 174
Victoria, Princess, later Queen 126
Victorian Arcade 240
Vikings 9
Viroconium (Wroxeter) 1-4
Visitor Economy Strategy, 2011 247
Vitalis, Ordericus 17, 18

Wakeman, Sir Offley 229
Wallace, Alfred 192
Ward, Arthur 83, 89, 211, 216, 218, 230
  Roger 72, 94
Warin, sheriff 20
Wars of the Roses 60-4
Watch, The 134, 136
water supply 86-87, 136-7, 179, 180, 197
Watur, Degory *57*
Weale's House 75
Weaver, John 113
Webb, Douglas 229
Welsh, wars with 34-9
Wenlock, Abbot Luke de 45
Wesley, John 131
West Midlands Agricultural Show, *see under* Shropshire and West Midlands
Wheeler's Tower *36*, 122
Whitehall 177
Whitehouse, Mary 167
Wightman, Mrs Julia 184-5, 192
Wilkinson, Ellen 213
William IV, King
  visit to Shrewsbury 123
William the Marshall, earl of Pembroke 35
Williams, John Bickerton 159
Williams-Freeman, Capt 197
Wilson, Harry 241
WI (Women's Institute) 223
Wood, Thomas 138
Woodville, Elizabeth 62
wool trade 31, 38, 39-41, 73, 76
Woolworth 231
Worcester, battle of 105, 106
workhouse (House of Industry) *128*, 129, 130, 188
Working Men's Club 227
Working Men's Temperance Hall 185
Wrekin, The 1, *1*
Wreocensaete 6
Wright, Thomas 122
Wroxeter (*Viroconium*) 1-4, *2*
Wulfere 6
Wyatt, James 151
Wycliff, John 53